Demetrio Aguilera-Malta
and Social Justice

Demetrio Aguilera-Malta and Social Justice

*The Tertiary Phase of Epic Tradition
in Latin American Literature*

Clementine Christos Rabassa

Rutherford • Madison • Teaneck
Fairleigh Dickinson University Press
London: Associated University Presses

Associated University Presses, Inc.
Cranbury, New Jersey 08512

Associated University Presses
Magdalen House
136-148 Tooley Street
London SE1 2TT, England

Grateful acknowledgement is given for the following translations quoted in this study:

Homer, *The Iliad*, translated by Richmond Lattimore. Copyright © 1960 by The University of Chicago. Reprinted by permission.

Homer, *The Odyssey*, translated by Richmond Lattimore. Copyright ©1965, 1967 by Richmond Lattimore. Reprinted by permission of Harper & Row, Publishers, Inc.

Vergil, *The Aeneid*, translated by James H. Mantinband. Copyright © 1964 by Frederick Ungar Publishing Co., Inc. Reprinted by permission.

Library of Congress Cataloging in Publication Data

Rabassa, Clementine Christos.
     Demetrio Aguilera-Malta and social justice.

     Bibliography: p.
     Includes index.
     /. Aguilera Malta, Demetrio, 1909-   ——Criticism
and interpretation.   I. Title.
     PQ8219.A36Z86   863   78-75193
     ISBN 0-8386-2079-5

Printed in the United States of America

**To my parents
Mary and Sotter Christos**

πάν μέτρον ἄριστον

Contents

7

Abbreviations

Aen.	*Aeneid*
Atomos	*No bastan los átomos*
Beo.	*Beowulf*
Caballeresa	*La caballeresa del sol*
Cid	*Cantar de Mio Cid*
Cruz	*Una cruz en la Sierra Maestra*
C.Z.	*Canal Zone*
D.G.	*Don Goyo*
Dientes	*Dientes blancos*
España	*España leal*
G.L.	*Gerusalemme Liberata*
Il.	*Iliad*
Inf.	*Inferno*
Infierno	*Infierno negro*
Isla	*La isla virgen*
L.Q.S.V.	*Los que se van*
Lus.	*Os Lusíadas*
Madrid	*¡Madrid!: reportaje novelado de una retaguardia heroica*
Mar	*Un nuevo mar para el rey*
Od.	*Odyssey*
P.L.	*Paradise Lost*
Quijote	*El Quijote de El Dorado*
Roland	*La Chanson de Roland*
Secuestro	*El secuestro del general*
7/7	*Siete lunas y siete serpientes*

Preface

The first work of Demetrio Aguilera-Malta to which I was introduced was *Don Goyo*, a novel about the *cholo* and *montuvio* inhabitants of Ecuador. It prompted the simplest response of approval—that of wanting to read more of the author's creations. To my pleasant surprise I found the range of his literature transcended the limits of most Latin American writers and that idealization of the native as hero was only part of a larger concern. There was an epic flavor about Aguilera-Malta's novels, short stories, and plays which necessitated a return to the poems of renown to find what specifically had stimulated the possible juxtaposition of a modern author and the poets of primary and secondary epic. As my research expanded, the topic of this study received sustenance from concepts propounded by notable figures who have dealt with related subjects.

First there is E. M. W. Tillyard, whose analyses went beyond the famous poems to novels, and whose statement in *The English Epic and Its Background* that "to consider a man an epic writer includes considering his general literary worth" (p. vi) proved highly motivating. I am also indebted to Brian Wilkie's *Romantic Poets and Epic Tradition*, in which he advocates using the broader term "epic tradition," a conclusion that revitalized the approach to my topic, and which served as a catalyst in determining that the epic spirit still persisted and more could be said about it. Then there are the works on mythology by Joseph Campbell, who for the very vastness of his studies has drawn the world closer together and shown that the hero has indeed "a thousand faces,'' all of which are fascinating. The fourth exegete whose commitment to literature is universal is Benjamin Carrión, who saw in his countryman's works an involvement with the technique and content associated with epos.

The inspirational acknowledgments include a deep appreciation for the guidance and practical assistance received from those who were instrumental in accomplishing this proposed literary union between the past and present. I extend my sincere gratitude to the faculty and administrative members of Columbia, University: Professor Andrés Iduarte, whose judgments, advice, and time were indispensable, Professor James F. Shearer, for his cooperation and encouraging comments, and Dean Ward Dennis, Professor Coleman Benedict, and Professor Kempton E. Webb for their intelligent criticism and suggestions.

Needless to say, I am extremely indebted to Demetrio Aguilera-Malta for the helpful, rapid responses to my queries and for making available those works which were inaccessible. I am also most grateful to Gloria Johnson and Thelma Nagasarian for their matchless efficiency in the technical preparation of the manuscript.

Finally, I offer a special thanks to my husband, Gregory Rabassa, whose knowledge and patience were invaluable in the course of my literary and historical adventures.

C. C. R.

Demetrio Aguilera-Malta
and Social Justice

1
Introduction

Milton: The Epic Hero Redefined

In his study of *Paradise Lost* C. S. Lewis emphasizes the continuous growth or evolution of epic heroes and their purpose when he asserts:

> Any return to the *merely* heroic, any lay, however good that tells merely of brave men fighting to save their lives or to get home or to avenge their kinsmen, will now be an anachronism. You cannot be young twice.[1]

Thus the hero of Western epic emerged from his Homeric surroundings to assume many transformations and roles during his literary existence. His originally egocentric orientation begins to change when Virgil establishes Aeneas's destiny as one of social, political, and religious magnitude in the founding of Rome. What is particularly striking in the development of secondary epic is the hero's gradual humanization contrasted with increased difficulties in overcoming obstacles and hardships along the road to glory.

The epic hero in his origins was a purely divine figure who challenged his peers for supreme power,[2] while the Homeric protagonists, when they were not demigods themselves, frequently received the direct protection of some deity.[3] Eventually the hero appeared in medieval and Renaissance garb as a totally mortal entity, but a man vested with heroic energy. Superior courage, prowess, and overall excellence in character and performance marked him as worthy of celebration and literary immortality according to the standards of the times. For the most part the same principles of honor exemplified by the warrior-hero of authentic epic still flourished under the guise of "religious" causes which were championed by heroes such as the Cid, Roland, Goffredo, and Vasco da Gama, all of whom symbolized the Christian ideal.

Milton's contribution to the development of epic tradition is significant not only for the quality of his work, but also for the innovative approach to his hero's portrayal. In the characterization of Adam the epic hero's evolution reaches a new level which distinguishes him from the vain or ambitious protagonists of earlier poems. The images of God begin their existence as privileged, sheltered, and immortal creatures who reflect the harmony of the Garden of Eden—an idyllic atmosphere soon to be transformed into a field of spiritual and verbal conflict. Adam in his post-lapsarian state is a new hero who bears little resemblance to the obdurate pursuer of fame and fortune epitomized by his epic predecessors. Out of the complex structure of *Paradise Lost* Milton creates a modern-day man whose feat will be largely one of endurance. With the First Couple's exile Milton fashions a hero to symbolize patient martyrdom[4] and condemns the once-celebrated Achillean attributes of pride and vengeance with their concomitants, war and violence. The active warrior-hero gives way to a humanized, rather inactive protagonist who represents suffering humanity as he goes forth to face a mortal future replete with misery, sorrow, and death.

The Epic Concern and Spirit

If the epic hero has undergone metamorphosis since the Homeric poems, the epic concern and spirit have remained essentially unchanged. In spite of variations within pagan or Christian epos, involvement with the human condition has been maintained. Life opposing death, and joy opposing sorrow, follow the hero's course toward his destined goal, and regardless of his success or failure, the ideal of virtue is constant. Traditionally, epics have asserted the positive values which the hero typifies. The tyrant who is generally evil incarnate cannot be eulogized. Despite the admirable qualities Satan exhibits in *Paradise Lost* (i.e., courage, fortitude, leadership, determination, etc.), he cannot be acclaimed as the hero because he demonstrates basically antisocial or anti-human characteristics which seek destruction over creation, perversion over perfection. Life still supreme over death, joy beyond sorrow, then, determine the celebration of a hero's survival in his struggle against his enemies or other obstacles which generally are embodiments of vice or evil.

Amidst all the violence and death accompanying the hero's course there is ever present the theme of survival, salvation, or regeneration, which is found in classical epic poetry as well as in the Christian tradition. When Odysseus succeeds in avoiding the whirlpool or in outwitting the Cyclops, such an accomplishment represents another extension of his existence. Aeneas during his bleakest moments of depression and disorientation sustains his men with an affirmation of their eventual success and survival in regenerative terms:

Now, through many perils and disasters, we steer our course for Latium where Fate has promised us a new abode, where a new Troy will rise again. So, persevere, and save yourselves for happier days.[5]

It is no small coincidence that Virgil's influence was evident in the epics of Tasso, Camões, and Milton. The spirit of revitalization which would manifest itself in seeking peace, reform, justice, and general social well-being was a concern of the epicists of the sixteenth and seventeenth centuries as well as for Virgil, who wrote his epic to celebrate the Augustan Pax Romana after a century of wars and internal strife. The Renaissance epic spirit inherently contains the elements of hope and a belief in the dignity of mankind, violence, and all of its manifestations notwithstanding. Lascelles Abercrombie has aptly synthesized the essence of this ideal:

> Man creating his own destiny, man however wearied with the long task of resistance, achieving some conscious community of aspiration, and dreaming of the perfection of himself: the poet whose lovely and noble art makes us a great symbol of that, is assuredly carrying on the work of Homer.[6]

Epic Method: The Role of Nature

The epicist in narrating the hero's tale of success or failure had recourse to a number of techniques which are part of epic tradition. Among these are formulas and similes, supernatural machinery, confrontations with obstacles or battles, visions, dreams, or omens, and other devices generally called "conventions." Nature's role in the epic is perhaps the least readily definable of elements in the tradition. Homer uses animals and natural phenomena to forge similes which may heighten the tension of the moment or serve as a relief from the pending action.[7] For Milton a feeling for nature juxtaposes his most lyrical passages.[8] Love and a bucolic setting are often intertwined in many an epic, and Virgil is perhaps the most sensitive of epicists in his appreciation of landscape and its effect on man's sentiments.[9]

But nature as a source of inspiration is as multifaceted as the epic itself and is intimately related not only to the epic method but to the epic concern as well. Homer's vivid portrayal of the physical confrontation of warriors in the

Iliad relies on comparisons between their activity and the violent characteristics of natural phenomena. Charging steeds, preying wolves, rushing cataracts, and raging thunder, all surround the heroes in symbolic reference when they are not actually challenged directly by these elements. Nor is it unusual for nature to illustrate in an expanded simile not merely the fury and wrath of a warrior felling his enemy but also to imply the power of divine will and the indomitable energy of a superior force that can destroy man's efforts towards progress:

He went storming up the plain like a winter-swollen
river in spate that scatters the dikes in its running currents,
one that the strong-compacted dikes can contain no longer,
neither the mounded banks of the blossoming vineyards hold
    it
rising suddenly as Zeus' rain makes heavy the water
and many lovely works of the young men crumble beneath
    it.[10]

Bestial entities on an associative plane often represent another significant concern of the epic—survival. Omens would hardly convey a positive or negative message without the symbol which most frequently assumes the form of some animal, particularly the eagle and the serpent. The hardiest and strongest of men are shaken and rendered almost helpless when both appear as a sign above the Trojans to portend disaster. But the rare man of the future, unaffected, not superstitious, asserts his faith in his god and himself:

But you: you tell me to put my trust in birds who spread
wide their wings. I care nothing for these, I think nothing
    of them,
nor whether they go by on our right against dawn and sunrise
or go by to the left against the glooming mist and the
    darkness.
No, let us put our trust in the counsel of great Zeus,
    he who
is lord over all mortal men and all the immortals.
One bird sign is best: to fight in defense of our country.
                    [Hector to Polydamas, *Il.* 12. 237-43]

Symbol becomes direct confrontation when, for example, Beowulf slays the dragon, tyrannical oppressor of his people. Nature's creatures, particularly in an aberrated form, can not only indicate an ominous forecast for the hero, but by opposing him may prove his very annihilation. A distortion of the natural order, especially in those epics whose theme is centered about Christian ideals and doctrines, signifies something evil, something demonic which is bent on conquering the hero's soul in addition to his soma.

Latin American Literature and Nature

The vastness of nature with its mysterious effect on man's destiny has been a major characteristic of Latin American literature that has preoccupied writers and critics observing the dynamic influence of the New World's geography since the Discovery. Chronicles, diaries, and letters since the time of Columbus described the rare surroundings and inhabitants of Latin America where epic feats of conquest and exploration were accomplished by those who dared to attempt the impossible. Nature was there to lure and to repel, to be dominated or to annihilate. Above all, it was there to be immortalized by the imagination of those who could translate their response to this inspiration into prose or poetry.

This unusual sensitivity to the natural environment has continued to manifest itself in the works of writers, and the hold is almost mystical if not totemic. The obsession with landscape is described by one critic in anthropomorphic terms which illustrate a progressive representation of existence from birth to death:

> El habitante de estas regiones ha tenido siempre el hechizo del paisaje que es al mismo tiempo su madre, su nodriza, su amante y su verdugo.[11]

Nowhere has topography been interrelated with man's destiny as it has in the literature of Latin America. For centuries nature has played a dominant role as a force believed capable of determining the mold of a hero's personality, character, and the success or failure of his mission. For the Argentine Domingo Faustino Sarmiento, who wrote *Facundo* (1851), the vast pampas symbolized a barbaric power which menaced his nation's social, cultural, and economic development. Sarmiento felt the topography of his land "como un ser vivo, como una fiera monstruosa que amenaza la vida argentina."[12]

As an essayist, Sarmiento documented the effect of geography on a historical figure, while, in the following century in *Doña Bárbara* (1929), Rómulo Gallegos creates the inhuman female version of a despotic character who reflects the ferocity of the landscape and is capable of consuming all those who come into contact with her. Santos Luzardo, the hero, struggles against his destructive enemy that Bárbara and the plains of Venezuela (*llanos*) represent as correlatives:

No era sino uno de tantos [enemigos]; a luchar contra la Naturaleza: contra la insalubridad que estaba aniquilando la raza llanera, contra la inundación y la sequía que se disputaban la tierra todo el año, contra el desierto que no deja penetrar la civilización.[13]

The hero of *Doña Bárbara* struggles to dominate and overcome the natural elements and the woman who reflects the *llanos*; his efforts eventually prove successful. The case is not always the same in the telluric novel of Latin America as is revealed in the first great work of this type, *La vorágine* (1924) by José Eustacio Rivera, in which the effect of the jungle on human beings transforms them into barbaric entities, uncontrollable, savage, and violent, then slowly oppresses them into a state of delirium in which reality loses itself in the process of annihilation. The jungle destroys man and beast alike, and those who survive destroy each other. There is no hope for man's salvation in this Green Hell.

So great has the influence of topography been on the writers of Latin America that it no longer is considered by certain critics to have *a* role in literature, but rather *the* role—that of hero in the epic feat of controlling the land for production:

> El héroe fundamental de la literatura hispanoamericana es el selva, el bosque, la pampa, el combate con los elementos adversos, la epopeya anónima del cacao que pinta Jorge Amado, o el ciclo de la caña de azúcar que reconstruye José Lins do Rêgo.[14]

This contest between man and nature in Latin American literature exists also on the analytic plane where critics and essayists have debated the primacy of one over the other. But the preoccupation with man's destiny and the many examples of socially oriented works, even though they may be telluric in content, still indicate a basic concern for the human element. Subjugated, defeated, rarely victorious, the hero and his survival are the crucial involvement of that tradition.

The Epic Hero in Latin America

The discovery of the New World introduced the role nature was to play as a major participant in Latin American literature and at the same time offered a new epic hero who would take his place among the idealized protagonists of literature—the Indian. He was to participate in the realization of the vision of war, pestilence, misery, and death forecast by the Archangel Michael after Satan invaded the Garden of Eden. Like Adam's epic feat, his also was destined to be mainly one of patience and endurance; and salvation for him too would depend on some greater power beyond himself. Although the Indian's literary development may have experienced changes, his actual lot remains, for the most part, essentially the same. The idealization of the autochthonous underdog has its roots in historical events which were documented from the moment of contact with the white man who came to conquer this new Paradise. Along with the discovery of the land came the exploitation of its inhabitants and their abuse, accompanied by an ardent defense of the aborigines as human beings by such committed spiritual leaders as Bartolomé de las Casas who denounced the injustices that flourished during this period.[15] Moral and social aspects of the Indian's predicament were revealed simultaneously in the literary production of the same era, and they continued through the centuries that followed both in epic poetry as well as in other forms of fiction and non-fiction.[16]

The Siglo de Oro or Golden Age of Spain was a time of great artistic achievements, and the historical reality of experience in America stimulated a renaissance in epic poetry. Although the production of epics celebrating heroic figures and events was extensive, few have survived the test of time and literary criticism[17] as has *La Araucana* (published in three parts: 1569, 1578, and 1589). Its author, Alonso de Ercilla y Zúñiga, a Spaniard who took part in the conquest of Chile, clearly indicates his admiration for the Indians who rebelled against their conquerors and fought for liberty. In the prologue to his poem, his eulogy of the so-called savages patently bears a negative reference to the Spanish host to whose ranks he belonged:

Que son pocos los que con tan gran constancia y firmeza han defendido su tierra contra tan fieros enemigos como son los españoles.[18]

Versified denunciation is included in a contrast between the two races with the white man emerging as a demonic bearer

of corruption, destroying existent virtue and sowing vice in its
stead:

> Pero luego nosotros, destruyendo
> todo lo que tocamos de pasada,
> con la usada insolencia el paso abriendo
> les dimos lugar ancho y ancha entrada,
> y la antigua costumbre corrompiendo;
> de los nuevos insultos estragada
> plantó aquí la cudicia su estandarte
> con más seguridad que en otra parte.[19]

The next significant surge of literature in defense of the
autochthonous inhabitants, as well as the masses in general,
appears in the nineteenth century to follow a course of
denunciatory *Dichtung* that attacked political tyrants
emerging from the chaotic state of new nations formed after
the independence of the Spanish colonies. As an example,
while the indigent population remained oppressed, Ecuador
continued producing despotic heads of state but also un-
daunted, crusading writers who were imbued with a concern
for humanity and justice. From Juan Montalvo and Juan
León Mera the literary path led eventually to the "Generation
of the Thirties" in the twentieth century and especially to the
"Grupo de Guayaquil." Montalvo's unrelenting condemnation of Ecuadorian dictatorships is impressively crystallized
in his image of the political monster, a classical Briareus,
whose tyranny can consume and destroy liberty:

> Tiranía es monstruo de cien brazos: alárgalos en todas
> direcciones y toma lo que quiere: hombres, ideas, cosas,
> todo lo devora. Devora ideas ese monstruo: se come hasta
> la imprenta, degüella o destierra filósofos, publicistas,
> filántropos; esto es comerse ideas y destruirlas. El tesoro
> nacional, suyo es; la hacienda de las personas particulares,
> suya es; la riqueza común, suya es: suyo lo superfluo del
> rico, suyo lo necesario del pobre.[20]

For Montalvo the Indian in particular suffered at the hands of iniquitous regimes. So, too, Juan León Mera, active in the politics of Ecuador, made his creative contribution toward vindicating the native in his poetic novel, *Cumandá* (1879). Despite the cumbersome sentimentalism of the story, it has nevertheless recently been recognized for its attributes: the excellent study of Indian customs and the censure of brutality as practiced by landowners who thrived on the lingering injustices of the Spanish colonial system. Mera's contribution stands as an exordium for the decades to come of *indigenista* fiction that would dominate the Spanish American narrative in the following century.[21]

Evolution of the Indian as underdog-hero takes a turn in the first third of the twentieth century when *indigenismo* becomes a literary movement, a style, an ideology almost, characterized by the demand for the native's redemption. The focal point of production and radiation is Ecuador; and this new spirit of Spanish American social humanism, as Jorge Icaza calls it,[22] found expression in a country whose history was comparable to that of most Spanish-speaking republics. In 1930 a volume of short stores was published in Ecuador by three young men who were to be the source of inspiration and controversy in the movement aspiring to improve the condition of the masses. *Los que se van*, the result of a collective venture which also symbolized the comradeship of the authors, Demetrio Aguilera-Malta (b. 1909), Enrique Gil Gilbert (b. 1912), and Joaquín Gallegos Lara (1911-1947), received, on the one hand, little favorable recognition from the Hispanic world with the exception of the Spanish critic Francisco Ferrandiz Albornoz and the Ecuadorian Benjamín Carrión. But it gained the admiration of Jean Cassou, Georges Pillement, and Valéry Larbaud in France. Its earthy realism was shocking for many, however, there were others who "felt" the stories with rare sensitivity; for them they were "contes ardents, sensuels et colorés, d'une chaude odeur de terroir."[23] As a prologue to the forthcoming *indigenista* literature which the three writers would subsequently produce, *Los que se van* had far less of the protest and denunciation which characterized the movement it set into motion; but in their surroundings the protagonists, the *cholo* and *montuvio*,[24] reflected the misery and poverty that were by-products of sociopolitical abuse and neglect. The new hero in his epic tale of suffering and endurance was beginning to emerge, barefoot, tattered, and squalid,[25] to take his place among the literary types who reflected man and his destiny.

This first union of regional writers in Ecuador was known as the "Grupo de Guayaquil" and it included two other men of artistic merit and equal preoccupation with the revindication of the masses, José de la Cuadra (1903-1941) and Alfredo Pareja Diezcanseco (b. 1908). They were soon followed by other young authors collaborating in the exposure of social injustice. Centered mainly about the university cities of Quito, Loja, and Cuenca, they were perhaps not so close in fraternal union as the five from Guayaquil, whom Pareja Diezcanseco described as "cinco dedos de una mano para golpear en la conciencia nacional,"[26] but they were just as fervent in sustaining the momentum initiated by the Grupo de Guayaquil. Nor was the underdog-hero limited to the Indian of the coastal regions and the highlands. In the plethora of fiction the proletariat of the city, black, white, and mestizo, could be found suffering the same exploitation. The decades that followed were filled with revolutionary literature demanding redemption for the indigent. In turn, many critics condemned the narration of violence as excessive; for others the constant moral theme of justice was too propagandistic.

The fact that epic literature is propagandistic, particularly in the hands of the great masters, has been noted as one of its prominent characteristics.[27] C. M. Bowra, in his study of literary epic, analyzes the epic's instructive nature and states how writers of this kind of poetry were "almost forced to point out a moral."[28] The *Aeneid*, the first epic of social commitment, is itself a perfect example, reflecting a background of ethical and spiritual revival.[29] For the Renaissance poets Camões and Tasso, the epic also was intended to serve as a vehicle for rallying the Christian forces of Europe and their respective countries against Islam. Even authentic epics such as the *Iliad* and the *Odyssey* indicate didactic intention within their plot since Homer includes the moral implication by demonstrating the difference between virtue and vice in wifely behavior.[30] *Paradise Lost* is perhaps the most notable expression of religious and moral conviction, for it would hardly be recognizable without its didactic character so evident in the visually demonstrative Book 11 and the aurally instructive Book 12. By the eighteenth century the epic poem becomes basically "a fervent confession of political, religious, and philosophical beliefs, a pamphlet, a polemic treatise, a moral code";[31] and in the nineteenth century the English Romantic poets believed, as Milton did, that the epic should be doctrinal and exemplary to a nation.[32]

The course, then, that epos seems to have followed is one of increased social, religious, or political import. The direction of epic tradition since the literary *Aeneid* indicates a determined commitment not merely to fulfilling the hero's destiny, but also to improving it. Therefore, reformation and edification are part of the epic purpose, and its didactic or exhortatory spirit was evident by Milton's time and vital after his time up to and including the nineteenth century, when epic poetry still found practitioners.[33] For the Latin American writer, this social commitment has always been present, and only the degree of intensity has varied. Agustín Yáñez, a contemporary novelist of Mexico, calls Latin American literature "edifying" for its tendency to diagnose national problems. Those works which do not have that orientation, that is, the social concern and consequent hope for amelioration, are atypical of the general trend.[34]

"Excessive," "violent," "radical," "extreme" were terms

used to qualify the fiction that found its center of radiation in Ecuador during the second quarter of the twentieth century. In its atavistic characters, motivated by wrath and vengeance, it resembled primary epic; in its apocalyptic vision it followed the measure set by Milton; in its scope it was universal. Above all, it fulfilled the choric requisite which is essential to epic literature[35] by presenting the major social concern of not just that moment, but also of previous centuries and of other Latin American countries. If this literature deserved to be qualified by the adjectives "excessive" or "revolutionary," the situation warranted such epithets. Subjugation of the downtrodden for centuries dictated radical denunciation and reform. There could be no limit to the exaggeration of evil and the bestial forms it could assume. Evil was a social and political reality, and the Satanic symbol was omnipresent in many guises ready to destroy, determined to pervert. Regarding this epic characteristic of Latin American literature, Arturo Uslar-Pietri has noted:

> Lo más de ella está concebido como epopeya primitiva, en la que el héroe lucha contra la naturaleza, contra la fatalidad, contra el mal. Es una literatura de símbolos y de arquetipos. El mal y el bien luchan con fórmulas mágicas. El novelista describe la epopeya de la lucha contra el mal que a veces no es sino la avasalladora naturaleza.[36]

And when nature was not the primary source of disaster, the evil element opposing the indigent colored masses, black or Indian, peasant or proletarian, was the political or social institution represented by a dictator, priest, landowner, or Yankee imperialist.

The product of the various literary groups in Ecuador who idealized the masses was indeed revolutionary literature. It forged a collective hero out of a grim reality and sought within a philosophy of Utopian or Marxist socialism the vindication of a figure whose mythification was excessive or fantastic for some critics, while for others the phenomenon was understood to be a continuation of the epic spirit:

La tendencia—natural, casi—en el período heroico de todo movimiento político, es la de crear personajes extraordinarios que sustraigan a las leyes comunes de la vida, esto es, héroes, idealizaciones humanas que se mueven en la esfera del mito. Pero, al fin y al cabo, ¿qué es un héroe sino una estilización unilateral, una descarnación, un desbrozo arbitrario, una parcelación del hombre en momentos y virtudes, una escogencia parcializada de aspectos que pueden servir de levadura al mito? De allí que a pesar de todos los escritores materialistas, la literatura épica revolucionaria tenga las cualidades de la literatura religiosa, fetichista y mesiánica.[37]

This socially oriented literature of Ecuador, with its political ramifications and spiritual fervor, has followed the course of the epic's evolution: for C. S. Lewis "the explicitly religious subject for future epic has been dictated by Virgil"; after the *Iliad* it was "the only further development left."[38] The course led most directly to Milton, whose theological subject still had political implications. The synthesis of politics and religion and the literary manifestation of their odd compatibility is aptly explained by Michael Fixler in the following manner:

Modern politics evolved out of millenial visions. As Karl Mannheim has pointed out, ideologies, in the modern sense, are rooted in the Reformation which established as a definable objective the realization of heaven on earth. Such apocalyptic dreams, the stuff of poetry and prophecy, not only gave form to spiritual yearnings but expressed among Protestants the demand of the dispossessed for social and economic betterment.[39]

Homeric Justification and the Tertiary Phase
of Epic Tradition:
Demetrio Aguilera-Malta

Paradise Lost was, by common consent, the last great epic poem. Epomania characterized the eighteenth century; and although admirable efforts were expended by the Romantic poets in the next century, there were no epicists who could stand the test of time as Milton and his predecessors had. The climax had been reached by the English bard, and the "epic purpose" had to "find some other way of going on."[40]

By the twentieth century the dilemma of the epic's destiny was resolved in the minds of those critics who viewed the type, genre, or tradition as having evolved into the novel. The "living organism," as Aristotle called the epic, had begun like the Homeric poems and had suffered the pangs of growth and modifcations of any vital phenomenon. The contemporary version of epic spirit and manner could be traced to its archetypal antecedents:

> It is in the *Iliad* that we hear for the first time the authentic voice of the Tragic Muse, while the *Odyssey*, with its well-knit plot, psychological interest and its interplay of characters, is the true ancestor of the long line of novels that have followed it.[41]

Although the close relationship between the dramatic and the epic manner is evident in the Homeric poems, the bond between these individual manifestations finds its source in the realm of spiritual and religious expression, for its antiquity is more remote than Western literature. Gertrude Levy notes the recitation of the Mesopotamian epic of creation, *Enuma Elish*, as part of the New Year's rites or ceremonies for renewal of kingship and the state.[42] Thus primary epic and the blend of Homeric elements to produce the innovation called "secondary epic," created by Virgil, are intimately related to drama and particularly to tragedy.[43] The two literary epics, the *Aeneid* and *Paradise Lost*, are perhaps the most ancient in the spirit of death and regeneration which permeates them and unites them to the original epic of creation: out of the ashes of Troy would emerge Rome, and man would be redeemed after Adam's tragic fall.

What may be termed the "tertiary phase" of epic tradition is, then, a return to the spirit of the great examples of epic literature which reveal the essential concern for man's destiny while he stands in the midst of death and misery. Works in the modern era which contain that epic spirit of heroic poems and reveal a certain grandeur in the sweep of the narration, that communicate the intensity of the dramatic moment, that possess the miscellaneous elements molded by the poet's imagination into the unique recounting of timeless truths, those works may be classified as belonging to the third stage of epic development. Many have been novels,[44] but the tertiary phase of epic tradition is such in scope that it can include the production of works by a group, as in the case of the Ecuadorian writers of Indianist literature, or as is the subject of this study, one author whose theater and prose fiction consistently exhibit the elements first manifested in the drama and narration of heroic figures in the *Iliad* and the *Odyssey* and in the literary innovations of epics since the Homeric poems.

When the Latin American critic Luis Alberto Sánchez commented, "Por las sendas de lo provincial se llega a lo ecuménico,"[45] he was unknowlingly predicting the course that Demetrio Aguilera-Malta was to follow after the publication of *Los que se van*. The volume which contains his short stories was his first major work of regional or *costumbrista* caliber, and together with the famous *Don Goyo* (1933) and *La isla virgen* (1942), they formed almost a saga depicting the life of the coastal and island Indian of Ecuador.

Aguilera-Malta's regional underdog-hero of Ecuador was soon joined by other individual or collective heroes who represented the downtrodden and oppressed beyond South America. During the five years that passed after the publication of *Los que se van,* two *réportage*-like novels appeared: *Canal Zone* (1935), and *¡Madrid!: reportaje novelado de una retaguardia heroica* (1936). The spirit of the first was one of protest similar to that which sought justice for the Indian in Ecuador's *indigenista* movement, only this time the mass hero was represented by the blacks of Panama and the republic itself struggling to survive the lengthy period of economic and spiritual rape which followed its independence from Colombia. Then in Spain, while witnessing the outbreak of the Spanish Civil War,[46] Demetrio Aguilera-Malta found inspiration in the courage of the liberal forces and their unparalleled but hapless defense of the capital against the overwhelming power of the Nationalists. The significance of these two réportages, *¡Madrid!* and *Canal Zone,* indicates more than a departure from the telluric, *indigenista* literature which was flourishing in that decade. What was revealed in their timeliness and style was a spirit and technique familiar to Hispanic epic tradition—a propensity for narrating events of actuality as the Spanish *jongleurs* did in the eleventh century, and not only those legends of remote history.[47] *¡Madrid!* particularly recalls the rhythmic assonance of the epic and ballad with their repetition of refrains and even the medieval convention of the *ubi sunt*:

¿Qué se han hecho las alegrías solares del Retiro, Rosales, la Moncloa, las grandes plazas bulliciosas, las amplias avenidas de compacta masa humana? ¿Qué se han hecho las parejas de novios de los cines, de los sitios confidenciales? ¿Qué se han hecho los bailes públicos de los locales descubiertos? ¿Qué se han hecho los desfiles domingueros a los campos sazonados de entusiasmo?[48]

With *España leal* (1938), whose heroine achieves the stature of a St. Joan in the Spanish Civil War, Aguilera-

Malta launches his career as playwright and dedicates his creative efforts almost entirely to the stage and cinema. The underdog-hero assumes many postures while his persecutors remain essentially symbols of evil in various forms culled from contemporary society: the sadistic students whose father has employed a teacher struggling to preserve his ideals (*Lázaro*, 1941), the perverted scientist who uses his genius to create genocidal devices (*No bastan los átomos*, 1954), the owner and audience of a nightclub where black entertainers are forced to accept verbal abuse (*Dientes blancos*, 1955), the jaguar or devil incarnate stalking his prey (*El tigre*, 1956), and the corrupt lawyer who has it within his power to destroy an entire family (*Honorarios*, 1957). Demetrio Aguilera-Malta's theater is universal in its theme of injustice, and his talents have undoubtedly contributed to the prestige of the dramatic arts in Latin America, where he has earned the respect of notable critics who consider him among the best playwrights of Ecuador and Spanish America.[49]

Since the 1950s, however, Aguilera-Malta has devoted his talents almost exclusively to the narrative. Of notable exception is an unusually imaginative play, *Infierno negro* (1967), whose theme of racial injustice is developed in a combination of expressionistic and classical techniques, incorporating as well excerpts from Afro-Hispanic and *Négritude* poetry. In 1960 another *réportage* novel is published about the Cuban Revolution, *Una cruz en la Sierra Maestra*, after which appear three historical novels, to the delight of those readers who lamented the dearth of historical or biographical fiction in Latin America.[50] *La caballeresa del sol* (1964) deals with Simón Bolívar and his mistress Manuela Sáenz; *El Quijote de El Dorado* (1964) recounts the adventures of Francisco de Orellana, discoverer of the Amazon River; and *Un nuevo mar para el rey* (1965) concerns Balboa, the Indian princess Anayansi, and the Pacific Ocean. In these episodes of Latin American history,[51] the journalist in Aguilera-Malta unites with the scholar to re-create the drama of two heroic epochs in history: the discovery and exploration of the New World and the fight for the American colonies' independence three centuries later. Aguilera-Malta, who has conveyed the significance of nature as he has experienced it, is equally adept at communicating the same spiritual function of topography regardless of the temporal remoteness in which these novels are set.

After the *Episodios americanos,* Aguilera-Malta writes two of his finest novels. The first, *Siete lunas y siete serpientes* (1970), cannot be categorized simply as "telluric," for it is more than a narrative about the inhabitants of coastal and tropical Ecuador. It is a blend of African, Indian, and Christian myths interwoven with the theme of man's survival in the perennial confrontation of good and evil. The typology of the novel, culled from the land and sea, primitive ritual, and Catholic doctrine, is consubstantially structured to determine the basic course to be followed for achieving salvation—love and harmony among human and beast, the only weapons that have some effect on Satan and his agents. The most recent novel, *El secuestro del general* (1973), is an original contribution to the currently popular narratives on Latin American dictatorships. Its uniqueness lies in Aguilera-Malta's uncanny talent for reducing economic and political tyranny to pristine representations: a head of state who is a skeleton that communicates with the nation by means of cassettes inserted in his thorax, and his Minister of War, a gorilla-like, barbaric general whose passion for a fruit leads to his kidnapping and eventual undoing.

In the panorama of literature created by Demetrio Aguilera-Malta, the epic spirit is pervasive. There is universality in scope whether the work is a short theatrical piece or a regional novel whose setting is a small island in the Guayas Archipelago. Protagonists range from the obscure *cholo* whose existence depends on the natural environment, to heroes of imposing historic stature such as Simón Bolívar, who regarded life and the realization of an ideal as correlatives. Like Milton, Aguilera-Malta's preocupation is with man and his destiny, and the intensity of each one's involvement with social and political forces has served to confirm a belief in man's essential nobility in the face of vilification or annihilation.

Aguilera-Malta, however, as much a product of his time and his nation's history as was Milton, combines a sense of the universal in epic tradition with the great influence of nature and its creatures—elements without which the epic of Latin America (which is still being written) could never have been conceived. For him the phenomena of the land and sea, which he understands and loves, have been more than inspirational in re-creating that epic spirit of New and Old World traditions. But Homer, too, saw the forces of nature assuming a fundamental role in determining his hero's destiny; and Virgil, long after Kronos had lost his throne and sought refuge in Italy, wrote his masterpiece with a sustained note of melancholy as he recalled a pastoral nation facing oncoming progress and civilization which would begin with Aeneas's victory.

This study proposes to discuss the dramatic and novelistic works of Demetrio Aguilera-Malta as a representative author of what I have called the "tertiary phase" of epic tradition, a phase which continues primary and secondary epic in a like, yet different manner. The emphasis will be placed on the role of nature and its components (topography, vegetation, and zoological phenomena) and will deal with the function of these elements in heroic poems of established fame and in the fiction of Aguilera-Malta. The epic concern will involve the familiar and perennial opposition of good and evil as they are manifested in the struggle of all heroes, individual or collective, in their quest for survival and justice.

Notes

1. C. S. Lewis, *A Preface to "Paradise Lost"* (London: Oxford University Press, 1960), p. 39.

2. See Gertrude Levy, *The Sword from the Rock* (London: Faber & Faber, 1953). Although the epic of creation *Enuma Elish* (3d millennium B.C.) is Near Eastern, there is substantial evidence that a link exists between the epics of that area and the Homeric poems. Other works of interest which trace the origins of Western epic are: Cyrus H. Gordon, *Before the Bible* (New York: Harper & Row, 1962), chap. 7; and T. B. L. Webster, *From Mycenae to Homer* (New York: Praeger, 1959), chap. 3.

3. The interrelationship of men and gods is analyzed by Cedric H. Whitman in *Homer and the Heroic Tradition* (Cambridge, Mass.: Harvard University Press, 1959), chap. 10.

4. Milton suggests this himself:

Since first this subject for Heroic Song
Pleas'd me long choosing, and beginning late;
Not sedulous by Nature to indite
Wars, hitherto the only Argument
Heroic deem'd, chief maistry to dissect
With long and tedious havoc fabl'd Knights
In Battles feign'd: the better fortitude
Of Patience and Heroic Martyrdom
Unsung. . . .

From John Milton, *Paradise Lost*, ed. Merritt Y. Hughes (New York: Odyssey Press, 1935), 9. 25-33. Future references to this work and edition will appear in abbreviated form directly after the citation (e.g., *P.L.* 9. 25-33).

5. *Aeneid*, trans. James H. Mantinband (New York: Frederick Ungar, 1964), 1. 202-7. Future references to this work and edition will appear in abbreviated form directly after the citation (e.g., *Aen.* 1. 204-7).

6. Lascelles Abercrombie, *The Epic*, 2d ed. (London: Secker, Ltd., 1922), p. 92.

7. Homeric similes and their function are analyzed by Whitman, *Homer and the Heroic Tradition*, pp. 223-39, 296.

8. Marianna Woodhull, *The Epic of "Paradise Lost"* (New York: The Knickerbocker Press, 1907), p. 46. This quality is also deemed "a truly English combination"—a point open to question since the blend of lyricism and nature could refer to Hispanic poetry as well.

9. Virgil's *Eclogues* (37 B.C.) and *Georgics* (30 B.C.) are clearly examples of this sensitivity which draws nature and man closer together. See Commager's "Introduction" to *Virgil: A Collection of Critical Essays*, ed. Steele Commager (Englewood Cliffs, N.J.: Prentice-Hall, 1966).

10. *Iliad*, trans. Richmond Lattimore (Chicago: University of Chicago Press, 1951), 5. 87-92. Future references to this work and edition will appear in abbreviated form directly after the citation (e.g., *Il.* 5. 87-92).

11. Uriel Ospina, *Problemas y perspectivas de la novela americana* (Bogotá: Tercer Mundo, 1964), p. 53.

12. Arturo Uslar-Pietri, "Lo criollo en la literatura," *Cuadernos Americanos*, 49 (1950): 270.

13. Rómulo Gallegos, *Doña Bárbara* (Barcelona: Araluce, 1929), p. 29.

14. Ricardo Latcham, "La historia del criollismo," *El criollismo* (Santiago, Chile: Ed. Universitaria, n.d.), p. 45. The same viewpoint is expressed by Pedro Grases in "De la novela en América," *Dos estudios* (Caracas: Talleres de la C.A. Artes Gráficas, 1943), p. 23.

15. Marcel Brion details the background of this period and the life of Las Casas in *Bartolomé de las Casas* (Mexico: Divulgación, 1953).

16. See Concha Meléndez, *La novela indianista en Hispanoamérica*, 2nd ed. (Rio Piedras: Universidad de Puerto Rico, 1961).

17. See Frank Pierce, *La poesía épica del Siglo de Oro*, 2nd ed., rev. (Madrid: Gredos, 1968).

18. Alonso de Ercilla y Zúñiga, *La Araucana*, intro. and notes by Juan Loveluck (Santiago, Chile: Zig-Zag, 1958), p. 31.

19. Ercilla y Zúñiga, *La Araucana,* Canto 36. 105-12.

20. Juan Montalvo, *Las catilinarias* (Paris: Garnier, 1929), I, 6.

21. See the analysis of Mera's novel and its literary and sociological value in Antonio Sacoto, *The Indian in the Ecuadorian Novel* (New York: Las Américas, 1967), pp. 37-62. For a detailed analysis of Ecuador's novel in the light of historical and sociopolitical events see Angel F. Rojas, *La novela ecuatoriana* (Mexico: Fondo de Cultura Económica, 1948).

22. Jorge Icaza, "Relato, espíritu unificador en la Generación del año '30," *Revista Iberoamericana* 32, no. 62 (1966): 212.

23. Georges Pillement, *Les Conteurs hispano-americains* (Paris: Delagrave, 1933), p. 18. See also Edmundo Rivadeneira, *La moderna novela ecuatoriana* (Quito: Casa de la Cultura Ecuatoriana, 1958), pp. 254-55.

24. This *cholo*, not to be confused with the *cholo* of the Andean highlands who was the subject matter of Jorge Icaza in *Huasipungo* (1934), is the indigenous inhabitant of the islands and coast of Ecuador. The *montuvio* also dwells in the lowland tropics, but his racial hybridism includes a large Negro strain in addition to the Indian. See José de la Cuadra, "El montuvio ecuatoriano" in *Obras completas* (Quito: Casa de la Cultura Ecuatoriana, 1958).

25. This unglamorous physical picture of a hero is not unusual. Joseph Campbell notes other famous gods and heroes (Wotan, Viracocha, Edshu) appearing as wandering mendicants who assume this posture as the prerequisite of anonymity before their rebirth. See *The Hero with a Thousand Faces* (Cleveland: World, 1956), p. 237.

26. In Icaza, "Relato, espíritu unificador en la Generación del año 30," p. 211.

27. Brian Wilkie, *Romantic Poets and Epic Tradition* (Madison-Milwaukee: University of Wisconsin Press, 1965), p. 44.

28. C. M. Bowra, *From Virgil to Milton* (London-New York: Macmillan, 1962), p. 16.

29. Ibid., p. 23.

30. L. A. Post, *From Homer to Menander* (Berkeley-Los Angeles: University of California Press, 1951), pp. 26-33.

31. Peter Hägin, *The Epic Hero and the Decline of Heroic Poetry* (Berne: Francke Verlag, 1964), p. 126.

32. Wilkie, *Romantic Poets and Epic Tradition*, p. 23.

33. Ibid., p. 49. The author also discusses the condemnation of war that Southey makes in his epic *Joan*, by using the technique of detailing a warrior's fight and death.

34. "El contenido social de la literatura iberoamericana," *Jornadas* (Mexico: Colegio de México, 1944) 14: 17.

35. E. M. W. Tillyard, *The English Epic and Its Background* (London: Chatto and Windus, 1954), pp. 12-13. This choric quality expresses the feeling of a large group of people living in or near the poet's own time. Tillyard also points out that the choric nature of epic allows for flexibility of form and does not necessitate verse.

36. Uslar-Pietri, "Lo criollo en la literatura," p. 274.

37. Antonio García *Pasado y presente del indio* (Bogotá: Centro, 1939), pp. 109-10.

38. Lewis, *A Preface to "Paradise Lost,"* p. 39.

39. Michael Fixler, *Milton and the Kingdoms of God* (Evanston: Northwestern University Press, 1964), p. 9.

40. Abercrombie, *The Epic*, p. 118.

41. E. V. Rieu, "Introduction" to the *Odyssey* (New York: Penguin Books, 1947), p. viii.

42. Levy, *The Sword from the Rock*, p. 23.

43. Aristotle in his *Art of Poetry* draws many parallels between tragedy and epic and notes that all the elements of the latter were to be found in tragedy. See *Aristotle*, trans. Philip Wheelwright (New York: Odyssey Press, 1951), p. 325.

44. See E. M. W. Tillyard, *The Epic Strain in the English Novel* (Fairlawn, N.J.: Essential Books, 1958).

45. Luis Alberto Sánchez, *Vida y pasión de la cultura en América* (Santiago, Chile: América, 1936), p. 131.

46. An excerpt from *¡Madrid!* is included in the anthology *Los que fueron a España* (Buenos Aires: Jorge Alvarez, 1966), pp. 123-27. The volume contains others such as Hemingway, Dos Passos, Neruda, Malraux, etc.

47. The Spanish epics were unique in their historicity or veracity as were also the romances or ballads, particularly the border ballads *(fronterizos)* of the fifteenth century which narrated events taking place in the last stronghold of the Moors, Granada. For a full explanation of this *ad informationem* or *noticioso* quality of Spanish epic and ballad see Ramón Menéndez Pidal, *Romancero hispánico* (Madrid: Espasa-Calpe, 1953), 1: 301-304.

48. *¡Madrid!: reportaje novelado de una retaguardia heroica*, 4th ed. (Santiago, Chile: Ercilla, 1937), p. 115. Future references to this work will appear in abbreviated form after the citation (e.g., *Madrid*, 115).

49. See Hernán Rodríguez Castelo, "Teatro ecuatoriano," *Cuadernos Hispano-americanos*, no. 172 (April 1964): 81-119; and Emmanuel Carballo's prologue to *Trilogía ecuatoriana* (Mexico: Andrea, 1959). Aguilera-Malta's theater has also

been the subject of a study by Gerardo A. Luzuriaga, *Del realismo al expresionismo: el teatro de Aguilera-Malta* (Madrid: Plaza Mayor, 1971).

50. Fernando Alegría indicates this gap in the literature of Latin America, but finds that the *réportage* is a substitute for the historical novel with the chronological perspective adjusted. See "La novela iberoamericana," in *Memoria del Quinto Congreso del Instituto Internacional de Literatura Iberoamericana*, ed. Arturo Torres-Rioseco (Albuquerque: University of New Mexico Press, 1952), p. 72.

51. The trilogy is part of a projected series of novels, *Episodios americanos*, whose themes and heroes represent great moments in the course of Latin America's development.

2
The Role of Nature in Epic Tradition: Topography

Nature in the course of epic evolution has manifested a complex role in the hero's destiny. From the anthropomorphic deity who represented the supernatural force challenging or destroying man in his impotent capacity as a human being, it has often been relegated to the position of setting or background. There, however, the natural phenomena have continued to fire the poet's imagination and to exert their influence upon the characters and action of the poem itself. As a vibrant, palpitating entity, the environment often has shared the joys and sorrows of the epic heroes. In Tasso's *Gerusalemme Liberata*, the successful deliverance of the Holy City is applauded by nature as Goffredo displays his banner upon the walls:

> La vincitrice insegna in mille giri
> Alteramente si rivolge intorno;
> E par che in lei più reverente spiri
> L'aura, e che splenda in lei più chiaro il giorno:
> Ch'ogni dardo, ogni stral ch'in lei si tiri,
> O la declini, o faccia indi ritorno:
> Par che Sïòn, par che l'opposto monte
> Lieto l'adori, e inchini a lei la fronte.[1]

In the earthly Paradise of Adam and Eve, the harmony and

happiness of the First Couple are also shared by the surroundings:

> . . .for Nature here
> Wanton'd as in her prime, and play'd at will
> Her Virgin Fancies, pouring forth more sweet,
> Wild above Rule or Act, enormous bliss.
>
> [*P.L.* 5. 294-97]

Topography is equally sensitive to the commission of the act of disobedience when Eve bites the apple (9. 782-84), and when the sin is compounded by Adam's participation in the rite of knowledge:

> Earth trembl'd from her entrails, as again
> In pangs, and Nature gave a second groan
> Sky low'r'd and muttering Thunder, some sad drops
> Wept at completing of the mortal Sin
> Original. . . .
>
> [*P.L.* 9. 1000-1004]

Luís de Camões, who himself knew the majesty and power of the seas and had experienced nature in the most exotic circumstances, animates landscape to heighten the loss of a great and virtuous king, Afonso Henriques:

> Os altos promotórios o choraram,
> E dos rios as águas saudosas
> Os semeados campos alagaram
> Con lágrimas correndo piedosas.[2]

Camões, indeed, as the other great masters of epic art, appreciated nature in its hylozoic expression, in all of its splendid majesty, as well as its devastating potential. Especially as a product of the Renaissance, Camões knew how to mold topography and its components into the ideal and idyllic background for the pleasures of love.

The Isles of Love

When Camões wrote his great epic, *Os Lusíadas*, he ended the poem in an atmosphere quite removed from the turbulence of the battlefield and the horrors of war. In contrast to the abuse which the Portuguese suffer at the hands of Bacchus, Venus protects them and rewards their heroism with a day's sojourn of feasting and sensual delights on the "Isle of Loves." Vasco da Gama and his men are surrounded by the beauty and attentions of the sea nymphs in the refreshing bucolic setting of fountains and greenery:

> Três fermosos outeiros se mostravam,
> Erguidos com soberba graciosa,
> Que de gramíneo esmalte se adornavam,
> Na fermosa ilha, alegre e deleitosa;
> Claras fontes e límpidas manavam
> Do cume, que a verdura tem viçosa;
> Por entre pedras alvas se deriva
> A sonorosa linfa fugitiva.
>
> [*Lus.* 9. 54]

Within a perfect blend of landscape and love, the warriors indulge themselves participating in the joys of living before returning to Portugal. Camões had been influenced by the presentation of sensual themes in the chivalric epics of Boiardo and Ariosto, yet restraint was demanded by the inherent seriousness of his epic purpose which accounts for his explaining the festivities of some seventy stanzas (18, when Venus decides to reward the heroes, through 87) as allegorical in essence. According to Camões, the frolicking, passionate activity represents honor and glory which the Portuguese heroes richly deserve[3]:

> Que as Ninfas do Oceano tão fermosas,
> Tétis e a Ilha angélica pintada,

Outra cousa não e que as deleitosas
Honras que a vida fazem sublimada.

[*Lus.* 9. 89. 1-4]

But the role of the nymphs is not limited merely to
providing entertainment for the men, for after a dinner of
sumptuous fare and conversation, one of the nymphs takes
up a musical instrument and midst her verses of prophecy for
Portugal, Gama, and the war against Islam, the didactic,
moralizing aim of serious epic poetry emerges, and the theme
of justice with its relationship to virtue appears:

Quem faz injúria vil e sem razão,
Com forças e poder em que está posto,
Não vence,—que a vitória verdadeira
E saber ter justiça nua e inteira.

[*Lus.* 10. 58. 5-8]

Torquato Tasso, a contemporary of Camões, also uses the
Isle-of-Love convention, but his technique is more closely
related to the writers of chivalric epic, Boiardo and Ariosto.
The purpose is still didactic and moral but the method is more
overtly allegorical. Armida, symbol of the evil that sorcery
and the Moslem faith represent, entices Rinaldo, the
Christian knight, and compels him to ignore the call of duty
by returning with her to her palace and beautiful garden. This
idyllic spot is located on the top of a mountain found on the
island of Tenerife off the coast of Africa. Ubaldo and Carlo,
the knights sent to rescue Rinaldo, are overwhelmed by the
charm of eternal springtime that the enchanted garden
possesses. Harmony is perfect even between the wind and the
birds:

Vezzosi augelli infra le verdi fronde
Temprano a prova lascivette note.
Mormora l'aura, e fa le foglie e l'onde

Garrir, che variamente ella percote.
Quando taccion gli augelli alto risponde;
Quando cantan gli augei, più lieve scote;
Sia caso od arte, or accompagna, ed ora
Alterna i versi lor la music'òra
[*G.L.* 16. 12]

Surrounded by the fragrant trees and flowers, the lovers sit by the lakeside exchanging sighs and embraces, oblivious to their observers. The atmosphere is described to reflect the mood of love and is in complete contrast to the symbolic, negative interpretation the knights are given when the Christian sage directs them to the island which he calls a "terra in paesi incogniti ed infidi" (14. 35: 4).

Armida's witchcraft suits her evil purpose, and deception is implied when the Sage refers to the garden's true character and function in his description.[4] Rinaldo's predicament delays his participation as Christian knight in the epic feat awaiting him outside the walls of Jerusalem, and the deadly sin of unheroic sloth is really what the false paradisaical garden symbolizes. Armida's reaction to Rinaldo's departure is a violent one: she destroys garden and castle and vows vengeance by any means. The rejected mistress will resort to her craft in combatting those virtues which strengthen the Crusader's commitment to duty.

In Homer's *Odyssey*, where the Isle-of-Love convention undoubtedly found its origin, the beauty of the environment is equally inviting. Hermes, sent on his mission to Calypso for the release of Odysseus, is as stunned as the Christian knights by the idyllic atmosphere which nature provides for the lovers:

There were four fountains, and each of them ran shining
    water,
each next to each, but turned to run in sundry directions;
and round about there were meadows growing soft with
    parsley

and violets, and even a god who came into that place would have admired what he saw, the heart delighted within him.[5]

Calypso is almost as bitter as Armida when confronted with losing her lover, but she cooperates at the behest of a higher command and even provides the materials which Odysseus will need to build his vessel and leave Ogygia. There is a feeling of equanimity and understanding as preparations are made for the Greek warrior's departure, and Odysseus to the very end treats Calypso with the consideration befitting his dedicated hostess. They spend one last night in each other's arms, and the following day the hero leaves the Isle of Love assured that the nymph is not planning "some painful trial" for him (*Od.* 5. 179)

In interpreting this episode of heroic inactivity, some critics dismiss it, as well as the Circean sojourn, as a temptation trial in which the female-obstacle convention familiar to most epics is used. Another theory revolves about the name of the goddess, which suggests concealment or cover,[6] thus relating the hero to a state removed from the world of activity, as if in a womb. This condition of withdrawal and isolation can grant him no fame; it is in fact equivalent to being dead.[7] The Ogygia experience, then, marks a point of passage from "unbirth" or death from whence the hero finally emerges, restored, rejuvenated, and capable of assuming the most important role of all—that of executing justice within his household.

Calypso's function primarily is to participate in Odysseus's rebirth; it is not instructional as is the part Circe plays which is highly significant in the change of his character and attitude toward the gods. Circe's island, Aeaea, unlike Calypso's, is not described in terms of a pastoral setting, for the attention is centered about the goddess' didactic role. After the swine metamorphosis episode, Odysseus and his crew are persuaded to stay and content themselves for a year on the island, feasting and relaxing. Circe, like Calypso, also shares her bed with Odysseus, regrets his departure, but decides to assist him and his men by offering advice which will prove essential to Odysseus's survival. The counseling is both religious and practical, and is in reality a fulfillment of the major function of the sorceress.[8]

The guidance that Circe gives the Sacker of Cities which will determine his salvation is one of abstinence. He and his men are to avoid the Symplegades (Roving Rocks), the Whirlpool, the monster Scylla, whom Odysseus would prefer fighting to losing six friends to her. When he proposes this to Circe, she answers:

> "Hardy man, your mind is full forever of fighting
> and battle work. Will you not give way even to
>   the immortals?"
>
> [*Od.* 12. 116-17]

Ultimately, all of the crew die after committing the sacrilege of slaughtering Helios's cattle. But their leader survives because he has followed the counsel of Circe and the prophet Tiresias, to whom he was also directed by the goddess.

The experience on the island of Aeaea and the subsequent ones stand as a contrast in adventures and character to the previous peripatetic trials. Here Odysseus loses his "recklessness" as Eurylochus labels his earlier pattern, and becomes more patient, more enduring, and less aggressive. He is in complete control of his passions, while his companions have revealed no change in their desires or behavior despite their mishap on Circe's island. For the worthy student, Odysseus, one year on this Isle of Love and the relationship with Circe determine a successful conclusion to his wanderings and adventures.

Most cases of the Isle-of-Love convention in epic poetry are episodic, and as doctrinal as their function might be, no example assumes a duration of significance as the one involving man's destiny in *Paradise Lost*. Milton's cosmology determines the setting of Eden as that of a "happy Isle" (*P.L.* 2. 410),⁹ whose idyllic harmony is a reflection of celestial Paradise. Bathed in an atmosphere of eternal springtime to juxtapose the First Couple's immortality, the Garden's perfection soon will be destroyed with the tasting of the apple. Their cycle of existence moves from bliss to suffering as transgression takes place, effecting their exile and determining the destiny of nature itself.

Within the isolated Garden lies another private realm which enhances the bond between nature and Adam and Eve—the Bower. The union of Adam and his wife is inviolable here, even for Satan, and nature's role is sensually decorative, while the surrounding elements and creatures join in concerted celebration as the lovers enter the Bower for the first time:

> . . .the Earth
> Gave sign of gratulation, and each Hill;
> Joyous the Birds; fresh Gales and gentle Airs
> Whisper'd it to the Woods, and from their wings
> Flung Rose, flung Odours from the spicy Shrub,
> Disporting, till the amorous Bird of Night
> Sung Spousal, and bid haste the Ev'ning Star
> On his Hill top, to light the bridal Lamp.
>
> [*P.L.* 8. 513-20]

There is a mutual involvement among the inhabitants of Eden and nature that reflects spiritual harmony and God's perfection. Disruption of this balance is a consequence of the act of disobedience and results not only in discord between Adam and Eve, but in a change in the behavior of natural phenomena as well. Verbal abuse exhibited by Adam in his disdain for his wife after her Fall is extended to physical violence between the once gentle creatures:

Beast now with Beast gan war, and Fowl with Fowl,

And Fish with Fish; to graze the Herb all leaving
Devour'd each other. . . .

[*P.L.* 10. 710-12]

The successive post-lapsarian events indicate not simply a
changed future for Adam and Eve; they corroborate the
prominent role nature will play in man's existence. Milton's
interpretation of topography and his use of animals stress this
interdependence of all God's creations. A serpent's body
camouflages the perpetrator of man's downfall, while a fruit
serves as the instrument of discord and destruction. The way
that man goes, so does nature; the rose will now sprout
thorns and the earth begins to experience pain with each bite
of the interdicted fruit. The isolated Bower must be
abandoned to the violation of the creatures heretofore denied
entrance, and the peaceful, verdant setting of Eden too will
fade with the new law of seasonal change.[10]
Such harmony was almost too perfect to survive indefi-
nitely. As in most isles of love, the stay in Eden was
temporary, and the world with its responsibilities must
eventually be faced. But for Eve, especially, the loss of Eden
is worse than her forsaken immortality:

O unexpected stroke worse than Death!
Must I thus leave thee Paradise? thus leave
The Native Soil, these happy walks and Shades,
Fit Haunt of Gods?. . .

[*P.L.* 11. 268-71]

Not only is the Garden a cherished entity of almost human
caliber, but the flowers themselves are addressed as if they
were Eve's offspring:

. . .O flow'rs
That never will in other Climate grow,
My early visitation, and my last
At Ev'n, which I bred up with tender hand
From the first op'ning bud, and gave ye Names,

[*P.L.* 11. 273-77]

Thus when Milton repeats the modifier "happy" in reference to Eden, he is summarizing what was once the perfectly integrated state of bliss—harmony and love between man and woman, their Maker, and the various elements of nature which functioned as part of the ideal union. Miltonic expressionism necessitated maximum participation of nature and its components beyond that of a purely decorative or antagonistic role. This synergetic performance was to appear again in literary currents of other lands where topography, vegetation, and the animal kingdom combined actively to influence the destiny of human beings who had inherited the lot of the first underdogs, Adam and Eve.

Demetrio Aguilera-Malta's Isles of Love perform many functions in his regional works, and nature as landscape and setting assumes various roles comparable to those portrayed in past epic literature. The Guayas Archipelago, located off the coast of Ecuador, is also the scene of the short stories in *Los que se van* and the three novels *Don Goyo, La isla virgen,* and *Siete lunas y siete serpientes*. Dependent on the sea that surrounds him and the imposing mangroves (*mangles*) that encircle his island, the *cholo* stands as a unique entity, heroic in his epic feat, which is mainly one of survival in the fight against natural and social menaces. Simple as his needs may be, his life is made more complex by the relationship he maintains with the atmosphere that is part of him. The vegetation in the supreme image of the mangrove tree protects him as it does the soil from the erosion of outside forces, provides him with a means of sustenance, and occasionally rebels when not respected.

The role of nature in these works of Aguilera-Malta goes beyond serving purely as a background or antagonist so familiar in the telluric fiction of Latin America. In *Don Goyo* earth and sea are dynamic forces even when they are introduced as a setting for lovers. Gertru, Don Goyo's daughter, and Cusumbo, her sweetheart, formerly a native of the higher *montuvio* region, escape to the shore to be alone, where they embrace sitting on top of the trunk of a mangrove tree. Nature's phenomena, curious and impatient, just as they observe Adam and Eve entering the Bower, begin an animated effort in favor of uniting the lovers:

> Se apretaban el uno al otro, como si estuvieran encrustados.
> Los mangles simulaban inclinarse sonrientes para oírlos. Soplaba el norte franco, torpemente, pegándoles la ropa al cuerpo, sacudiéndoselas, tal que si quisiera desnudarlos.[11]

In another instance, the Isle of Love begins as a setting for an encounter between former sweethearts. In the short story "El cholo que se vengó," Melquíades returns to take his revenge against Andrea, who had left him for another. The sea reacts in symphonic approval to the monologue of revilement, the *cholo*'s only weapon:

> La playa se cubría de espuma. Allí el mar azotaba con furor. Y las olas enormes caían como peces multicolores sobre las piedras. Andrea lo escuchaba en silencio.[12]

Having suffered violence and abuse at the hands of the man for whom she rejected Melquíades, the *chola* listens to a recapitulation of her own and her children's misery without saying a word while the sea contrasts her silence and immobility:

> Una ola como *raya* inmensa y transparente cayó a sus pies interrumpiéndole. El mar lanzaba gritos ensordecedores.
> [L.Q.S.V. 137]

As Melquíades' verbal attack comes to a close, the sea follows his measure and slowly withdraws, and the elements of nature return to their normal function in the background:

El frío era más fuerte. La noche más oscura. El
mar empezaba a calmarse. Las olas llegaban a desmayar
suavemente en la orilla.

[*L.Q.S.V.* 138]

Nature in "El cholo que se vengó" is raised to the highest
plane of a humanized entity which could be interpreted as
Melquíades' alter ego, the other part of him which would like
to strike Andrea physically and execute all the violence
suggested by the raging waters. This sensitive performance of
the water and the silence of the *chola* result in an exchange of
roles, relegating Andrea to the position of background or
setting, while the natural forces involved assume the
proportions of a major character. It has been noted in this
much acclaimed short story that the fury and subsequent
calm of the sea suggest a pattern of sexual activity in the most
primitive sense by the element itself.[13] Sexual performance by
natural phenomena is by no means unusual in literature.
Milton himself in his frequent parallels between man and
nature describes in unmistakably anthropomorphic terms
creative or procreative activity:

> . . .While now the mounted Sun
> Shot down direct his fervid Rays, to warm
> Earth's inmost womb. . . .

[*P.L.* 5. 300-302]

The impression is the same when Raphael describes the act of
creation to Adam:

> The Earth was form'd, but in the Womb as yet
> Of Waters, Embryon immature involv'd,
> Appear'd not: over all the face of Earth
> Main Ocean flow'd, not idle, but with warm
> Prolific humour soft'ning all her Globe,
> Fermented the great Mother to conceive,
> Satiate with genial moisture. . . .

[*P.L.* 7. 276-82]

Nor is topographical syngenesis unusual in the works of Aguilera-Malta. Myth and imagination combine to depict the islands and the mangrove trees in the midst of an act of love that will insure perpetuation of the isles:

> Era una fiesta extraña la de estas agitaciones nupciales. Se estiraban los maridos nervudos. Jadeaban estruendosamente, en un desbordamiento de virilidad. Parecían catanudos verticales, catanudos tornados remezón de lujuria y furor de correntada. Después el espasmo, la semilla, la semilla humilde, loca, que iría a flotar, abandonada sobre el océano, hasta encontrar otra isla madrehembra, a la cual pudiera sacarle vida para regarle con la lluvia de la savia que adquiriera.
>
> [*Don Goyo*, 85]

The island setting has traditionally been utilized as a haven for the pleasures of love or the tranquility of the individual, and its isolated structure enhances the mood of security that is intrinsically related to the harmony of earthly paradises. Its very structure, however, paradoxically converts insular topography into a realm more vulnerable to and more radically affected by intrusion. The unexpected invasion of the island may cause the separation of the lovers as in the case of Hermes's sudden arrival on Ogygia, or the appearance of Ubaldo and Carlo in Armida's garden; or the visitor may dramatically alter the course of the destiny of those whose privacy has been disturbed, as happens when the Supreme Intruder enters Eden. Comparable impact through such a disruption occurs in Aguilera-Malta's novel *El secuestro del general*. The refuge, "Los Cuatro Gallinazos" (named for the buzzards that fly overhead), is introduced in insular fashion, that is, at midpoint in the course of the narrative. Depending on one's perspective, the island can be considered an isle of either love, neglect, or destruction. Here can be found the home and family of the sequestered general, Jonás Pitecantropo, who has isolated them from any visitors from the sea by surrounding the island with floating mines. More of an "islote" than an "isla,"[14] it can only be reached by helicopter. The barbaric Minister of War has thus succeeded in protecting his wife and five sets of female triplets from civilization and politics until the sudden discovery of the island by a resourceful newspaperman disturbs their tranquility and safety. When the women are brought to the mainland and the general's secret private life is exposed by his captors, he demonstrates rare sentiments that reflect signs of a rudimentary kind of human love. In his verbal explosion there are overtones of Edenic bewilderment after the Intrusion and the inevitable, subsequent repercussions:

> Ni eso respetaron. ¡Malditos!. . .Pensé que estarían a salvo en esa isla. . . .Creía que la maldad de los hombres nunca les llegaría. ¿Por qué no me hacen a mí todo lo que quieren? Ellas son inocentes. ¿Por qué tienen que pagar culpas ajenas? ¿Por que?
>
> [*Secuestro* 167-8]

The revelation of the kidnapped general's feelings toward his loved ones, perhaps the only evidence of his humanity, simultaneously produces a physical transformation. Visibly shaken, his emotional outburst is accompanied by restoration of human characteristics emerging from the depths of his bestial primitiveness.

When Satan is exiled from Heaven, seeking revenge, he initiates his function as perpetrator of sin and evil by assuming the body of a serpent in order to seduce Eve. Milton's epic, based on Judeo-Christian myth, parallels the novel of Aguilera-Malta, *Siete lunas y siete serpientes*, which also finds inspiration in these same myths and contains a demonic character whose tyrannical pattern of vice and destruction begins much like the Fallen Angel's. Candelario

Mariscal, because of his mysterious origin and rebellious behavior, foments the legend that he is the son of Satan. Reared by the priest Cándido, he bears few markings of the Christian principles he has been taught, and his excesses eventually culminate in setting fire to his godfather's humble church. Cándido's wrathful castigation is exile, which prompts the offender's career of limitless violence, selecting the inhabitants of Daura as his first victims.

The island of Daura is inhabited only by the Quindales family, whose eldest daughter, Josefa (La Chepa), is destined to be Candelario's passion and the cause of mass devastation. His desire to pursue and possess her drives the youth into an uncontrollable state of frenzy interpreted by expressionistic transformations. As satanic conversion finds its most frequent manifestation in the serpent, Candelario's bestial metamorphosis is set by the tropical environment to be appropriately that of an awesome reptile. Just as the Fiend swims through Chaos to reach the "happy isle," Candelario Mariscal, as a crocodile,[15] makes his way to the island to see Josefa. Like Satan, he plays the *voyeur*, watching the girl as she approaches the shore. Her rejection, however, continues to inflame his passion, until one night he appears again on the island, completely obsessed and intoxicated, to satisfy his lust. Neither man, beast, nor any element of nature can control his fury:

> Huracán sensorial, arrasaría con cuanto se interpusiese. Aunque los árboles cruzaran sus marañas de troncos, ramas y hojas. Aunque la casa retorciera sus paredes y entretejiera sus puntales y varengas. Aunque los seres— reales o ficticios—anudaran sus garras y colmillos. Aunque los arpones, hachas y machetes se ataran entre sí cadenas deslumbrantes. Caiman visible e invisible, subiría los peldaños de la casa de Josefa Quindales.[16]

There is no defense possible. All of nature and man must yield to the hurricane force of his desire. Josefa is saved because of her absence; but enraged at the trick fate has played on him, Candelario slaughters her parents and then rapes her adolescent sister, Clotilde. Then his departure:

> Después, metamorfosis del caimán. Saltando en trébol de corazas verdes. Arremolinándose contra los árboles. Tumbándolos con la cola. Destrozando el tronco con las fauces. Estriando la corteza con las garras. El caimán está loco. ¡Ay de la montaña! ¡Ay de las hojas! ¡Ay de los animales mínimos cuya aurora les estalló en las entrañas! El caimán está loco.
>
> [7/7 71-72]

The crocodile-gone-mad destroys with his jaws, claws, and tail. On land and in the water, the indomitable king of the tropical river devastates nature and all of its creatures. Thus the harmony of the island Daura has been destroyed by the demonic figure of the man-crocodile driven by lust. The unit of peace and love in its isolation no longer exists, and Candelario commences his reign of terror on the seas and on the mainland as bandit, pirate, and assassin. So unholy a creature has he become that he derives particular pleasure when his violence finds its target in the underdog. As he says, "Me gusta joder a los de abajo" (p. 121). If he is not Satan, as rumor has it, he must be one of the Devil's agents or perhaps his son.

The other island which will complete the cycle of Candelario's course of love in its various forms is Balumba, home of the medicine man Bulu-Bulu and his family. The theme is almost the same as that which concerns the events taking place on Daura. The dominant force is again the sexual drive, in this case consuming the flowering Dominga, daughter of the warlock. The interpretation of her desires and fears seeks as expression another reptile, the snake, and in the legendary dwarfs, the Tin-Tines. The parallel between Dominga and Josefa is clearly drawn, for both are pursued and desired. The strange creatures who lust after Dominga arrive at night as a pair, fight one another for the right of possession, and then the victor is bitten by the serpent, who also seeks the young girl. In a repeated pattern of seven nights the ritual performed in a somnambulant state is pagan and phallic in orientation. Dominga strangles the snake each night and buries it, after which she can sleep. Like Candelario, she must destroy in order to find some respite. Her parents, who found their love and peace on the island of Balumba, sense the need for the wholesome relationship with a marriage partner. Salvation, then, becomes the theme as Candelario seeks Bulu-Bulu for advice.

Candelario's problem at this point is having to contend with a ghost. The ghost is Josefa, the only member of the Quindales family who escaped his violence but who has since died. The irony of their union now is based on her over-whelming cooperation as a partner in sex, and her attentions for two years have been Candelario's torment. For his crime of massacring her parents, he suffers the physical annihilation associated with his infamous reputation; but in Candelario's case, destruction will be accomplished by sexual means.

If, as Clotilde Quindales says, "the devil is in every man" (p. 95), then he must be exorcised. But salvation for Candelario will depend on his capacity to repent, which is implied in the fantasmagoric projection of his conscience, and is presumed in his confession and appeal to the exotic and competent spiritual adviser, Bulu-Bulu. The latter will indicate the course toward survival as Michael does Adam, and Circe, Odysseus. The essential element must be a wholesome love, and the proposed marriage between Dominga, the medicine man's daughter, and Candelario Mariscal will form a union that should stand firm against any evil trespassers.

The insular setting of *Siete lunas y siete serpientes* provides a background for the critical turning points in Candelario's life, where action and conscience are presented in surrealistic and expressionistic imagery inspired by the natural environment. The village of Santorontón on the mainland also enters to complete the geographic trinity of the character's wanderings; but the islands of Daura and Balumba are especially significant in that they mark the location and means for Candelario's fall and redemption.

Topography as an Antagonistic Force

Topography reaches human proportions in the novel *La isla virgen* when an island plays an antagonistic role and is instrumental in determining the main character's destiny. Néstor, the white *patrón* who has bought San Pancracio, becomes obsessed with conquering the soil and making it produce as he desires. What begins as a financial concern is transformed into a personal challenge as the island defies the owner and refuses to accept his domination. Néstor is compelled to pursue his course despite the fact that his fortune and attitude are unlike those of Don Goyo, who settled in the archipelago in his youth and courted the isles that eventually yielded to his will:

> De pronto las islas se dieron. Fue una entrega de hembras lujuriosas. Quisieron resarcir al hombre que había luchado tanto con ellas y que había vencido por fin con su fe y su tesón. Empezaron, poco a poco, a mostrársele tales cual eran. Lo guiaron con sus deseos intangibles por los lugares más secretos que tuvieron. Se volvieron propicias a todos sus esfuerzos. Lo empezaron a querer, en su despertar de sueños milenarios.
>
> [*D.G.* 127]

Néstor, however, fails in his efforts to subjugate the untamed virgin land. He is basically inexperienced in agricultural matters, and his impatience and inflexibility prevent him from transforming the capricious land into an Isle of

Love. The Virgin Island rejects his every advance: crops fail, the *cholos* who are in his employ run away, die of malaria or by violent means; and he himself contracts the fever, which unleashes his frenzied imagination, converting his obsession into his doom.

The island has earned a reputation for being damned, and all failure can be attributed to predetermined supernatural causes and forces. In this manner the novel follows the fatalism of most telluric works of Latin America. Nature confronting man is a consuming monster which he can never hope to dominate, and thus emphasis is placed on the futility and insignificance of human endeavor. This, however, is not the entire role nature plays in *La isla virgen*, for the outcome is conditioned by Néstor's attitude and his character. The rational approach to the problem is represented by the overseer Guayàmabe, whose loyalty to his *patrón* is unquestionable, and whose counsel is often solicited but rarely followed. Guayamabe, like his predecessors who have guided the heroes of epic tradition, indicates the way toward Néstor's salvation. The solution of raising cattle is offered but rejected by Néstor since it would take too many years to accumulate a large enough herd to achieve substantial profits. The land must be made to produce rapidly. Guayamabe believes success is possible. The island is there for cultivation; only one thing is needed:

—Hay que tener paciencia. La tierra sólo es de los que tienen paciencia.[17]

The female who has charmed and defied Néstor can be conquered, but patience is the weapon, as are respect and love—the basic components of any fruitful union. A rejection of such an ethic in any relationship will have disastrous consequences, particularly when violence is substituted for patience and abuse replaces understanding. What results in Néstor's case is the creation of an aberration—a monster that will succeed in annihilating the hero.

As the island develops into an implacable enemy, salvation appears in the form of a woman, Esperanza, who represents the ideal mate for Néstor. Vibrant, exciting, challenging, and human, she too must be conquered, not by violation, but through love and understanding also. In epic tradition she is familiar as the classical false omen predicting the successful conclusion to previous events or portending the desired outcome for the hero, but Néstor's destiny is now irrevocable; the end is near and his future is immutable. Nestor's past transgressions against man, not nature this time, are recalled when Pablo Melgar returns to the island to avenge his father's death. Pablo's story, one of several sub-plots in *La isla virgen, now reaches a climax as the author* connects it to the main narrative in fulfilling Nestor's destiny. Pablo kidnaps Esperanza and the impact of her loss compounded by the fever he is sustaining as a victim of malaria, drives the *patrón* into a frantic search for the woman he loves. The pursuit involves a blend of three elements which summarize the essence of his existence—the Virgin Island, Esperanza, and his fate. Néstor, feeling the lure of the first, makes his way toward the jungle, the womb of the island.

In his delirium, Néstor establishes the solution to harmony and peace between man and his environment—a physical union which will come about ironically through death. In that brief moment of enlightenment before he meets his end, the white man understands he has been wrong in his treatment of the island and that he also lacked compassion for his fellowman. Without unity, love, temperance, and all the principles of justice, survival indeed is impossible. At this point the Virgin Island has conquered him, and the vanquished hero is content to be absorbed in her forever:

—Soy de ella. Sólo de ella. Por fin, me ha vencido para siempre. He estado ciego. Todos los míos han estado

ciegos. La lucha con mi casta ha terminado. Los que ven-
gan en pos de mí nacerán de la tierra. Fluirán lo mismo
que un río, lo mismo que la savia de los árboles.

[*Isla* 403]

In the creation of the Virgin Island, Aguilera-Malta has
utilized familiar techniques of epic tradition[18] in establishing
a major character that resembles a supernatural phenomenon
and challenges the hero. Simultaneously, by humanizing the
island, he also has presented a female obstacle such as Dido
or Armida for the hero to overcome. As a third aspect of epic
continuity, this relationship between Néstor and his environment in *La isla virgen* reflects the trend in Latin American
regional fiction which raised nature to the plane of a basic
force affecting the destiny of the protagonist.

Thus nature with its inspirational malleability can perform
the function of an Isle of Love or can become an Isle of
Purgatory. At worst, it can be transformed from a tropical
paradise into a green hell. If the element acquires anthropomorphic properties, the result is a monstrous phenomenon
which is rarely conquered. One of the most impressive examples of earth and surrounding waters joined to create an
awesome aberration of nature is Adamastor, the animated
version of Africa's Cape of Storms in *Os Lusíadas*.
Appearing to confront and destroying hundreds of travelers
who took the route around the tip of South Africa to the East
Indies and the China Sea, Adamastor would tell his tale of
woe and metamorphosis and the cause of it. His sin was a
double one, for he was one of the Giants who defied Jupiter
and then dared to fall in love and pursue Thetis, queen of the
Nereids and mother of Achilles. For his efforts he was turned
into earth and doomed to this spot eternally to be abused by
the tumultuous waters around him. His only respite is offered
when ships attempt to sail around the Cape and are subjected
first to a recounting of his story, then to their own destruction. His appearance in and of itself is horrible enough to

wreak havoc and the description Camões gives is indeed fitting:

> De disforme e grandíssima estatura
> O rostro carregado, a barba esquálida,
> Os olhos encovados e a postura
> Medonha e má, e a cor terrena e pálida,
> Cheios de terra e crespos os cabelos,
> A boca negra, os dentes amarelos.
>
> [*Lus.* 5. 39. 3-8]

Aguilera-Malta's Virgin Island is also an ominous composite figure based on tropical topography, marine creatures, and vegetation:

> Y de improviso le parece que la Maldita cobrara forma humana, que se convirtiera en una mujer. Claro que una mujer extraña, inverosímil. Su melena es de víboras enfurecidas. Los ojos parecen dos puñales. Las manos de crustáceos se alargan potentes, amenazadoras. En la boca, le agoniza un tiburón recién nacido. Los senos son nidos de gavilanes y de lechuzas. Cefalópodos raros se tuercen en su vientre. Tiene el torso áspero y verde, como el lomo de un cocodrilo. En sus pernas alojan hacinamientos de mangles y de raíces adventicias. En sus vellosidades profundas crecen algas marinas y moluscos oscuros.
>
> [*Isla* 211]

These monstrosities created by Camões and Aguilera-Malta have their symbolic significance. Bowra explains Adamastor as a natural barrier beyond which the Portuguese sailed, in defiance of the ancient belief that no man could safely travel past the Pillars of Hercules.[19] By exceeding this limit the Portuguese paid in lives lost at the Cape, just as Néstor's Promethean gesture of attempting to violate the Virgin Island or Mother Earth results in his tragic end.

The seas and natural waterways persecuting heroes have frequently been stirred into motion by the wrath of the gods as epic tradition reveals, and Odysseus is undoubtedly the prime example of fortitude and endurance in such predicaments, particularly when survival is complicated by the juxtaposition of two monster-like entities. While Scylla looms over him and his men, nearby Charybdis threatens certain annihilation for the entire vessel and crew. Charybdis is another distortion of nature, purely elemental in structure, which can and should be avoided like the Syrtes or the Roving Rocks. The hero is usually doomed if he challenges the natural monster and therefore makes every effort to bypass the area. But there is little hope of salvation when the elemental force leaves its geographic confines. Such is the case when humanization of aquatic substance occurs in the *Iliad*. Xanthus (Scamander), one of the two rivers by the gates of Troy, resents his waters' being darkened by the blood of those Trojans who have fallen victim to Achilles's vengeance. Xanthus rebels and is stirred up in rage against Achilles, who ignores the river's request to do battle elsewhere. Leaving the banks of his enclosure, Xanthus continues his pursuit of the hero on land and finally traps him:

> He spoke, and rose against Achilleus, turbulent, boiling
> to a crest, muttering, in foam and blood and dead bodies
> until the purple wave of the river fed from the bright sky
> lifted high and caught in its waters the son of Peleus.
> [21. 324-27]

Achilles finally does escape, but only through the intervention of Hera, who calls upon Hephaestus to counteract the waters' effect by burning them back to their source.

The river as a supernatural entity could prove catastrophic for Achilles; but even in its natural behavior the element has had a devastating effect on epic characters. Seeking retribution for the loss of Roland and his men in the pass,

Charlemagne pursues the Saracens who have caused the tragedy. Approaching the Ebro River, the infidels are barred from their retreat:

> Mult est parfunde, merveilluse e curant;
> Il n'i ad barge ne drodmund ne caland.
> Paien recleiment *Mahum* e Tervagant;
> *E Apollin que lur seient aidant.*
> Pois, saillent enz, mais il n'i unt guarant.
> Li adubet en sunt li plus pesant,
> Envers le funz s'en turnerent alquant,
> Li altre en vunt encuntreval flotant,
> Li mielz guarit en ont boüt itant,
> Tuit sunt neiet par merveillus ahan.[20]

The episode is not entirely devoid of supernatural intervention. Prior to the confrontation of the two armies, nightfall approaches and Charlemagne prays for God's intercession to restrain not the heathen enemy, but the sun itself, thus making pursuit possible. The pagan deity, Tervagant, obviously does not respond to the Saracens' invocation and those who are not slaughtered by the Franks encounter death by drowning. Even the elements are on the side of justice which the Christian forces represent.

To confront or antagonize a river, whether in the form of a natural topographical entity or as an actual deity is a perilous gesture for the hero; but when the waters reach oceanic proportions and they are challenged by mere earthly creatures, the effects on man are even more tragic. Such is the case in Aguilera-Malta's *Canal Zone*, where the mutilated earth and two enslaved oceans take their revenge on an entire society. *Canal Zone* is the first novel by Aguilera-Malta which deals with a subject other than the Ecuadorian *cholo*. It attracted readers for its condemnation of United States imperialism[21] and for the exposé on injustices suffered by the black underdog of Panama who was caught up in the economic and moral crisis produced by the epic engineering feat. The theme of injustice steeped in an atmosphere of corruption accompanies the peripatetic adventures of Pedro Coorsi, who is both an individual and a collective symbol of the oppressed masses. The obstacles challenging his existence include the effect of his origin which is half black, the loss of a job during the depression that followed the prosperity of rapid economic growth, extreme sensitivity to decadence surrounding him, and the physical presence of the monster that represents the cause of his condition and his eventual annihilation—the Panama Canal.

Before him, Pedro's father had challenged the earth and the two oceans and participated in man's conquest of the elements with drills, explosives, and steam shovels, drawn by the author in a portrait that sensorially humanizes technology as it ravages the land:

> Se oía la ronca voz de la dinamita, el jadeo lejano y angustioso del agua esclavizada, el suspiro de los montes heridos, el relinchar de las portentosas máquinas febriles. Y, por sobre todo, la tierra que se abría como una flor de colosales pétalos; la tierra, que propiciaba el puente líquido. . . .Después—entre el canto del hierro y del cemento—las dragas, que extendían sus manos monstruosas para arañar el fango de los fondos marinos.[22]

But the earth takes its revenge. Abandoned by the peasants who cultivated its soil and harvested its crops, the land lay fallow while the Panamanian farmers flocked to the city to profit from the epic feat of building the Canal. Plundered by machines and dynamite, the earth began to consume the workers who participated in the construction of the monster as a black woman relates to Pedro her husband's fortunate but temporary exception:

> Se había logrado escapar de la primera época. Cuando se escribieron con sangre y con plomo homicida las primeras páginas de ese poema de cemento, mar y acero;

cuando el alarido de la dinamita se mezcló al de los
hombres pulverizados; cuando las fiebres traidoras mordi-
eron la negra carne sin protección, y, en racha mortal,
la barrieron incesantes; cuando volaron los cerros y, en su
vuelo estrepitoso, se llevaron ramilletes de existencia.
[*C.Z.* 38]

The woman's mate ultimately encounters his death leaving
a family alone to continue the struggle for existence. When
Pedro's father dies, the boy with a promising future is forced
to abandon his studies and to grow up in an atmosphere of
corruption and decadence, witnessing abuse of the masses by
social and political forces typified by bureaucrats, landlords,
and opportunists in general. In the background looms, omnipresent, the monster, product of the chained oceans, son of a
ravaged earth, and stepchild of business exploitation. The
canal is the cause of an additional conquest of the nation by
the United States fleet. Pedro serves the sailors who in turn
are victims of financial profit, but his obsession with the
canal and its unholy devastation of the country's moral and
spiritual fiber leads him to his doom. His violent end behind
the wheel of an automobile is not even commented on; it is
not even mentioned by the newspapers. Society's final gesture
to the departed underdog is one of complete indifference.

Totemism and Consubstantiation

The *Aeneid* is without doubt the epic in which nature is
alloted a predominant role in the narrative and where its
functions are so varied. The earth "groans" (9. 709; 120,
713); Aeneas carries the golden bough to Hades as a talisman
(6. 136ff.); Turnus is revitalized when he plunges into the
Tiber (9. 815-18); and the deities of the woods and rivers
participate actively to determine the outcome of Trojan and
Italian destinies. The land ruled by Saturn (Kronos) in the

Golden Age was tended by an agricultural society, and with the advent of the Trojans the end of peace and harmony in pastoral Italy draws near.[23]

For both the forces of Aeneas and the combined armies that oppose them, the tree functions as a spiritual symbol, often associated with the practical concern of the moment. The king of Latium, whose mother was a wood nymph, consults the sacred laurel which responds in the voice of his father, Faunus (Pan), a protecting deity of shepherds and agriculture. It is also not unusual to encounter warriors whose stately or imposing stature reflects their dendritic origins:

> Pandarus and Bitias, sprung from Idaean Alcanor,
> whom the wood-nymph Iaera bore in Jupiter's grove,
> youths as tall as their ancestral firs and hills.
> [*Aen.* 9. 672-74]

Partial to Aeneas are the pines of Ida, while Turnus receives protection from another tree. In the final battle scene between the two great warriors, Aeneas throws his spear at his enemy, who is temporarily spared by the remains of a sacred olive tree which had been removed from its spot by the irreverent Trojans:

> But the Trojans, with no respect, had cut away
> the sacred trunk to clear a space where they could
>   fight.
> Here the spear of Aeneas stuck, where its impetus
> had carried it, holding fast in the tough and stubborn
>   root.
> [*Aen.* 12. 770-73]

Turnus's prayers to Faunus and Mother Earth are efficacious enough until Venus intercedes and dislodges her son's weapon, which eventually finds its intended target.

The *Odyssey* contains far fewer references to tree imagery

and totemic implications, but there is one impressive example which bears noting. At the end of the poem Penelope is still dubious that the beggar-turned-hero is Odysseus, even after he has punished the suitors and cleaned his house. She cleverly tells Eurycleia to set his bed outside of the chamber—the bed he himself built. Odysseus confirms he indeed is the husband whose talents designed and constructed the magnificent bed:

". . .I myself, no other man, made it.
There was the bole of an olive tree with long leaves growing
strongly in the courtyard, and it was thick, like a column.
I laid down my chamber around this, and built it, until I
finished it, with close-set stones, and roofed it well over,
and added the compacted doors, fitting closely together.
Then I cut away the foliage of the long-leaved olive,
and trimmed the trunk from the roots up, planing it with a brazen
adze, well and expertly, and trued it straight to a chalkline,
making a bed post of it, and bored all holes with an auger.
I began with this and built my bed, until it was finished,
and decorated it with gold and silver and ivory."
[*Od.* 23. 189-200]

Odysseus, through the combination of the olive tree and bed, has united as well the spiritual or religious essence of matrimony, conception, birth, and death—the cycle of man's existence. In a civilized society Eden's bower is restored to reflect again the stability of a harmonious union between two people whose love has stood the test of time.[24]

In *Paradise Lost* the tree assumes maximum significance. Satan initiates his campaign against the inhabitants by executing his first act of sacrilege and defiance on earth; he takes as a point of observation the Tree of Life, where as a cormorant he sits "devising Death / to them who liv'd" (*P.L.* 4. 197-98). When in serpent disguise he begins his conquest of Eve, the dramatic content of the scene is charged with a combination of ritual and hierophantic monologue in front of the Tree of Knowledge:

> O Sacred, Wise, and Wisdom-giving Plant,
> Mother of Science, now I feel thy Power
> Within me clear. . . .
>
>   [*P.L.* 9. 679-81]

Lucifer's remarks directed at the tree which supposedly gives him such mysterious, intellectual superiority stimulates Eve to imitate his act of homage after she bites the apple:

> O Sovran, virtuous, previous of all Trees
> In Paradise, of operation blest
> To Sapience, hitherto obscur'd, infam'd.
>
>   [*P.L.* 9. 795-97]

C. S. Lewis in his analysis of the Fall comments on Eve's continued descent in planning homicide by giving Adam the fruit. Referring to the act of worship in front of the tree and the "low Reverance done" (9. 835), he notes her ritualistic gesture disparagingly:

> She who thought it beneath her dignity to bow to Adam or to God, now worships a vegetable. She has become "primitive" in the popular sense.[25]

In his commentary Mr. Lewis appears to minimize the importance of totemic relationships and their role in all cultures, including Christianity: a "totem," which will be introduced again in *Paradise Regained*, will have the greatest impact on mankind since either tree in Eden—the Crucifix.

Individual and tree become more consubstantially related when the hylozoic properties are replaced by the presence of the soul or spirit of a person magically encased within the trunk. Tasso makes excellent use of the Germanic tradition of the haunted woods when the devils and demons inhabit the forest and drive the Crusaders from the frightening surroundings. To strike the tree is doubly sinful in Tancredi's case: he will repeat his act of violence against Clorinda, the warrior-maiden he has killed, and simultaneously cut down a member of the woods that were once sacred to pagans before the Christians arrived. A voice that he believes is Clorinda's soul speaks to him after his first blow, warning him that all the trees contain the souls of fallen Christian and pagan knights as well:

> Son di sensi animati i rami e i tronchi
> E micidial sei tu, se legno tronchi.
>
> [*G.L.* 13. 43: 7-8]

Rinaldo, on the other hand, must cut down the huge myrtle that stands in an idyllic setting of the same forest. A demon duplicating Armida, his former mistress, pleads with the knight to spare the tree. Embracing the trunk, she cries:

> Deponi il ferro, o dispietato, o il caccia
> Pria ne le vene a l'infelice Armida:
> Per questo sen, per questo cor la spada
> Solo al bel mirto mio trovar può strada.
>
> [*G.L.* 18. 34: 5-8]

Since reason now prevails over passion, he is moved to pity neither the form that resembles Armida nor the myrtle she is protecting. Unlike Tancredi, Rinaldo cannot be aroused by any natural phenomenon which is metamorphosed or spiritually animated. Although the woman then changes into a monster while thunder, lightning, and hail besiege him, he strikes the tree and fears none of the souls groaning as the totem falls and spirits flee. Thus the spell of the enchanted woods is broken.

The tree is also developed as a major symbol of human destiny and existence by Aguilera-Malta on the islands of the Guayas Archipelago, where most of the action of his regional novels takes place. The author surrounds his *cholo* with the majestic and powerful mangrove trees (*mangles*). Totemism is based primarily on economic dependence and the constant companionship between the woodcutters and the tree which provides sustenance and shelter for the peasant while protecting the island itself from erosion by the sea. Although there is no formally practiced dendrolatry, the tree is regarded with respect and superstitious awe propagated by the years of symbiosis and the myths the human mind is capable of creating. The mangrove in *Don Goyo* holds much of the same significance noted in epic tradition: it symbolizes strength and stability in a primitive society, just as the olive represented the same for Odysseus and Penelope. It behaves in any number of hylozoic ways and demonstrates sensitivity to the plight of the *cholo*, particularly to Don Goyo's destiny; like the natural phenomena of the Garden of Eden, the tree will reflect or follow the course of the characters' capitulation to an evil force.

Don Goyo has his own special mangrove that functions somewhat like the sacred tree of Faunus in communicating with the patriarch of the islands and prophesying the future. The ancient tree, as old as Don Goyo himself (legend has it that he is 120 years old), knowing that the time is approaching when the primitive society in its innocence will be sacrificed to the exploitation of the white man, affectionately inclines its massive trunk and foliage toward Don Goyo's canoe:

Sus hojas verdinegras parecieron tocar al cholo anciano en gesto de caricia. Su corteza abrió como una flor gigan-

tesca. Sus nudos agrietados se dijeran entrañas desgarradas. Y—en medio del asombro de los siglos, hecho inquietud de dolor y vida—el mangle más viejo de las islas—con voz extraña y triste—habló:
—Nos vamos, Goyo. Nos vamos.

[*D.G.* 77-78]

But beyond the totemic relationship exists a more intimate one that the *cholo* believes is the physical as well as the spiritual result of their coexistence—the absorption of *mangle* properties or a blending of man and tree. This strange consubstantiation is explained by one of the older *cholos* to the young men listening:

—El mangle lo llevamos dentro.
Y trató de explicar.
Se había ido metiendo, en una posesión tenaz, rotunda, silenciosa, sin que ni ellos—posiblemente—se dieran cuenta. Es que los mangles tenían extrañas fuerzas desconocidas de los hombres; una especie de ramazones elásticas e invisibles, que se adentraban sobre la carne de todos, por los ojos, por la boca, por los cabellos, que se enraizaban en la vida; que los pegaban—como enredadera —sobre la piel dormida de las islas. ¡Ah, los mangles!

[*D.G.* 83-84]

The younger *cholos*, in spite of their superstitious nature and their great respect for Don Goyo, find it difficult to believe that the mangroves are indeed part of them or that they should follow the wish of the oldest tree and look to the sea for their livelihood so as not to permit the white man's exploitation of the mangrove wood. The Tree of Life in Eden was not intended for Adam and Eve, nor can the ancient emblem of the islands continue to reflect Don Goyo's immortality. Just as the oak once sacred to Faunus gives way to the new invaders of Latium, so shall the mangrove fall, forecasting conquest by the white foreigner and taking with it the tribal leader, who symbolized the simple perfection of tropical isolation.

In the novel *Siete lunas y siete serpientes*, topography, flora, and fauna no longer assume the once prominent role they had in Latin American regional writing. The *cholo* is not described as he formerly was in his daily confrontation with the phenomena of nature while obtaining his livelihood from the sea or the mangroves, and his battle with the elements withdraws to concede the plot to the perennial war between good and evil in their Christian and medieval pristine representations. Aguilera-Malta's use of the tree symbol, nevertheless, maintains its totemic and consubstantial significance as it did in his first novel, *Don Goyo*. The most readily definable and perceptible of the arboreal structures is the Crucifix, and the second is a rosebush that has taken root in the palm of a boy who is promised a pony for tolerating the pain he must endure as the bush grows. Both plants in turn are governed by their respective symbols of virtue and vice. The cross is occupied by a wooden Christ who descends when he so desires to participate in the action. The rosebush is watered with sedulous care by Don Chalena, a man who has made a pact with the Devil for wealth. In the fascinating interplay of Christian myth and allegorical expressionism the two symbols perform a totemic function for the men who play a major role in determining the destiny of the people in the village of Santorontón.

The Crucifix is the constant companion of the priest Cándido, who through it found his own salvation (literally) when he was invited by its occupant to climb aboard the wooden vehicle after they both had been tossed into the sea by pirates. At times the cross serves as a mast for his canoe; at others, it becomes a weapon ready for defense or attack. In the days when rumor had it that Satan roamed the village sowing discord and violence, when the victims of homicide strangely disappeared from the beach, Cándido took his crucifix and paraded through the town to drive Lucifer back to his abyss. Even more effective is the crucifix held like a mace by its master:

El Hijo de María se había desclavado de la Cruz. Sostenía la Cruz con ambas manos. Levantaba la Cruz en esfuerzo increíble. Mazo descommunal la Cruz. Alzada sobre sus cabezas la Cruz. La Cruz ciclópea. La Cruz punitiva. La Cruz arma. Amenazadora. Implacable.

[7/7 119]

The fantasy of the rosebush follows the same course as the tree to represent power, evil this time, which Don Chalena incarnates. The villagers' need for water is exploited by this man who has given his soul to the Devil and whose lust for power, mostly financial, is demonstrated by planting the bush in the child Tolón's palm as he dreams of a pony and his physically mute mother (La Muda) stands watching. Aguilera-Malta presents an unusual counterpoint between the procedure of cultivation and dialogue exchanged by Chalena and the *santoronteños* concerning his monopoly of the water supply and what he will next demand in payment for its distribution:

Como todos los días—ante ellos—seguía regando su rosal. Su rosal en la mano extendida de Tolón. Potro-Rosal. Rosal-Potro. Tolón-Potro-Rosal. Seguía regando su Rosal.

—Tal vez, nuestras casas, ¡Don!
—. . .Hombre, no estaría mal. No, no estaría mal.
Continuaba regando el Rosal. Ante ellos—cuerpo reseco ojos resecos ostiones difuntos—ante ellos. Tolón soñaba—dormido o despierto—con el Potro. Chalena soñaba—dormido o despierto—con el Rosal. La Muda soñaba—dormida o despierta—con Tolón florecido. Los santo-rontenos—dormidos o despiertos—seguían soñando con agua. Agua. Agua.

[p. 143]

As Chalena gains complete domination of their lives and families, the rosebush takes root and the pain becomes overwhelming for the boy. Desperate as well are the women who

defy their husbands and decide to accept Chalena's terms for
satisfying visually his prurient appetite in exchange for water:

> —Aunque ustedes no quieran, ¡veremos a Don Chalena!
> Don Chalena regando el Rosal. ¡Maldito Rosal! El Potro
> de Humo. ¡Maldito Rosal! La raíz en la carne. ¡Maldito
> Rosal! Tolón medio loco. ¡Maldito Rosal! La muda
> clavada con manos y pies. ¡Maldito Rosal! enraizado en la
> tierra. En la mano. En los sueños. ¡Maldito Rosal!
>
> [p. 147]

The rosebush, Don Chalena's plant of immortality, is an
appropriate reflection of what he does not possess—the
healthy virility of a young man. He is obese, batrachian-
like, and impotent. The flowers he hopes will blossom
represent youth, desire, and love ("gather ye rosebuds while
ye may"), and their anxiously awaited plurality complements
the demonic figure's gluttony and avarice. As the bush produces its thorny extensions, a mother stands silently by,
accepting the situation much like the villagers' toleration of
Chalena's abuse and exploitation. But the two totems are
juxtaposed in religious significance. Tolón, surrounded by
thorns and nailed to his rosebush, is the instrument of
Chalena's redemption. A silent Mary stands near her son
while he experiences Christ's pain for the salvation of the
"unjust." The image of the projected flowers and the cross
combine in rosary fashion to synthesize the innocent, the
pure, the beautiful at the mercy of satanic corruptibility.

Fusion between man and nature in the works of Aguilera-
Malta is not always so painful as the rosebush experience of
Tolón. Madness or delirium offers the character some relief,
but not total. In *La isla virgen*, a sense of fusion with nature
eases Néstor's grief as he begins to lose touch with reality. He
feels the power of absorption that the island has and his
physical transformation in a uniquely sensitive response to
the land and its vegetation:

—Noto que los pies y las manos se me alargan. Me crecen bejucos en las puntas de los dedos. Bejucos, que poco a poco, me van atando a estas tierras. ¡Si tú supieras, Guayamabe! Las pisadas que ahora doy en la montaña me suenan adentro, como si fueran latidos en mi propio pecho. Cuando suben las mareas en los esteros, siento que sus corrientes me crecen en la sangre. El último yerbajo que se corta empieza a dolerme como si fuera parte de mí mismo.

[*Isla* 371-72]

At the end of the novel, when he is beyond saving, consubstantiation between Néstor and the topography is almost complete. He is insensitive to pain, and he welcomes his own annihilation. But Néstor's union with the island is not purely a hallucinatory resolution to his psychic dilemma. The consubstantial cycle of man's course was begun by Adam and is continued in such novels as *La isla virgen*, where nature's relationship with the hero is as intimate as it is in *Paradise Lost*. Adam is equally desirous of returning to his material source to find peace. There the torments resulting from his fallen state will disappear in the inevitable merging of once-conscious matter and the earth:

. . .how gladly would I meet
Mortality my sentence and be Earth
Insensible, how glad would lay me down
As in my Mother's lap? There I should rest
And sleep secure. . . .

[*P.L.* 10. 775-79]

As a technique of classical and primitive as well as Biblical precedence, the blending of human and elemental substance or the creation of mortals from topographical material becomes a means of enhancing the basic interdependence of the two reconcilable oppositions, nature and man.[26] To have dendritic origins was not unusual for Virgil's characters, and the contemporary hero, though somewhat reluctant, is drawn as well to a past that may reveal his arboreal ancestry:

> A ratos me parece que hubiera nacido en estos sitios. Me grita el ancestro en una forma vegetal y extraña. ¿No será que antes tenía raíces adventicias, como las de los mangles? ¿Alguna fuerza antihumana me separó de las ramas y los troncos?"
>
>   [*Isla* 89]

Unlike Néstor, who has been molded by an urban environment, the hero or heroine who lives close to the soil and cultivates it can accept his origin as part of the Divine scheme which formed the universe out of the abyss and then linked it substantially with mankind:

>   . . .he form'd thee *Adam*, thee O Man
> Dust of the ground. . . .
>
>   [*P.L.* 7. 524-25]

Hardly displeased with the means by which he was created, Adam confirms his terrestrial composition ("That dust I am," 10. 770), and knows his destiny will be fulfilled when he returns to the earthy matrix where he and Eve will "mix" with their "connatural dust" (11. 529). It is the same attitude that sustains and consoles our First Parents and the characters of literary tradition who seek refuge in the maternal haven in which they were formed. Whether human existence is menaced by annihilation, abuse, or any traumatic experience requiring decision and change, topography serves to translate the basic fears and anxieties that pursue the mortal figure. In *Siete lunas y siete serpientes* Clotilde, the girl whose home became the forest in which the animals helped her to survive, transforms sexual violence into the tree image as she looks to the soil for protection:

¿Dejarán de llegar los árboles? También ellos querrán

clavar sus raíces en mí. Crecer en mí. Gozar en mí. Vivir en mí. Sacudir sus cabelleras verdes mientras danzan en mí. Sólo soy tierra. Un pedazo de tierra.

[7/7 270]

Procreation and death in the womb of Mother Earth also have an elemental alternate in the sea, which functions as a protective, generative, or annihilating substance.[27] The irenic sanctuary for Balboa surges in the imagination of the Indian princess who is helpless in preventing the discoverer's execution. Praying to the nature deities whom she forsook to worship a Christian God, Anayansi's only hope for the Spaniard's salvation is a fantasy restoring him in natural and human confluence to the sea he discovered:

> Por un instante, Anayansi imaginó que eso no tendría lugar; que él recibiría la ayuda del Dios en que ambos creían o de los dioses aborígenes en que ella había creído antes y a los que ahora se aferraba, de nuevo, con más fe; y que éstos, cuando los hombres menos lo advirtieran, lo harían desaparecer, para reintegrarlo a ese Mar del Sur que descubriera.[28]

The sea affords comparable refuge for Anayansi's autochthonous brothers who populate the coastal areas of Ecuador and are recreated by Aguilera-Malta in the short stories of *Los que se van*. Deriving sustenance from the waters that protect their insular and littoral world, the characters of these tales on occasion find consolation by meeting their end in the dark abyss which mysteriously weaves an aqueous shroud around the despondent hero. There is the young *cholo* rejected by the beautiful and glamorous city who finds solace in death by drowning ("El cholo que se fue pa' Guayaquil"), and the conscience-striken, aging protagonist of "El cholo del tibrón," who disappears among nocturnal waves in the sea that years before was the setting for his crime. There is also Clotilde Quindales, who vacillates between the two elements to seek death either by fleeing to the mountains which once protected her or by seeking a watery grave:

¿Dónde hundirme para recuperarme? Sólo en la muerte.
La buscaré dentro del mar resonante ataúd líquido. O
iré a la montaña. ¿Llamaré a los tiburones o a las
víboras?

[*7/7 274*]

But like Adam and Eve, the peasant girl cannot choose the
hour of her departure from the world of mortals. Flinging
herself into the sea, Clotilde is miraculously lifted by the
waves she sought for destruction and is returned to the canoe.
As if revitalized by the element, she paddles anxiously toward
the shore and a new life, represented by the voice of the man
who beckons:

—¡Clotilde! ¡Clotilde!
Incendiada—otra vez incendiada de vida—respondió:
—¡Voy, Juvencio! ¡Voy!

[*7/7 278*]

Water as a creative and generative substance also has its
human equivalent which functions in propitiatory context to
redeem or resurrect mankind:

The blood of Bulls and Goats they may conclude
Some blood more precious must be paid for Man.

[*P.L.* 12. 292-93]

It is for the martyr to express the sacrificial rite in terms of the
life-sustaining liquid, as the heroine of *España leal* explains
to her father:

La sangre que hoy se riega es una sangre sublime. Es
como si estuviéramos sembrando. . . .¿Te acuerdas, pap-
aíto, cuando trabajabas en el cortijo del amo? ¿Te
acuerdas como echabas la semilla sobre la tierra húmeda y
fértil? Pues así están haciendo los hombres. Están regando
su sangre como una semilla roja. ¡De allí saldrá la nueva
España, la nueva humanidad![29]

Paca Solana adds to the union of earth and water/blood, the image which completes a generative trinity in the rebirth of Spain and humanity—the seed. The seminal factor in the process of redemption is given maximum significance in *Paradise Lost*, where human, divine, and natural elements converge to establish a typology of salvation:

> This ponder, that all Nations of the Earth
> Shall in his Seed be blessed; by that Seed
> Is meant thy great deliverer.[30]
>
> [*P.L.* 12. 147-49]

Adam's joy at the knowledge of his role in the redemptive process is that of any human being who participates in creating his own immortality. So too a glorious future is revealed to Rinaldo, whose seed ("'l buon germe roman," *G.L.* 17. 79, 7), will produce the House of Este and a line of illustrious descendants:

> Veduto hai tu de la tue stirpe altera
> I rami e la vetusta alta radice;
> E, se ben da l'età primiera
> Stata è fertil d'eroi madre e felice,
> Non è, né fia di partorir mai stanca;
> **Ché per vecchiezza in lei virtú non manca.**
>
> [*G.L.* 17. 86, 3-8]

Unlike Crisóstomo Chalena, who must artificially plant and irrigate a rosebush that cannot bloom because of the destructive forces that surround it, Rinaldo is destined to initiate the cultivation of a tree whose copious foliage will thrive on its own vitality and the generative strength of his virtuous progeny.

As germination and growth are depicted in the symbols water-earth-seed, the synergetic association between man and nature frequently is accompanied by a form of pantheistic exhilaration. The way the forecast of descendants affects

Adam and Rinaldo, so too in *Don Goyo* the direct impression of sound, color, and odor excites the boy Cusumbo, who is about to cross the threshold of manhood—a time when he also will participate in the rite of procreation as the world about him does yearly. His irrepressible joy is expressed in the desire to commune with all of nature and mankind by means of a wish to be converted into a rice plant, whose germinal extension contains the mystery of nature's vitalizing force:

> —¡Si yo fuera arrozal!
> Dar alegría a los montes, alimento y cobijo a los hombres. Sentirse uno y muchos. Grano de arroz entre los dientes, paja de arroz sobre las chozas y las balsas.
> ¡Ah, las espigas![31]
>
> [*D.G.* 15]

In the works of Demetrio Aguilera-Malta the interaction of man and his topographic circumstances is marked, on the one hand, by the generative force as demonstrated by the seed image, and on the other, by annihilation or the final return to an originally creative substance. However, the intertwined structure of natural and human factors persists throughout the character's existence, frequently reflecting his physical or spiritual state or affecting his destiny. Culling from his own environment, the author forges his metaphors or similes, like Homer, from a familiar landscape. The peasants of Cuba appear to be fashioned from living clay,[32] while the discoverer of the Amazon River, Francisco de Orellana, has a face which has assumed the texture of vegetation.[33] Don Mite, the dying *cholo*, projects a profile in which his beard resembles the briar that is woven about the mangroves of the islands (*Isla*, 115), and the soldier-priest Andrés de Vera is compared to the bamboo plant, tall and dry, that flourishes in the tropics of Panama (*Mar*, 133). Manuela Sáenz, Bolívar's beautiful and devoted companion in love and war, follows the Liberator across the Andes, resolute, determined as never before to accept the role she plays in his life. As a member of the troops, she follows the mountain course whose topography seems to have been absorbed by her physically and emotionally as well:

> Ella seguía inconmovible. El rostro hermoso se le había endurecido. Algo de la estructura pétrea de las montañas y de la pujanza de esos ríos empezaba a incorporarse a su existencia. Avanzaba. Avanzaba, sabiendo que ya no dudaría más, que ya no vacilaría más, que acompanaría para siempre a Bolívar, a su ejército, a sus ideales.[34]

The woman who once fought against the deep involvement with Bolívar now reflects the solidarity of her commitment to herself and to him by assimilating those properties that belong to the Andean range. As the mountains stand firm, so will she in her loyalty to the Liberator; as irreversible as the river's current is Manuela's love and dedication to the cause.

One of the more modern techniques of blending nature and man is a type of photographic consubstantiation which Aguilera-Malta employs to emphasize the hero's obsession with his destiny or goal. The vastness of the land or sea lends itself to that form of imaginative interpretation as Balboa observes the Panamanian jungle on the brink of encountering the Pacific Ocean:

> Miraba hacia adelante. Le obsesionaba el mar presentido. Muchas veces le parecía que la misma selva no era otra cosa que ese mar, que se había vuelto verde. En lugar de mirarlo quieto y tranquilo, lo veía revolverse, como si esos árboles, sus ramas y sus hojas fueran verdes olas que lo atraían más y más.
>
> [*Mar* 132]

But the impression is complicated as well by his love for the

Indian princess Anayansi, who is as much a part of his life as the natural surroundings:

> Y lo curioso era que, como en doble exposición, fre-cuentemente se le aparecía Anayansi. Se diría que las dos imágenes—la de ella y la del mar—eran parte de una misma obsesión.
>
> [*Mar* 132]

What actually occurs is a tripartite, kinetic superimposition which represents three vital symbols of the discoverer and his new world: the sea, the jungle, and the woman who synthe-sized glory through her faith and love for the hero. Well-versed in the technique of cinematography and an artist him-self, Demetrio Aguilera-Malta uses this method along with those previously discussed to consolidate the elements of nature and man in the struggle for survival or in the pursuit of a specific goal.

The land, sea, and topographical elements as they are reflected in epic tradition have performed a function that transcends purely rhetorical or scenic limits. The relationship of man and his natural milieu has been an intimate one as has been noted by the poets, and their reciprocal influence is still part of the epic concern itself. The changes in the individual's spiritual condition will affect the soil he cultivates and the waters that sustain him:

> Curs'd is the ground for thy sake, thou in sorrow
> Shalt eat thereof all the days of thy Life;
> Thorns also and Thistles it shall bring thee forth
> Unbid. . . .
>
> [*P.L.* 10. 201-204]

Modern man, who often ignores the ethical and moral code in his civilized world, has also continued violating the phenomena of nature in the desire to subjugate them as he has his fellowman. The reaction of topography has been interpreted as a conversion of the element into an aberration ready to consume the human violator. There is little difference between the river Xanthus, who leaves his banks to pursue Achilles, the polluter of his waters, and the Virgin Island that rejects coercion or domination by the white man. Considered as part of the fatalistic character of Latin American regional fiction, this antagonistic response, however, is determined by man himself as Guayamabe tells his *patrón*, Néstor. The solution of compatibility does not lie in the union of men or native and colonizer against nature, according to the belief of some critics,[35] but rather in a radical change in values—a standard which is borne by the ecologist today in the current dilemma of man versus his environment. As Paul Ehrlich has stated:

> Our entire system of orienting to nature must undergo a revolution. And that revolution is going to be extremely difficult to pull off, since the attitudes of western culture towards nature are deeply rooted in the Judeo-Christian tradition. Unlike people in many other cultures, we see man's basic role as dominating nature, rather than as living in harmony with it.[36]

The exhortation to action and reform prevalent in much of epic literature is not only applicable to man's social problems but to his treatment of the surroundings that sustain him, for there is no doubt that humanity's destiny is as inextricably woven with nature's now as it was in the Garden of Eden.

Notes

1. *La "Gerusalemme Liberata" di Torquato Tasso*, ed. Severino Ferrari; new rev. ed. by Pietro Papini (Florence: Sansoni, 1940), Canto 18, Stanza 100. Future references to this work will be abbreviated (e.g., *G.L.* 18. 100).

2. *Obras Completas*, ed. Hernâni Cidade (Libson: Sá da Costa, 1947), 4 (*Os Lusíadas)*, Canto 3.84. Future references to this edition will be abbreviated (e.g., *Lus.* 3. 84. 1-4). C. M. Bowra notes these verses and discusses nature's mourning of the king, which hints at "some deep companionship between landscape and man." See *From Virgil to Milton* (London-New York: Macmillan, 1962), p. 106.

3. The entire island episode, however, is far more intricately related to the total structure of the poem than Camões states. See my article "Cynegetics and Irony in the Thematic Unity of the "*Lusiads*" in *Luso-Brazilian Review* 10, no. 2 (Winter 1973): 197-207.

4. A Bartlett Giamatti analyzes the opposition City-Salvation/False Garden in his study *The Earthly Paradise and the Renaissance Epic* (Princeton: Princeton University Press, 1969).

5. *The "Odyssey" of Homer*, tr. Richmond Lattimore (New York: Harper & Row, 1968), 5. 63-64. Future references to this work will be abbreviated (e.g., *Od.* 5. 70-74).

6. See Howard W. Clarke, *The Art of the "Odyssey"* (Englewood Cliffs, N.J.: Prentice-Hall, 1967), pp. 50-52. Mr. Clarke finds little significance in the seven-year confinement but does mention the episode in connection with the sin against the sun god: "In the days when all myths were interpreted as solar myths this was taken as the period in the progress of the year-spirit when he [Odysseus] is hidden, his powers enfeebled, waiting only for his time to return" (p. 51).

7. See George E. Dimmick, Jr., "The Name of Odysseus," in *Homer: A Collection of Critical Essays*, ed. George Steiner and Robert Fagles (Englewood Cliffs, N.J.: Prentice-Hall, 1962), p. 111.

8. Richmond Lattimore summarizes the experiences on the islands of Circe and Calypso as not being symbolic or allegorical, although they lend themselves to a morality which demonstrates the temptation of comfort and beauty. These adventures dramatize the test by which a person established his quality. When the men are changed into swine, Lattimore explains it simply as a "fairy-tale trans-formation" (*The "Odyssey" of Homer*, p. 15). The function of the goddesses is, however, more complex.

9. Medieval tradition considered the location to be on top of a mountain which was surrounded by the waters of Noah's flood. Dante places the earthly Paradise at the summit of the mount of Purgatory (*Purgatorio* 28), and the island was generally considered to be Tenerife.

10. Even before the Fall, Eden's landscape (and particularly the trees) communi-cates a sense of "inherent sorrow." See William Empson's analysis, "Milton and Bentley: The Pastoral of the Innocence of Man," in *Milton: "Paradise Lost," A Collection of Critical Essays*, ed. Louis L. Martz (Englewood Cliffs, N.J.: Prentice-Hall, 1966), pp. 38-39.

11. *Don Goyo*, 4th ed. (Buenos Aires: Platina, 1958), p. 71. Future references to this work will be abbreviated (e.g., *D.G., 71-72)*. John S. Brushwood discusses *Don Goyo* as a landmark in the evolution of the Latin American novel and notes this passage in particular where personified nature "deepens the emotive quality of the characterizations without destroying the simplicity of the characters." See his study *The Spanish American Novel: A Twentieth-Century Survey* (Austin: University of Texas Press, 1975), p. 100.

12. In *Los que se van. Cuentos del cholo y del montuvio*, 2nd ed. (Quito: Casa de la Cultura Ecuatoriana, 1955), p. 137. Future references to this work will be abbreviated (e.g., *L.Q.S.V.* 137).

13. See Seymour Menton's *El cuento hispanoamericano. Antología crítico-histórico*, 2nd ed. (Mexico: Fondo de Cultura Económica, 1966), 2: 69.

14. *El secuestro del general* (Mexico: Editorial Joaquín Mortiz, S.A., 1973) p. 122. Future references to this work will be abbreviated (e.g., *Secuestro*, 122).

15. The American crocodile or cayman is called *caimán* in Spanish America.

16. *Siete lunas y siete serpientes* (Mexico: Fondo de Cultura Económica, 1970), pp. 67-68. Future references will be abbreviated (e.g., *7/7* 67-68).

17. *La isla virgen*, intro. by Angel F. Rojas, "Consideraciones sobre *La isla virgen*," 2nd ed. (Quito: Casa de la Cultura Ecuatoriana, 1954), p. 208. Future references to this work will be abbreviated (e.g., *Isla* 209).

18. The novel itself has been called "an epic book from beginning to end" by Angel F. Rojas. (*Isla* xxii.)

19. C. M. Bowra, *From Virgil to Milton*, p. 125.

20. *La Chanson de Roland*, ed. Léon Gautier (Tours: Alfred Mame et Fils, 1884), 2466-74. Future references to this work will be abbreviated (e.g., *Roland* 2466-74).

21. For versified censure of imperialism in connection with the Canal, see José Santos Chocano's "La epopeya del Pacífico," and "En el Canal," in *Alma América*, prol. by Miguel de Unamuno (Madrid: Gen. de Victoriano Suárez, 1906).

22. *Canal Zone*, 2nd ed., rev. (Mexico: Andrea, 1966), p. 12. Future references to this work will be abbreviated (e.g., *C.Z.* 12)

23. See Steele Commager's "Introduction" to *Virgil: A Collection of Critical Essays*, ed. Steele Commager (Englewood Cliffs, N.J.: Prentice-Hall, 1966), pp. 10-11.

24. Howard W. Clarke adds the observation: "Like Antaeus, the mighty wrestler and giant who was invincible so long as he was in contact with his Mother Earth, the marriage of Odysseus and Penelope has a primal strength—it is secure, fixed in time and place, yet alive, natural, capable of further growth." *The Art of the "Odyssey"* (Englewood Cliffs, N.J.: Prentice-Hall, 1967), p. 78.

25. *A Preface to "Paradise Lost"* (London: Oxford University Press, 1960), p. 126.

26. For an analysis of additional synergetic combinations in *Paradise Lost*, see Frank L. Huntley, "Before and After the Fall: Some Miltonic Patterns of Systasis," in *Approaches to "Paradise Lost,"* The York Tercentenary Lectures, ed. C. A. Patrides (London: Edward Arnold, 1968), pp. 1-14.

27. For an interesting study of Satan's voyage through the Abyss to Earth interpreted as a birth process, see Michael Lieb, "Prolegomena: The Dark World," *The Dialectics of Creation. Patterns of Birth and Regeneration in "Paradise Lost"* (Amherst: University of Massachusetts Press, 1970).

28. *Un nuevo mar para el rey; Balboa, Anayansi y el Océano Pacífico (Episodios Americanos,* 3) (Madrid: Guadarrama, 1965), p. 280. Future references to this work will be abbreviated (e.g., *Mar*, 280).

29. *España leal; tragedia en un prólogo y tres actos, el último dividido en dos cuadros* (Quito: Talleres Gráficos de Educación, 1938), p. 17. Future references to this work will be abbreviated (e.g, *España*, 17).

30. Milton's allusions to the germinative symbol are frequent in the final message to Adam in Book 12: "A Son, the Woman's Seed" (327); "The Seed of Woman" (379); "In thee and in thy Seed" (395); "So in his seed all Nations shall be blest" (450); "The Woman's Seed" (543); and "The great deliverance by her Seed to come/(For by Woman's Seed) on all Mankind" (600-601).

31. This passage is one of many examples in the telluric works of Aguilera-Malta which particularly represents the consubstantial union of man and nature. In *La isla virgen* the theme is evident in the titles of the three parts comprising it: "La tierra" (Book 1), "El hombre" (Book 2), and "La fusión" (Book 3). The blend of human and natural elements is what Luis Alberto Sánchez notes as a striking characteristic of the author's technique: "Exhibe cuadros tan duros, tan descarnados, en que el ser humano y la naturaleza se compenetran de tal manera, que separarlos sería destruir la obra en sí." *Proceso y contenido de la novela hispano-americana* (Madrid: Gredos, 1953), p. 322.

32. *Una cruz en la Sierra Maestra* (Buenos Aires: Sophos, 1960), p. 86. Future references to this work will be abbreviated (e.g., *Cruz*, 86).

33. *El Quijote de El Dorado: Orellana y el Río de las Amazonas (Episodios Americanos,* 2) (Madrid: Guadarrama, 1964), p. 141. Future references to this work will be abbreviated (e.g., *Quijote*, 141).

34. *La caballeresa del sol; El gran amor de Bolívar (Episodios Americanos,* 1) (Madrid: Guadarrama, 1964), p. 259. Future references to this work will be abbreviated (e.g., *Caballeresa* 259).

35. This conclusion is proposed by Angel F. Rojas in his introductory study of *La isla virgen (Isla* xii).

36. The quote is included in an article on the same theme by Peter A. Gunther, "Mental Inertia and Environmental Decay: The End of an Era," *The Living Wilderness,* 34, no. 109 (Spring 1970): 5.

3

The Role of Nature
in Epic Tradition:
Fauna

> And the great dragon was cast out, that old
> serpent, called the Devil, and Satan, which deceiveth
> the whole world: he was cast out into the earth, and
> his angels were cast out with him. [Revelation 12:9]

When the harmony of Eden was disrupted, the creatures
who once cooperatively shared the routines of Adam and Eve
were compelled to initiate hostility among themselves while
men in turn showed no procrastination in undertaking the
new venture involving pursuit and consumption of nature's
beasts. As moving entities with the capacity to defend themselves and to destroy, they could inspire fear more often than
admiration. These nonstatic phenomena with the instinct to
survive posed more of a threat to Adam's scions than
topography and its vegetation which passively awaited
climatic changes or divine will to stir them into ominous
motion.

Serpents

Serpents have played a considerably impressive role in the
development of myths and folklore throughout the history of

man. They have served to attract or repel, frequently with a combination of awe and fear, and in many instances have been typologically integrated into the philosophical and religious structure of certain cultures. For example, the Hindu deity Shiva appears with bracelets, armbands, ankle rings, and brahminical threads which are living serpents that represent the mysterious creative energy of God and immortality.[1] The encircling snake again appears in Germanic cosmology as the Midgard Serpent that holds the middle of the universe (Earth) with its infinite coils. Still powerful, yet ominous, is the role of the serpent in the Egyptian Book of the Dead, which was read at the time of burial and accompanied the deceased on his journey through the Underworld. Here the reptile represented a peril to be generally avoided.[2]

Ophidian imagery and inspiration flourished with the mythology of the Western world, and literary epics after Homer refer to his creations and also to the awesome monsters that Hercules encountered during the fulfillment of his twelve labors. The most fascinating creatures which populate the epic field since the Classical period are generally composites and often include within their structure a serpent element. Cerberus, the three-headed canine which guards the gates of Hades, has snakes encircling each neck (*Aen.* 6. 419), while the Furies, or Eumenides, fly about the epic stage shaking their horned-snake locks. In *Gerusalemme Liberata*, Tasso's Hell is replete with strange supernatural entities that include several seven-mouthed Hydras to enhance the nightmarish atmosphere of the Underworld (*G.L.* 4. 5. 4).

Snakes as prophecy appear on occasion in the *Iliad* to symbolize the destruction of the Trojan army (2. 308ff., 12. 208-209). But in the *Aeneid* maximum use of serpent imagery is made by Virgil. Laocoön, the Trojan priest of Neptune, meets his death along with his sons as he succumbs to the venomous bite of his attackers emerging from the sea (*Aen.* 2. 212-24), while Allecto rouses Turnus by raising two serpents among her viperous tresses (*Aen.* 7. 450). Queen Amata's fate, the war between Turnus and Aeneas, its outcome, and subsequent founding of Rome can all be attributed to a snake. The entire plot is complicated by Allecto's sending a viper at Juno's behest to bite the queen and cause a form of insanity resulting in her favoring Turnus as a choice for Lavinia (*Aen.* 7. 341ff.). Queen Amata becomes mad and begins to run through the woods beckoning all Latin mothers to join her in her cause against Aeneas.

The serpent becomes even more repulsive when multiplied and attached to a human being as some sort of appendage. Medusa's viperous locks serve to petrify anyone casting a glance upon her, and even in death the venomous effect can be felt. In Lucan's epic he relates how Perseus ran across the Libyan desert carrying the severed head of the Gorgon, from which drops of blood fell to form snakes of poisonous character.[3] The poet selects several of the types and immortalizes them in his *Pharsalia*. As Cato's troops cross the desert, some of his men are bitten by vipers, and the agonizing death of each is a memorable tribute to the species:

> . . .A burning prester's fang
> Nasidius struck, who erst in Marsian fields
> Guided the plough. Upon his face there glows
> A redness as of flames; the skin is stretched
> On one vast tumour past the growth of men;
> A gory juice puffs out upon the mass
> That hides his body, and his corslet plates
> Burst with the monstrous bulk. Not to such height
> In brazen cauldron boils the steaming wave,
> Nor in such bellying curves does canvas bend
> To western tempests. Now the pile of flesh
> No more contains the limbs; the shapeless trunk
> Burdens the earth; and there, untouched by fowl,
> To beasts a fatal meal, they leave the corse;
> Nor dare to place, yet swelling, in the tomb.[4]
> [*Pharsalia* 9. 790-804]

The threat of physical harm and potential death that accompanies the snake lends itself to usage in metaphoric expression in literature as in the case of Paris when he shrinks back upon seeing Menelaus (*Il.* 3. 30-37), or Androgeos when he encounters Aeneas (*Aen.* 2. 376-82); but as the epic evolves and is influenced by the Judeo-Christian tradition, the ophidian image beings to carry with it not simply the threat of physical destruction, but potential spiritual corruption and annihilation as well. The relationship of anthropophagy and the reptile becomes closer, and the complexity of attributes encompasses a combination of bestiality and treachery to threaten man's immortality. The serpent at his worst represents the lowest form of God's creatures, the least to be admired, and the last to be trusted.[5]

The "Epic of the Serpent," *Paradise Lost*, reveals even Satan's revulsion at utilizing the body of a snake. He himself is quite aware of the demeaning image that is projected by the creature:

> O foul descent! that I who erst contended
> With Gods to sit the highest, am now constrain'd
> Into a Beast, and mixt with bestial slime.
>
> [*P.L.*9. 163-69]

The technique of degradation by deformity[6] continues when Satan returns to Hell to share his success with the other fallen angels whose shouting and applause are converted into "A dismal universal hiss, the sound / Of public scorn" (*P.L.* 10. 508-509), and whose once-celestial bodies are transformed into a miscellany of reptilian forms.

So too, Adam, when betrayed by his wife, crystallizes her degradation in the select epithet he uses:

> Out of my sight, thou Serpent, that name
> Befits thee with him leagu'd, thyself as false
> And hateful; nothing wants but that thy shape,

Like his, and colour Serpentine may show
Thy inward fraud, to warn all Creatures from thee.[7]
[*P.L.* 10. 867-73]

Most of the serpent references in epic poetry can be found
in Aguilera-Malta's works as well. Although confrontation
with the reptile is an expected occurrence in the tropical
setting of his regional fiction, the major part of symbolic
allusions connotes anthropophagous qualities in nature or in
human beings and what they produce in their societies. The
image conveys a message of destruction, implied or patent,
that threatens the hero's survival. Modern warfare has produced weapons of almost reptilian structure which lend themselves readily to metaphorization. Aguilera-Malta dedicates
two of his works to the Spanish Civil War: the tragedy
España leal and the *réportage-novel ¡Madrid!: reportaje
novelado de una retaguardia heroica.* The tragedy contains
ballads where the imagery is quite impressive for the melee of
steel, lead, fire, and death which is made all the more
terrifying by the use of snake symbolism:

Cantan ametralladoras
haciendo coro a los máuser.
Y serpentinas de plomo
manotean en el aire.

[*España* 24]

In *¡Madrid!* the approaching bombers are announced by
another instrument produced for dispensing terror: the siren.
The author intricately weaves a series of surrealistic images
that culminates in an uncontrollable fury of serpent
references that portend chaos and destruction:

La sirena aúlla larga, prolongadamente.

Se trepa en la noche como una enredadera. Multiplica
acrobacias inesperadas sobre los edificios bañados por una

débil luna. Se sorbe íntegros los pisos más distantes. Y sus ramos de víboras desparramadas hurgan los oídos soñolientos de todo el vecindario.

[*Madrid* 95][8]

The snake as a portent of doom in literary or authentic epic is frequently introduced by some external power that controls the destiny of the hero. But reptilian imagery can also communicate the imminent destruction of the hero, often self-imposed. One of the first dramas of Demetrio Aguilera-Malta is *Lázaro*, the tragedy of a teacher who is duped into signing a document renouncing his ideals, without which his life becomes a farce. Under the influence of alcohol, the human equivalent of the serpent's venom, Lázaro's tongue is loosened, his ambitions and desires expressed, while Julia, the woman he has secretly loved, listens. His spiritual destruction begins with self-deprecating imagery that is a miscellany of ophidian symbols to reveal his deep-rooted frustration and agony. The tension and pitch of the drama fluctuate erratically as does the mood of the protagonist, and are stabilized in serpent allusions that reflect Lázaro's judgment of his own worth. Calling himself a "dragón con alas de mariposa,"[9] Lázaro intensifies the pathetic impression of his dwindling dignity. In the grotesque image, the dragon symbolizes a wish to have power and respect instead of being an underdog who is ridiculed; but the butterfly's wings, the delicate and sensitive soul he possesses, can never bear lifting the burden to heights above his oppressors. He attempts to fight the battle of self-containment but cannot restrain the words of love he has guarded for so long. After arduous combat with his emotions, Lázaro finally succumbs:

Aunque no quiera, las palabras me brotan en los labios. ¡No puedo contenerlas!. . .¡Es como si no fueran mías mis palabras!. . .Se me atropellan aquí, en la garganta. . .

como un puñado de cordones eléctricos, como un puñado de víboras enloquecidas. . . .Soy impotente para contenerlas.

[*Lázaro* 15]

He finally sinks to the earthly level and reflects the scorn directed at him and which has its source also within him by using another undulating image associated with destruction as he dubs himself a "gusano con sueños de héroe" (p. 15).

The heroine of *La caballeresa del sol*, Manuela Sáenz, is perhaps the novelistic modernization of Virgil's Dido. Each woman plays a significant role in relation to the hero's goal and destiny; and both also stand as obstacles despite the great love that motivates their behavior. Society's influence is just as strongly felt in the Latin epic as it is in the story of Manuela and Simón Bolívar. The manifestation of censure and gossip is a sufficiently anthropophagous instrument without transformation into a bestial entity being needed; but in both tales of love and war, verbal persecution is converted into a teratoid representation to intensify the potentially catastrophic effect that slander can have. In the *Aeneid* the awesome figure of Rumor flies about. It is a plumed creature with innumerable tongues, pricked-up ears, and hissing mouths, one for each feather that bears an eye.[10] But for Manuela it is the snake that represents the evil propagation of calumny:

Quisieron hacerle daño, con los medios que estaban al alcance de sus manos. Especialmente, la defamación y la calumnia, que empezaron a envolverla, como anillos de una invisible boa viscosa.

[*Caballeresa* 190]

Viperous tongues indicate one aspect of the serpent imagery that is used in *La caballeresa del sol*. In addition, Manuela's emotional state and that of her volatile and

devoted maid, Jonatás, are described in ophiomorphic terms.
When Jonatás is highly enraged or excited:

> Los labios y los pómulos parecían hinchársele, como le
> habían contado que ocurría con ciertas víboras coléricas.
> [*Caballeresa* 28]

The snake, however, does participate actively in Manuela's
drama. Upon learning of the Liberator's death, she attempts
suicide, not using a man-made instrument of destruction as
Dido does with Aeneas's sword, but the reptile itself, whose
symbol so adequately presented the means for conveying a
message of evil that constantly surrounded Bolívar and his
mistress. No longer able to continue the battle against
society, Manuela offers herself, like Cleopatra, to the viper's
fangs, but is unsuccessful in her efforts.

The serpent appears in *La isla virgen* to function in one of
the subplots as a complex entity performing several roles to
determine the destiny of two characters, Tejón and Márgara.
Much in the same way as snake imagery is utilized to unify
the second book of the *Aeneid*, here also the reptile portends
disaster, acts to destroy, and symbolizes the eventual revitalization or rebirth of the people involved. Tejón, a *cholo* who
is employed by Néstor on the Virgin Island, is bitten by a
rattlesnake. A young man of exceptional fortitude and
courage, he raises his machete, strikes a heavy blow to begin
the process of extracting the poison from his leg. But
infection sets in, and, as he lies thinking of the past, the
dubious future, and the girl he loves, he begins to consider
the possibility of losing his leg:

> ¿Y si le pudriera la pierna? ¿Y si estuviera condenado a
> no andar más sobre sus propios pies? Por un momento,
> se imagina con una pata de palo, o arrastrándose, como
> un reptil, sobre la panza de los cerros. ¿Cómo trabajará
> entonces? Y—esto mucho peor, aún—¿cómo hará para
> portarse como un hombre con la Márgara?
> [*Isla* 24]

In the very normal, very real considerations the image of the
serpent has been compounded to parallel Tejón's infected
leg, the possible wooden one if he loses his own, or none at
all, which would mean ambulation comparable to that of a
snake—crawling—and finally, concern for his masculinity,
which involves the sexual act and contains the phallic echo of
the serpent.

In Tejón's subsequent thoughts the serpentine image
evolves into the symbol of actual death and decomposition
—the worm. The *cholo* begins to visualize his worsening state
in connection with his own past experiences when he applied
medication to the deteriorating tissue of other bodies:

> Muchas veces, personalmente, tuvo que echarles creolina.
> Observó, de cerca, la materia infectada. Era a modo de
> una gran rosa abierta sobre la carne viva. Insoportable
> hedor giraba en torno. Hubo ocasiones en que pudo ad-
> vertir las tripas colgantes, los huesos descubiertos, o,
> sencillamente, los músculos rojiblancos. De ellos, surgía
> la pus espesa, untosa, repugnante. Y—al fondo—más
> repugnantes aun, los vermes.
>
> [*Isla* 25]

The phenomenon of living decay is without doubt a reality in
the tropics, and Tejón's fear is justified as he too begins to
notice the gruesome transformation of his own leg: it has now
become infected with vermin.

When Márgara is aware of his condition, she comes to tend
Tejón, and he is restored to health through a combination of
nursing skills and love. The fortuitous circumstances
brought about by the snake's bite result in a determination to
flee the island and the *patrón*. The odds are against the
lovers; few have survived the hardships that are presented by
nature and its creatures. As they struggle through the tropical
vegetation, they encounter many a threat to survival,
including ominous vipers, which now, oddly enough, seem to
avoid contact with Tejón:

Lo que se ve a cada instante son culebras. Sallamas, sobre-camas, papagayos, bejucos. De las buenas, sí muy pocas. Una chonta que se hinchó al advertirlos, enfurecida, pero que huyó en seguida; una coral, que el Tejón mató. Y nada más.

[*Isla* 177][11]

Tejón comments on his mysterious new power which has converted him into an implacable enemy of the reptiles:

—Es que desde que me picó la equis, ya las demás me respetan.

[*Isla* 177]

Their escape from the island is successful. A resurrected Tejón, charged with new energy, strength, and optimism, goes forth to begin what promises to be a better life on the mainland.

Tejón, the only one to escape from the Virgin Island, leaves an atmosphere that recalls the second book of *Aeneid*, whose structure is based on serpent and fire imagery and reflects the theme of death and violence. The twin serpents come out of the sea to destroy Laocoön and his sons (199-227); Androgeos, upon encountering Aeneas, is compared to a man who shrinks back in horror as he unexpectedly treads upon a snake (378-81), and Pyrrhus, the son of Achilles, before he kills Priam is also likened to the reptile (469-75). Out of the death and conflagration that envelope Troy, however, Aeneas exits to re-create the Ilium that perished in the forthcoming conquest of Latium, his marriage with Lavinia, and the eventual founding of Rome by his scions.[12] Similarly, a new Tejón emerges from the devastating experiences on the island to face a brighter future with Márgara by his side.

The most varied combination of reptilian imagery is concentrated in the novel *Siete lunas y siete serpientes*, which begins in the midst of Dominga's nightly ritual to calm her sexual anxiety. From her bed, in an almost paralyzed state, the young girl watches the satyr-like dwarf[13] who must now do battle with the approaching serpent. After the mythical creature is fatally bitten by the snake, the attempted seduction of Dominga continues with the reptile as suitor reaching her bed and slithering about her:

> Un escalofrío la recorrió. De los pies a la cabeza. El ofidio siguió avanzando. ¿En qué forma podría detenerlo? ¡Si le fuera dable hacer algún movimiento! Imposible. Tenía la impresión de que se estaba convirtiendo en una estatua. Fría. Inmóvil. Mientras la X-Rabo-de-Hueso continuaba reptando encima de ella. Envolviéndola. Subiendo—en incontenible anudamiento—hasta su cuello.
>
> [7/7 14]

But Dominga survives to strangle the serpent and bury it in the ground, only to repeat the ceremony for seven successive nights.[14]

An impressive example of serpent imagery used to forecast doom is found in an episode reminiscent of the *Aeneid*'s twin serpents, which come out of the sea from Tenedos to kill Laocoön and his sons—a scene which also portends Troy's destruction. The doubly monstrous symbol as an omen represents the treacherous Greeks and the violence that will accompany the fall of Troy. In *Siete lunas y siete serpientes* there are two "armies" that stand in opposition to each other. One consists of the priest Cándido, the doctor from the city, Juvencio Balda, who has extracted the rosebush from Tolón's hand, and Clotilde Quindales, the girl who did not escape Candelario's violence during the night of her parents' massacre. The other host is made up of the men who are bent on exterminating anyone who challenges their absolute control of Santorontón. They are represented by the military, civil, and church figures led and dominated by Crisóstomo Chalena, the evil financial and economic power. Juvencio lies in Candido's hut recuperating after a merciless

beating by Chalena's henchmen because he extracted the
rosebush from the child's palm, and the hiatus in violence is
much like that granted Troy after the Greeks seem to have
departed. The priest watches an approaching canoe which
suddently appears carrying an ominous-looking crew:

> De improviso, se levantó la arena de la orilla. Empezó
> a girar con rapidez vertiginosa. La arena de la orilla.
> En medio de ellos. Arropándolos. Envolviéndolos. En olas
> ascendentes de tirabuzón de dientes, ojos, cabellos, torsos,
> manos, pies. . . .Poco a poco, se fue integrando, en primer
> plano, la figura de una víbora tricéfala.
>
> [7/7 113]

The tricephalic serpent is the chief of police and his men,
who have come to arrest Juvencio. But one reptilian symbol
of evil and destruction is succeeded by another familiar
tropical monster, the crocodile, which follows the serpent to
the shore:

> Atrás del ofidio de aspecto tridente, daban vueltas cinco
> cabezas de caimán, sin cola. Cinco cabezas de caimán
> unidas por el tronco. Cinco cabezas de caimán con dos
> patas. Cinco cabezas de caimán que andaban como un
> carrousel, girando sobre el eje de su unión. Cinco cabezas
> de caimán horrible estrella viva de cinco puntas.
>
> [7/7 113-14]

The five-headed cayman is Chalena and the remaining
maleficent figures of power who will complete the forces that
have come to arrest the doctor for a murder he did not
commit. The ominous portents of violence assume their
anthropomorphic structure and continue their pattern of
destruction which will be temporarily suspended when the
symbol of salvation—the wooden crucifix—intervenes.

But the serpent which is used in the novel to connote death
and violence eventually finds its redemption by participating
in the rebirth of Santorontón. To combat the periodic

drought and Chalena, who has stored water which is withheld from the animals but rationed out to those humans who can pay for it, the technological skill of man combines with the collaborating physical resources of the animals to construct a primitive reservoir that will provide the necessary supply for the villagers. The serpent sheds his treacherous skin and participates with the other beasts, ferocious and docile alike, in a communal endeavor to save themselves and the village. In this context of harmony, the snake recalls his first role in the Garden of Eden. The "subtl'st Beast of all the field" (*P.L.* 7. 495) is "not noxious, but obedient" (*P.L.* 7. 498), as are the other creatures, and he too is capable of joining the battle against the forces of evil.

Water Monsters

For the seafaring heroes of the Mediterranean epics, Poseidon's wrath transferred to tormented waters was not the only threat to survival. Lurking in the deep were strange monsters mothered by Amphitrite or descended from Oceanus, and neither divine nor mortal being was entirely secure in or near the element. Hippolytus, cursed by his father Theseus, meets his doom while riding his chariot along the coast when his horses, frightened by sea beasts appearing near the shore, overturn the chariot and drag the youth along the ground, and Hercules, as is related in the *Iliad* (20. 145-48), was forced from the shore to seek refuge on higher land when a sea monster began to pursue him. The inhabitants of the waters were often inspirational models for the ships which reflected the ferocity of the warriors preparing to invade foreign shores:

> . . .the mighty "Triton" that terrifies the sea
> with dark blue conch, his shaggy front swims in the waves
> like a man down to the waist, but with a fish's belly.

Beneath the monster's breast the waves are churned to
    foam.

[*Aen.* 10. 209-212]

But traveling across the colder northern seas the heroes in
search of adventure also had to contend with the awesome
creatures that surged from the murky abyss:

Above the water many of the dragon
Race, the strange sea-dragons who explored
The tides, and likewise nicors lying on
The headlong slopes; sea-serpents and sea-beasts
Who often in the morning slip along
The sail-road on a journey sorrowful
To men. These rushed below, wrath-puffed
And bitter, for they heard the call, the war-horn
Singing. . . .[15]

Homer, however, for the most part ignores fabled
monsters of the deep and assigns the major role of destruction not to any aberration that inhabits the waters, but rather
to the normal species found in rivers and the seas, and the
reference is generally of religious or moral import. Vengeance
was not complete with the death of the enemy; to be denied
proper burial and the funeral pyre was tantamount to
dishonor. The worst fate a hero or the common individual
could meet was to be left as carrion for nature's beasts. The
warriors of the *Iliad* are particularly conscious of such a
dishonorable death, and this concern is brilliantly realized in
Book 21, where aquatic imagery and participation are most
skillfully employed. Achilles, son of the sea-goddess Thetis,
slaughters numerous Trojans in the River Xanthus. His fury
finds many a target as his enemies fall into the current. When
Achilles, still seeking revenge for Patroclus's death, encounters Lykaon, he finds no mercy in his heart to spare this
son of Priam. After striking Lykaon with his sword, the
Greek warrior dispatches him to his fluvial tomb and rapid
extermination:

"Lie there now among the fish, who will lick the blood
　　away
from your wound, and care nothing for you, nor will
　　your mother
lay you on the death-bed and mourn over you, but
　　Skamandros
will carry you spinning down to the wide bend of the
　　salt water.
And a fish will break a ripple shuddering dark on the
　　water
as he rises to feed upon the shining fat of Lykaon."

[*Il.* 122-27]

　　The carnivorous marine species that inhabit the tropical
waters of Aguilera-Malta's islands function both in a literal
sense by destroying the native and also as symbolic inspiration to intensify moral or social aberrations. The shark,
supreme in the equatorial seas, finds little challenge from the
less powerful creatures that share his environment.[16]
Aguilera-Malta, for the most part, uses the shark in
metaphysical representations of evil as he would any monster
that challenges a hero with annihilation. For Panama the
invasion of the sharks is symbolized by the United States fleet
on maneuvers in the second part of *Canal Zone*, where
battleships assume the properties of thousands of selachian
creatures grouped together:

　　Eran 40,000 y habían llegado en numerosos barcos. Ahora
　　en la tarde, se veían los escualos de acero arrimando sus
　　panzas formidables a los muelles rechinantes. Erizados de
　　cañones y corazas, se dijeran monstruosos triceratopos
　　milenarios. Desafiaban a los hombres, a la tierra y al mar.
　　Se alineaban en filas aplastantes sobre la espalda oblicua
　　de las cosas humilladas.

[*C.Z.* 78]

Pedro Coorsi feels the futility of his existence confronted on
one side by the monster the canal represents, and on the
other, by the colossal marine beasts docked in the harbor.

The dogfish image dominates *Una cruz en la Sierra Maestra*, where the military figure Sergeant Padilla symbolizes maximum tyranny in abusing the people who are his captives. A former fisherman, now representative of the dictatorship which has ruled the nation, Padilla is aptly represented by the shark in his ferocity and thirst for blood. The reflection of the marine beast, however, is sustained psychologically in the reality of the soldier's past and is echoed during the critical hours he spends in the hamlet terrorizing the peasants. Padilla recalls his brother's face—a face which has tormented him for years because of the memories it can resurrect of the time when he loved a woman and was rejected. Coralia, he believed, abandoned him for Raúl, his brother. Obsessed with revenge, uncontrollable and determined, Padilla sets fire to the boat which shelters, he thinks, the lovers. From a distance he witnesses the Dantesque image of flames and disoriented figures in the twilight tropical sun while the sea and the wind join the *danse macabre*. The only escape is to fling themselves into the shark-infested sea. The entire episode is ironically drawn, with fire consuming the boat while the surrounding waters serve merely as a haven for their executioners. The sharks can be vaguely distinguished by Padilla as they dart about flashing a triangular symbol of destruction to parallel the three-sided relationship which the sergeant believes exists. The sounds of the wind and the sea smother Padilla's repentant call to his brother and the woman to wait and not jump into the sea; he is on his way to save them.

The entire recollection complements the futility of the peasants now at his mercy: the woman who perished with Raúl was not Coralia. The experience of that day results in Padilla's breakdown, the subsequent obsession with fire and water, and the eventual return to a life of destruction as a military tyrant. By the time he discovers the fugitive rebels whose whereabouts he perceives "as a shark senses blood"

(*Cruz* 100), his own mental condition is irremediable. At the end of the novel the sergeant contemplates burning the hut and the people within while a blazing sun shines on him. Finally he turns his gun upon himself to face the same violent method of annihilation that he employed in destroying so many others.

The Cephalopod and Tentacles

Less common in epic poetry as a monster of the deep is the octopus. When it does appear in Homer, the image is used in connection with survival during Odysseus's final bout with Poseidon's fury. As he struggles to avoid being crushed against the rocks, he seizes one to escape the great wave sent by the Earthshaker:

> . . .This one
> he so escaped, but the backwash of the same wave
>   caught him
> where he clung and threw him far out in the open water.
> As when an octopus is dragged away from its shelter
> The thickly-clustered pebbles stick in the cups of the
>   tentacles,
> so in contact with the rock the skin from his bold
>   hands
> was torn away. . .
>
> [*Od.* 429-35]

The tenacity of the mollusk is the core of the simile, and the characteristics of strength, suction, and grip are conveyed to parallel the Ithacan king's contact with the rock which means his salvation. In reverse manner, but developing the same attributes of the marine creature to connote death, destruction, and violence, Aguilera-Malta uses the octopus image.

In *Canal Zone* the cephalopod is used to describe the technological monstrosity of the twentieth century, the Panama Canal, which seems to grow in proportion to the protagonist's despair:

> Se lo imaginaba como un pulpo colosal, de tentáculos innumerables. Se lo representaba su imaginación con su rechinamiento de compuertas, con su vomitar continuo de torrentes de agua, con su parpadear de grúas y su bufar de barcos, creciendo día a día. Sorbía la sangre de todos: de los que pasaban, de los que vivían en su derredor, de los que soñaban, desde lejos, en conocerlo y en cruzarlo. Lo veía monstruoso, inaudito, poco a poco, iba tomando más forma en su mente el sombrío delineamiento del pulpo. Desaparecían de sus ojos la ciudad, la calle, los hombres, los escaparates. Allí—frente a él—creciendo a cada rato más y más, se le aparecía, más bien el horroroso habitante de los mares, moviendo, en remolino trepidante, sus adherentes látigos enormes.
>
> [*C.Z.* 33]

With the arrival of the United States fleet on the mainland, intent on conquering the bars and houses of ill repute, sea imagery continues depicting the absorption of human beings by the canal and the nightclubs function in their own distinctive way:

> Las cantinas parecieron llamar. Y las cantinas llenaron. Como inauditos cefalópodos atraparon íntegros los hombres.
>
> [*C.Z.* 77]

Alcohol and the octopus again join forces in *La isla virgen* to annihilate the underdog. Don Celeste provides Don Merelo with *cholos* to work on the islands, for which they receive negligible recompense. The *cholos* have accumulated debts in Don Celeste's store and they are pressed to accept the arrangement as a means of payment. To establish the mood which would be conducive to their willing departure, the

Indians are given drinks and are eventually intoxicated. As the scene progresses and their stupor increases, the effect is one of discord, imbalance, and incoherence, until they withdraw to the square to await boarding the vessel that will carry them to their doom:

> La noche sigue adentrándose en el ambiente. En la plaza oscurecida difícilmente se pueden distinguir los perfiles humanos. Sólo es una gran sombra batida, agitada, verdadero pulpo de innúmeros tentáculos.
>
> [*Isla* 334]

The imagery of the octopus is complex in meaning. The swirling agitation of the tentacles portends the movement of the sea, where the *cholos* will soon disappear. It also suggests by the consubstantial blend of vague human outlines and mollusk-like shadows a visual preview of the Indians' death. Finally, there is a reflection of the sea beast's gelatinous quality in the inebriated condition of the victims, which has rendered them all too flexible and amenable to their predetermined fate and the nefarious plans of their exploiters.

In the novel *Siete lunas y siete serpientes* the octopus appears again as a symbol of death, this time within its own element. Padre Cándido, on one of his frequent visits to his more distant parishioners, is caught up in a whirlpool from which there appears no escape. In the midst of an attempted rescue by dolphins, the whirlpool begins to assume the properties of the powerful creature of the deep:

> Le parecía que la líquida espiral volvíase zoomórfica. Era un pulpo enorme. Un gigantesco pulpo verde. Que lo había apretado entre sus innúmeros tentáculos. El "ojo" del remolino constituía su cabeza. Los expirales de olas, cada vez más débiles, eran las extremidades que se le iban aflojando al cefalópodo. Segundo a segundo, se veía más lejos.
>
> [*7/7* 38]

Cándido's fantasy involves the opposition of marine symbols to represent good and evil: the cephalopod, a diabolic anthropomorphic entity threatening destruction, and the amiable, clever cetaceans, which succeed in saving the priest from the whirlpool. Once out of the vortex, Cándido, who has no means of propulsion (he has lost the paddle of his canoe), is aided by another creature related to the sea, the pelican. A group of five pulls the vessel to safety while Cándido marvels at the occurrence. He considers the possibility of free will among animals as well as humans, and his speculations recall God's commentary to Adam that the beasts "also know, / And reason not contemptibly." [*P.L.* 8. 373-74]

The Amphibian Monster

The monsters of the deep stimulate sufficient terror when in their element, but there are those creatures endowed with amphibian characteristics that enable them to depart from their native waterways and initiate an equally violent career of destruction on land. Sea serpents and nicors were insignificant when compared with Grendel's mother, "the cursed monster of the depths, the mighty mere-wife" (*Beo.* 80), who could leave her domain, roam and ravage the earth, finally to meet her end at the hands of Beowulf.[17] Zoomorphic or anthropomorphic, the invaders out of the sea rarely symbolized noble or virtuous forces. They were almost invariably enemies. The foreign beast in twin-serpent form destroyed Laocoön and his sons and prefaced Troy's downfall; no less ominous are the ships that carry Yuçef to oppose the Cid in Spain or Baligant to fight the Franks.[18] And the conquerors who landed in the New World undoubtedly presented a fearsome impression of metallic creatures emerging from the ocean.

The awesome king of the tropical river, the crocodile, appears in his native surroundings to crowd the shores and mud banks while indifferently observing the vessels that pass. The saurian menace in Latin America is frequently present in Aguilera-Malta's historical novels whenever aquatic mishaps occur. As if revived in the current, the beast quickly dismisses terrestrial lethargy for enthusiastic participation in the unexpected banquet of Indians and Spaniards alike within a few moments after a boat has capsized *(Mar* 110, 126). However, in *Siete lunas y siete serpientes* the human crocodile, Candelario Mariscal, unlike his zoological counterpart, is equally efficient on land and in the water. The creature's anthropophagous characteristics in particular are applied symbolically to the ignoble colonel's satanic attributes and his impulse to consume the weak and helpless underdog.

Candelario, whose life of violence has earned him the reputation of being Satan's son, slips into a canoe whose occupants are forced to carry him at the risk of losing their lives if any opposition is shown. Candelario, Man-Crocodile, confirm his notoriety by killing one of the men while the other, almost paralyzed with fear, begins to comply with his every wish. As the distance between the canoe and the shore grows greater, "El Coronel" (as Candelario now calls himself) performs two acts that add to the legend of his occult powers. With no provisions aboard to satisfy his hunger, Candelario reaches into the calm sea and, as if responding to his summons, a school of mullets hastens to the canoe and they offer themselves to the Colonel, who gathers them up with his hands. His terrified companion, Canchona, speculates about a means of escape but is interrupted by the crocodile smile of Candelario, who has read his thoughts and will continue tormenting him until he no longer has use for his services. The Crocodile's sardonic grimace, now accentuated, connects the Miracle of the Fishes with the following episode which convinces Canchona that Candelario is indeed the son of Satan:

—Lo único que tienes que hacer es obedecerme.

—Sí, mi Coronel.

Sin agregar palabra, Candelario Mariscal se arrojó al agua. Apenas la tocó, caimán. Regresó la cabeza. Ya verde. Trompuda. Horrible. Se abrieron sus fauces colmillos colmilludas colmillonarias. Espantosas.

—¡Súbete en mi espalda!

El Tuerto tartamudeó:

—¿Qué? ¿Qué dice?

—Lo que oíste. ¡Apúrate!

[*7/7* 104]

Canchona, rendered helpless by fear and the superior force that commands him, jumps onto the back of the Cayman to join him in a career of destructive adventure.

But Candelario Mariscal also has his turn to be smiled upon by the crocodile, and it occurs on the eve of his marriage to Bulu-Bulu's daughter, Dominga. Alone, pondering his future with a wholesome, attractive, and most important of all, human bride, he is not surprised to see his nightly visitor, the ghost of Josefa Quindales. As usual Candelario's nightmare of making love to the girl who has been buried for two years is as intensely passionate as his desire was for her the night he killed her parents. Now, when Colonel Mariscal has abandoned his life of violence, now, after he has sought release from the macabre pattern of orgy with a dead woman, Josefa (Chepa) returns to satisfy his desire and continue her revenge of sexual annihilation. The retired villain's concern while the session of lovemaking continues is whether or not he will be virile enough for his bride, Dominga, the next day. But Josefa has read his mind much in the same way that the Man-Crocodile could penetrate the thoughts of his victims, and she warns her lover of his impotence on the wedding night. Furious at Josefa's plan to intrude after he is married and the scandal it would cause, he rushes at the departing ghost:

—¡Ya lárgate y no me jodas más!
Esqueleto. Esqueleto en la puerta. Risa calcárea. De
pulidos maxilares. Esqueleto. Luz en las cuencas vacías.
Luz mortuoria. De velones taciturnos. Esqueleto riendo.
Risa calcárea. Al propio tiempo, risa de caimán al engullir
su presa. Calcárea.

[7/7 364-65]

Sensual delight turns into cold horror as Josefa's threat is
reflected in her conversion into a skeleton and strengthened
by the evil laugh of the saurian beast ingesting its prey.

Satan, who can assume any form in his campaign of
destruction, has not overlooked the innocuous-appearing
batrachian. The Fall begins when the Fiend is observed

Squat like a Toad, close at the ear of *Eve*;
Assaying by his Devilish art to reach
The Organs of her Fancy;. . .

[*P.L.* 4. 800-802]

Just as he entered the serpent's mouth and acquired his most
notorious appearance, so too the forces that aligned themselves with evil were released in the same way to roam the
universe:

And I saw three unclean spirits like frogs *come* out of the
mouth of the dragon, and out of the mouth of the beast,
and out of the mouth of the false prophet.
For they are the spirits of devils, working miracles, *which*
go forth unto the kings of the earth and of the whole
world, to gather them to the battle of that great day of God
Almighty.

[Revelation 16:13-14]

In *Siete lunas y siete serpientes* Demetrio Aguilera-Malta
also assigns the form of a frog or toad to the primary
demonic character, Crisóstomo Chalena, who has made a

pact with the Devil to become the wealthiest man in the village. As his control of the water supply and the people increases, so do his batrachian properties:

> El hombre había cambiado de un día para otro. Tenía fajas verde-amarillas sapo gigante. Los brazos y piernas se le habían enmagrecido y encogido. El vientre capar-azón de quelonio se le agitaba, fuelle vivo. Casi no podía abrir los ojos—ojillos, ojales, ojículos—. Lo que le seguía creciendo era la boca.
>
> [7/7 134]

Chalena's amphibiotic development is also like that of his ancestors, for he too spent his youth in one element and later settled on land during his adult years. Abandoned by his mother, Chalena traveled on a ship piloted by his father, a rather despicable character who left an indelible mark on his offspring's psyche. Though his father's scorn foments hatred for mankind in general, it also stifles young Crisóstomo's masculinity, which, like the tail of the tadpole, slowly recedes and finally disappears. Sexual activity becomes internalized in thought as his virility is smothered by the waves of adipose tissue. Chalena rests in his hammock after disposing of Tolón and his mother, La Muda, devising his next scheme; and like the frog, he emits croaking sounds that vibrate in the folds of what barely resembles a neck:

> Sa-u. Po-cug. Sapo-ucug. Sapo verde. Sapo negro. Sapo amarillo. Sapo hinchado. No sapo chico-jambatu. Sapo grande-ucug. Tirado en su hamaca. Sin Muda meciendo. Sin Tolón venteando. Sapo sapeando. No jambatuando. Ucugando. No jambatu. Ucug. El sapo Chalena. Chalena no jambatu. Chalena ucug. ¿Rurruillag Chalena? ¿Chal-ena capón? ¿Rurruillag Ucug? ¿Sapo grande capón? Chalena capón. Auto capón. Por hundirse en sí mismo. Por hundir dentro de él sus partes viriles. Por filo-auto-atrofiarse. Por minimizar todo aquello que le aminorase su sed de poder. Su hambre de plata.
>
> [7/7 255]

Aguilera-Malta, in creating Crisóstomo Chalena, patterns him physically after the cold-blooded animal, to degrade and expose his particular vice. Chalena's lust for wealth supersedes any other passion; his drive is directed toward a cold, lifeless, metallic substance. The name "Crisóstomo" alludes to the golden composition of his mouth, which grows to accommodate limitless amounts of the material while his sexuality diminishes. Removed from the human desire for contact and warmth, his virility is of no consequence, and thus his characteristics of masculinity atrophy. Chalena is rendered, by his own will, into a sort of eunuch, incapable of participating in normal sexual pleasures and eternally denied the love of any woman.

The Crustacean and the Claw

Among the smaller inhabitants of the sea that sally forth to conspire actively or symbolically in the destruction of the hero is the crustacean. The creature, quick to withdraw when confronted by man, is unusually tenacious when his claws have grasped the enemy. When nature joins the antagonistic forces opposing the inhabitant of Aguilera-Malta's islands, the crab participates along with the other zoomorphic monsters of the tropics. In the novel *Don Goyo*, the *cholos*, following the advice of the old patriarch, decide to abandon their basic means of livelihood, which is cutting wood from the mangrove to sell to the white man. Don Goyo, in communion with the largest and oldest tree of the island, believes they should look to the inhabitants of the water for sustenance. The *cholos* encounter little success in what appears to be another rebellion of nature against man; for fish, oysters, clams, and crabs, in all their abundance, flee their pursuers. The crustacean, with his weapon of destruction, the claw, faces the *cholo* fearlessly, makes his attack from the hollow trunk of a tree, and succeeds in hitting his target:

Levantó el cholo la mano, sacándole de un tirón desde el hueco en que la tenía metida. Y entonces todos vieron, atónitos, que un enorme crustáceo de carapacho azul le colgaba. Gruesas gotas de sangre caían al suelo. Medio advirtieron una tenaza dentada cerrándose sobre uno de los dedos del pobre hombre.

—¡La sin boca!

El cholo, en esfuerzo loco, estrelló el animal contra una varenga de mangle. El crustáceo se agitó pesadamente unos segundos. Y después, quedó inmóvil, rígido, con las patas abiertas; pero sin aflojar el dedo mordido, colgando siempre, en un baño de sangre, de la carne del cholo, con los ojos levantados, como dos periscopios diminutos.

—¡Me ha fregado!

[*D.G.* 112-13]

Perhaps the most famous claw in epic tradition is found in *Beowulf*, and the havoc it causes results in the death of many brave men. The valiant hero faces Grendel, who is part giant, yet also a sea monster which dwells in the murky waters of the mere. Although the anthropophagous prowler manages to depart after battle with the leader of the Geats, he leaves behind the trophy of Beowulf's victory and proof of his imminent death. All those gathered in the hall of Heorot gaze upon Beowulf and the synecdochic symbol of his triumph as the scop describes the motionless claw:

Each socket of the nails was most like steel,
each handspur of the heathen champion a horrid
spike; all said no excellent sword's iron of the bold
could so lay on that it would cleave the monster's
bloody battle-hand. . . .

[*Beo.* 64]

Aguilera-Malta often uses the properties of the crustacean or its pincers to describe the annihilating characteristics of the jungle (*Quijote* 53) and a parasitic plant (*Isla* 51); the flaming extensions of fire reaching toward the sky find metaphorization as well in the claw (*Cruz* 133; *7/7* 206). But when the natural appendage is modified by an artificial substance created by man, the impression is more psychological or sociopolitical. In the play *Lázaro,* the hero, who is threatened by forces surrounding him, interprets reality—the corrupt society in which one's principles must be sacrificed in order to survive—as an entity attacking him with its claw of lead (p. 16); the claw destroys both dreams and the idealist who is capable of creating them. Succumbing to the stifling, over-powering pressure indicated by the heavy metal, Lázaro wins the woman he has loved, and simultaneously becomes an economic and social success. The price is himself, or the "other" Lázaro, who believed in nobler things. Obsessed with the "murder" he has committed in his fantasy, he is compelled to confess the secret which has been plaguing him. His fiancée, Julia, unaware of his spiritual deterioration, listens to his frenetic struggle to tell her:

> Tengo que decírtelo mismo. . . .Es un secreto que todo este tiempo me ha quemado los labios; que ha arañado las vértebras con su garra de vidrio.
>
> [*Lazaro* 28]

Lázaro's anguish cannot be alleviated, for although he has not killed the person he claims he has, his ideals, once compromised, can never be restored. The image of the glass claw carries with it the crystal-like quality of his private thought, his sensitive character, and the irreparable damage that has been done to his spirit.

Weapons of war and their metallic composition readily find their symbolic translation in the crab and its chelae as in the tragedy of the Spanish Civil War, *España leal.* Since description is limited because of the genre employed, Aguilera-Malta's lyrical interpretation of the drama is largely found in the three ballads recited in the play. The *romance* dedicated to one of the heroes of the war, Antonio Coll, is recited and the symbolism of the country's destruction is intensely manifested in the imagery which blends weapons of metallic substance and the creatures of nature. The tank, ominous in and of itself, acquires even more of a teratoid character when the crustacean figure becomes the metaphor:

> Crustáceo de gris acero
> con caparazón de sangre
> marcha bebiendo distancias
> en los botijos del aire.

[España 57]

But the claw, associated generally with the crawling shellfish, is reserved for another creature of power and destruction, the lion, whose historical trajectory is appropriately drawn to express the slaughter of a multitude of people. The familiar bullring of Spanish tradition becomes the scene of mass annihilation during the war and recalls the more barbarous aspect of Roman culture displayed in the Coliseum. In the ballad dedicated to the workers of Badajoz, Aguilera-Malta describes the massacre of the inhabitants who were herded into the bull ring to face their death by machine-gun fire:

> Los minutos se estremecen
> en los párpados del Sol.
> se dijera que la arena
> es un inmenso reloj.
> La angustia sube a los cuellos
> como la garra de un león
> y panderetas de sangre
> se elevan, en surtidor.

[España 44]

The simile of the lion's claw is an imposing one because of the three circular images—the arena, the clock, and the tambourine, a musical instrument which adds to converting the episode into a scene of macabre, sadistic entertainment.

Aguilera-Malta combines the modern with the most ancient forms of destruction, and compounds the horror of sophisticated weaponry by paralleling it with a primitive means of slaughter and enhancing it all with the perennial enemy of man—time.

Creatures of the Air

The clawed monster emerging from the sea to pursue its quarry on land has a winged equivalent in the flying species whose performance is just as disastrous for humans and whose presence in epic tradition is as frequent as the violence of warfare. In the form of eagle, hawk, or vulture, the bird of prey functions as a bearer of evil tidings, or in a simile to describe a mighty hero destroying his opponent. Even the lesser entomological creatures can do significant damage, a fact of which Homer was aware when he compared the plight of the suitors to that of a herd of cattle pursued by a horse fly:

and they stampeded about the hall, like a herd of cattle
set upon and driven wild by the darting horse fly
in the spring season, at the time when the days grow longer.

[*Od.* 22. 299-301]

The carnivorous nature of the flying predator and the havoc winged zoomorphic entities can cause are firmly established in Greek mythology. Both Tityos, for attempting to violate Leto, and Prometheus, for stealing fire from the gods, encounter the torment of vultures feeding upon their livers. The Harpies and the Eumenides play their part in punishing mortals for acts contrary to the laws of social and religious behavior. The Harpies, originally attractive goddesses,[19] evolved through myth and literature into the repulsive alar monstrosities that dwelled on the Strophades Islands and persecuted Phineus for divulging a secret. The powerful Erinyes, however, were born of the blood of Ouranos when Kronos unmanned him,[20] and their origin seems to predict a career closely associated with violence, discord, and hate. Their early function as the avenging deities was one of the punishing acts of violence and disobedience toward parents, the aged, hosts, and suppliants. By the time Virgil wrote his epic, the Furies were related primarily to fostering evil by stimulating disunity and strife. Their home was found in Tartarus, which they shared with many other aberrations of the natural order. Allecto, the most notorious of the serpent-tressed sisters, is given a major role in the *Aeneid*, where, upon the instigation of the frustrated Juno, she departs from her underworld habitat to sow the seeds of hatred and violence, affecting the once-peaceful Italian nation. Tasso, who found great inspiration in the *Aeneid*, adopts the flying deity and compiles a list of vices that the avenger is capable of creating or stimulating within the Christian camp:

> Rota Aletto fra lor la destra armata,
> E co 'l foco il venen ne' petti mesce.
> Lo sdegno, la follia, la scelerata
> Sete del sangue ognor più infuria e cresce.
> [*G.L.* 8. 72. 1-4]

For the Greek and Latin epicists the taloned creature served more than as a threat to characters confronting death and bodily destruction. Hector threatens Patroclus (*Il.* 16. 836) as the suitors do Odysseus (*Od.* 21. 30). In the Renaissance epic *Gerusalemme Liberata*, Adrasto swears that the same end is in store for Rinaldo, Armida's former lover. Fear of the human body's desecration or abuse by the ravages of vultures is familiar as well in the epics of the medieval period. The Cid's daughters are ruthlessly beaten by their husbands and then abandoned to the mercy of the wild beasts in the forest:

> Leváronles los mantos e las pieles armiñas,
> mas déxanlas marridas en briales y en camisas,
> e a las aves del monte e a las bestias de la
> fiera guisa.[21]

In the *Chanson de Roland*, Charlemagne has a dream which forecasts the battle with the Saracen troops to be led by Baligant. He sees his army besieged by hurricanes, lightning, and thunder, and then by strange flying monsters:

> Grifuns i ad plus de trente milliers,
> Nen i ad cel à Franceis ne se giet.
>
> [*Roland* 2544-45]

The aerial monsters capable of killing or devouring the hero are not always awesome in appearance. They can even be insignificant in size. Thetis finds her son, Achilles, weeping over Patroclus not only because he mourns the loss of a dear friend, but for his body itself, which will soon begin to deteriorate. The goddess promises to preserve the body for a year and protect it from the scavengers: " 'the swarming and fierce things, / those flies, which feed upon the bodies of men who have perished,' " (19. 30-31).

In Milton's *Paradise Lost*, the winged zoomorphic image alludes primarily to evil that corrupts man's soul, that is, Satan, but the physical extinction of human beings also is represented in the activities of Satan's son, Death. At liberty to wander about the earth once Adam and Eve have sinned, he too reacts like a vulture to olfactory stimulation:

> . . .With delight he snuff'd the smell
> Or mortal change on Earth. As when a flock

Of ravenous Fowl, though many a League remote,
Against the day of Battle, to a Field,
Where Armies lie emcampt, come flying, lur'd
With scent of living Carcasses design'd
For death, the following day, in bloody fight.
[*P.L.* 10, 272-78]

Lucifer runs the gamut of symbolic metamorphosis by assuming the lowest form of animal in the serpent, which to him is demeaning, to the highest entity that soars through the element where he is supreme as "Prince of the Air" (*P.L.* 10. 185). The Fiend is compared to a vulture (3. 431) as he contemplates his vengeance from exile, while the lesser fallen angels who join him in ravaging their quarry are likened to locusts (1. 341). But as he visits Eden for the first time, the Tyrant chooses the tallest plant, the Tree of Life, and sits "like a Cormorant" (4. 196), observing the details of the setting for his crime. There is, however, less of the scavenger in Satan than the image conveyed by the carnivorous vulture. Consumption is left to his son, Death. Satan's role is one of infecting, or partial annihilation by temptation and contamination, inspiring awe more than fear and organizing the rest of his demons, ethereal spirits, and evil creatures in the campaign to destroy mankind.

Aguilera-Malta's world of aerial beings includes most of the imagery of epic poetry and some modifications in keeping with the fauna of the New World. The traditional eagle and the species peculiar to the American continent, the condor, combine to describe Simón Bolívar, the Liberator, in a context of historical and cultural import in *La caballeresa del sol* (pp. 32, 340). Both Bolívar and the condor as symbols of freedom are juxtaposed by Aguilera-Malta to enhance the spirit of independence and to echo the Liberator's dream for unity among the Andean nations of South America. The relationship of Bolívar and the condor is intensified by another device of imaginative narration—legend. After the decisive victory at Junín, Bolívar seems to become part of the vast Andean background. Somewhat more than human for his relentless, messianic devotion to the cause for liberty, Bolívar becomes almost a spiritual entity moving about the mountains and presenting himself unexpectedly. The people's fantasy begins to forge a mysterious hero who appears nightly over the scene where the battle took place:

> Decían que, por las noches, Bolívar, en su caballo blanco, recorría al galope el Lago de los Reyes. A veces, parecía flotar sobre éste. De improviso, aparecieron miríadas de aborígenes. Que ellos, con equino y todo lo ataban a los cuellos de decenas de cóndores. Y que, al final, estos, en un raudo vuelo, se elevaban sobre los Andes con su preciosa carga, para ya no volver hasta la noche siguiente.
>
> [*Caballeresa* 255]

Bolívar, indeed, inspired myths that raised him on his Pegasus to celestial heights, only to fall as angels before him, perhaps for his own hubris, to the abyss which would hold him eternally.

Of less noble stature, the image of the vulture is used conventionally in the same novel to signify or portend disaster and death. The fight for independence in South America, as in most other Spanish American countries, was fatricidal by nature, and Aguilera-Malta's presentation of both liberal and royalist forces is equally favorable when he draws those truly heroic figures of either side whose courage and pride merit special recognition. One such character was General Rodil of the Spanish Army, who refused to yield the fortress at Callao to Bolívar's troops. Through months of barricading themselves, they preferred to end their lives by famine and pestilence rather than surrender. The fortress, a symbol of strength and endurance, becomes infested with disease, and many soldiers accept dying as they originally vowed they would. The bird of prey benefits by their determination, for the eager flying scavengers can be seen hovering over the fort to create a grimly decorative image:

> El número de cadáveres que continuaba cayendo al Océano Pacífico aún era elevado. Constantemente, por eso, la Fortaleza del Callao tenía un penacho oscuro de aves de rapiña y una impalpable bufanda de hedor insoportable.
>
> [*Caballeresa* 301]

Aguilera-Malta forms a parallel between the familiar Spanish trait of uncompromised honor in the grotesque but tragic outline of a proud warrior crowned in vulture's plumage and draped with an illusory, albeit soiled and contaminated scarf which neither has protected him against the inclemencies of starvation and disease, nor can guard him from the ineluctable course of Spain's destiny.

At times Aguilera-Malta chooses to gather and spread his winged beings throughout a novel presenting them in a variety of forms to function constructively as well as destructively. In *El secuestro del general*, whose setting is populated by many teratoid humans and numerous anthropomorphic beasts, vultures glide over the mine-infested waters surrounding the insular domicile of the Pitecantropo family (p. 122) as noble condors magically transport the lovers, María and Fúlgido, to freedom away from the persecution of the townsfolk of Laberinto (p. 91). There is also the ludicrous image of the Dictator on his flying ass making the rounds to sample public opinion (p. 194), while giant parrots act as emissaries miraculously repeating messages in exact duplication of the human voice (pp. 168-69).

There are other instances in which the novelist concentrates on aerial images and winged entities for the sole purpose of conveying disaster or death. Such is the case in *La isla virgen*, where spirits and alar creatures serve as unifying markers in the narrative. Participating in the destruction of Indian and

white man alike, the birds of prey join forces with the
entomological species in an atmosphere populated by ghosts
and other ethereal phenomena that are created by the fancy
of the common people. The Virgin Island for many is
damned. The *patrón*, Néstor, in his struggle to disprove this
superstition, without being aware of the consequences of his
defiance, is surrounded by several ominous indications that
his efforts to subject the island to his will can end only in
disaster. The bearer of death finds its support in the
mosquito, whose unimpressive size is deceptive for the
malignant disease it carries.[22] The basic action of the novel is
neatly wedged between the two cases of victims succumbing to
malaria—Don Mite, one of the older *cholos*, whose death is
preceded by a wild explosion of delirium that draws a parallel
between man and his bestial qualities when he loses his
rationality (Book 1, chapter 6), and the final disappearance
of Néstor into the jungle, similarly raving at the height of his
fever (Book 3, chapter 6).

Intermittent deaths of *cholos* lead to the disappearance of
Néstor's sloop *La Sulinterma*, whose cargo consists of the
duped Indians. While their oppressors, Don Merelo and Don
Celeste, settle accounts and prepare their victims for a life of
bondage working off mythical debts, the wives of the *cholos*
wait outside of the store where negotiations are taking place.
Their movements, set against the background of night, are
compared to those of bats:

Afuera, merodean las mujeres.
Algunas portan sus críos. Dan vueltas y vueltas; como
murciélagos encandelillados. Acaso quieren decir mucho,
hacer mucho. Pero las detiene el miedo. Por eso, se
contentan con hablar entre ellas. O con llorar,
mansamente, quietamente, ante lo inevitable.

[*Isla* 340]

The simile, introduced by a verb associated with scavenging

(*merodear*), connotes death and recalls Homer's image of the shades of the suitors killed by Odysseus (who were like scavengers themselves while he was away), when they are gathered and prodded on by the staff of Hermes as he delivers them into Hades:

> . . .Herding
> them on with this, he led them along, and they
>   followed, gibbering.
> And as when bats in the depths of an awful cave,
>   flitter
> and gibber, when one of them has fallen out of his
>   place in
> the chain that the bats have formed by holding one
>   on another;
> so, gibbering, they went their way together.
>
> [*Od.* 24. 4-9]

Confusion, frustration, and a sustained note of fatalism characterize the two scenes which emphasize the helplessness of the women and the suitors while the method of grouping them together or herding denotes an underlying resignation to a superior power. The Indian women portend disaster; for the vessel carrying them and their families across the waters will never reach any terrestrial destination.

The pilot of the ship, Modesto Chamaidán, will end his Charonian vocation on this final trip as well. For years he has served as ferryman transporting souls to the islands where the peasants were subjected to potential annihilation by both nature and the white man. On the sloop that carries its human freight of inebriated natives in the hold, Don Modesto begins remembering the past, which is mottled by incidents such as this one. Guilt seizes control of the pilot as his fantasies determine the course that his ship and destiny will take. After rejecting the plea of one passenger to return to his dependent parents, Don Modesto sees the *cholo* withdraw obediently but now less human in form and more like a phantom. As the pilot's emotional crisis reaches its climax, so do the eery sounds and motions of the creatures into which the Indians have been converted:

> Ahora, los barqueados le estiran la mano, en súplica infinita. Hacen gestos de llamada inenarrable.
> Y avanzan.
> ¡Avanzan hacia él!
> Se trepan sobre el aire, como sobre escaleras invisibles. Suben a la borda. Caminan por la ramada. Se pegan a la mayor. Flotan entre las maderas y los cabos.
> Tienen los ojos inmóviles. Los pelos desordenados. Los dientes traqueteantes. Están en apinación monstruosa. Hablan confusamente, desordenadamente. Sin que les pueda entender una sola palabra.
>
> [*Isla* 358-59]

The Prince of Air begins his domination of the events occurring on the *Sulinterma* as the atmosphere becomes the province of demons, spirits, visions, and fantasy,[23] unleashed by the evil enterprises of Don Celeste and his business associates. The ship never reaches the Virgin Island; a mysterious gust of wind carries it off to the horizon to meet an unknown fate. Superstition and rumor also complicate any investigation leading to the whereabouts of the vessel. Some *cholos* refuse to mention the name *Sulinterma*, for others the names of the people who manned it become taboo; still others report occasional and unexpected materialization of the sloop in the distance, only to see it vanish. A young boy reports on what he has heard of the vultures' behavior when the apparition again disappears:

> —Algo nos han contado, don Néstor. Dizque afuerisima han visto una gallinazada. Parece que iba trepada sobre una balandra que andaba ligerísima. Cuando se han acercado, la balandra se les ha hecho humo. Los gallinazos sí dizque seguían revolteando, como locos, casi a flor de agua.
>
> [*Isla* 388]

The harbinger of death also announces the inexplicable disappearance of Don Merelo, whereupon his daughter, Esperanza, goes to Néstor for protection while the island itself seems to become invaded by evil spirits who come at night to frighten the inhabitants that still remain. The "ethereal creatures" are not agents of Satan, but rather the henchmen of Pablo Melgar, who has returned to avenge his father's death[24] by kidnapping Néstor's hope for the future, Esperanza.

Néstor's imminent downfall is predicted by the classical flying omen of doom, here used in a metaphor conversationally and ironically expressed by the *patrón* of the Virgin Island himself when Guayamabe, his loyal majordomo, tells him that total ruin of the cotton crop often is preceded by mild frosts. Néstor, who planted the fields with cotton against the advice of his overseer, nervously retorts:

—Pareces un pájaro de mal agüero. Siempre andas vaticinando desgracias.

[*Isla* 376]

The crop shortly thereafter is frozen as Guayamabe predicted, and Néstor's final battle with the island is lost. At that moment shots are heard; Pablo Melgar has succeeded in abducting Esperanza, and, along with her, Néstor's only chance for survival. The work of the miniature flying monster, which maintained Néstor in a state of suspension between the world of reality and his delirious fantasies, now draws to a conclusion. Driven by his love for the woman, the *patrón* plunges into the jungle, where he will undoubtedly meet his end as carrion for some birds of prey whose ominous image has been echoed throughout the narration of the story.

In *Siete lunas y siete serpientes,* Aguilera-Malta manipulates imagery of the aerial realm as he does in *La isla virgen* to reflect violence or death and its evil perpetrators. From Josefa Quindales, an ethereal entity with very human behavior, who participates after death as a ghost, to references describing the batlike qualities of the village women working cohesively to prevent a sanctified marriage between Candelario Mariscal and Bulu-Bulu's daughter, the symbolic parallels between human, alar, and unearthly entities are effectively drawn. Most impressive is the bat par excellence as created in the imagination of the people—the superstitious, naïve, uneducated makers of myth and legend who will perpetuate it until it is reshaped and recorded by the cultured poet. The supreme bat is constructed by the villagers, who have heard of Colonel Mariscal's crimes and have decided that he is Satan or Satan's son. There is no limit to the variations of attributes assigned him:

—Tiene siete mil cachos.
—¿De veras?
—Y siete mil rabos.
—No ha de ser tanto.
—De los ojos le salen ríos de chispas.
—¡Ah! ¿y tiene alas?
—Dos veces siete mil alas.
El sabihondo extendía las manos, tratando de abarcar un gran espacio. Agregaba:
—Asisotas.
—Ha de dar miedo, ¿verdad?
—¡Imaginate!
—Las orejas le terminan en punta, ¿no?
—Claro. Como si en ellas le crecieran unas afiladas.
—¿Y las manos y los pies?
—Allí las garras son como puñales. Con los dedos encontrados. Por eso, puede colgarse boca abajo de cualquier rama o de cualquier techo.

[*7/7* 127-28]

If Candelario Mariscal is Lucifer's son, his characteristics have legitimate antecedents:

Oh, quanto parve a me gran maraviglia

quand'io vidi tre facce alla sua testa!
L'una dinanzi, e quella era vermiglia;
l'altre eran due che s'aggiugníeno a questa
sovresso il mezzo di ciascuna spalla,
e si giugníeno al luogo della cresta;
e la destra parea tra bianca e gialla;
la sinistra a veder era tal, quali
vegnon di là onde el Nilo s'avvalla.
Sotto ciascuna uscivan due grandi ali,
quanto si convenía a tanto uccello:
vele di mar non vid'io mai cotali.
Non avean penne, ma di vipistrello
era lor modo; e quelle svolazzava
sí che tre venti si movean da ello.[25]

Dante's bat image of Satan also depends on a mystical number—three—and revolves around three pairs of wings, three faces, three winds, and the three-lined verse form, terza rima. Aguilera-Malta's number is seven, which is made even more mystical by multiplying it by a thousand to produce seven thousand horns, seven thousand tails, seven thousand wings, etc.; this is a popular method for intensifying an impression or reaction, in this case, horror and fear stimulated by Candelario Mariscal's demonic behavior. The entire effect is one of earthy realism circumscribing the peasant's world of fantasy.

The flying image presents itself again in connection with Chalena's architectural master plan for subjugating the people of Santorontón, which involves the assistance of Satan's agents to complete the arrangements on monopolizing the water supply. By means of ducts leading from the rooftops of some villagers who have cooperated with Chalena, rainwater will be gathered, kept under lock and key, to be sold by the oligarch to those who can pay. One night while the inhabitants of Santorontón are asleep, buckets of water are dropped on the chosen houses by strange alar beasts. One courageous witness describes the birdlike creatures to his neighbor in simple, but colorful detail:

El no pudo distinguir—¡la noche estaba tan obscura!
—si tenían colas y cuernos—¡Dios nos libre de los siete
mil cachos!—, aunque sí podía jurar que vio las alas,
los baldes y el agua. Y, también, que echaban fuego
por los ojos. Pero, ¿no hay aves que echan fuego por
los ojos? ¿O serían murciélagos?

[*7/7* 87-88]

Whether the winged monsters pouring water from buckets
onto the roofs were bats, birds, or devils, Satan has fulfilled
his end of the bargain with Chalena, who is competent
enough to administer the supply in his own perverted fashion
and for his own benefit.

Chalena himself is not excluded from the miscellany of
aerial creatures. Enraged by the capacity for organization
and cooperation that the *santoronteños* have exhibited in
finally constructing their own reservoir, the liparoid, batrachian monster fumes, swells, sputters, and swears vengeance.
The Fiend must come to his aid again. At sunset the people,
gathered in the square, chattering and bewildered, anxiously
exchange comments on the latest supernatural act performed
by Satan's follower:

¡Carajo! ¿Ustedes vieron lo que nosotros vimos? ¿Quién
no lo vio en el pueblo? ¡Cómo volaba don Crisóstomo!
¿No? Volaba sin alas. Como una pelota que acabaran
de patear. ¿De qué otra manera podría volar el Des-
graciado? Han de haberle pateado la panza. Con patada o
con alas—o, ¡quién sabe con qué!—cierto es que el
Maldito se elevó.

[*7/7* 354-55]

Chalena flies away, only to return clutching some mysterious
object. Dynamite for the reservoir? Poison for the water? In
Santorontón, "where the Devil still dances on the tip of his
tail" (p. 308),[26] good and evil move about in the open and not
only as symbols. The battle is just beginning.

The creatures of land, sea, and air populating the epic stage function in various ways that involve the survival of the hero. Although characteristics of majesty, nobility, or prowess found in animals are compared in similes or metaphors to the great warriors of tradition, the basic role of nature's beasts is to convey some form of obstacle or threat of destruction. As an aberration of the once-perfect natural order, the monster, particularly in the Christian epic, represents evil, specifically evil of Satanic origin. Distortion of the human or angelic form by bestial reference or metamorphosis is a method of degradation, or it may serve as a warning which portends disaster for the hero opposing some malevolent force. The concern for the individual is one of salvation, although in the Renaissance or medieval epics the salvation of the soul takes precedence over physical survival. Aguilera-Malta's use of animal imagery combines the classical concern for the hero's soma as he confronts institutions and people whose moral deformity is indicated by those zoomorphic properties which represent treachery, violence, and annihilation.

Notes

1. Joseph Campbell, *The Hero with a Thousand Faces* (Cleveland: World, 1956), p. 129.

2. Ibid., p. 370.

3. *The "Pharsalia" of Lucan*, tr. Sir Edward Ripley (London: Arthur L. Humphreys, 1919), 9: 700-733

4. The contemporary Ecuadorian novelists have often been accused of excessive naturalistic analysis in their works. Lucan would probably be open to the same cricitism for detailing, as in this and subsequent passages, the gruesome physical changes that take place when the soldiers are bitten.

5. Treachery has been associated with serpents as far back as the Gilgamesh myths of Mesopotamia (third millenium B.C.). One episode relates how the hero falls asleep after finally encountering the plant of eternal youth. While he sleeps, a serpent steals the plant, eats it, and gains the power of sloughing off its skin and renewing its youth, thus cheating Gilgamesh of his immortality. See Campbell, *The Hero with a Thousand Faces*, p. 187.

6. See John M. Steadman, *Milton and the Renaissance Hero* (London: Oxford University Press, 1967), pp. 180-81. Mr. Steadman notes that Renaissance literary

theory required that the deformities of evil be exposed and castigated and that they meet their due reward of misery and shame. In this manner both the demands of poetic justice and those of divine retribution were fulfilled.

7. Rarely is serpentiform reference complimentary. Similes are striking for that reason when the hero or epic character is likened to a snake physically and his attributes are thereby enhanced. Such is the case in *Gerusalemme Liberata*, when the aging Raimondo has his wish granted to fight Argante in Tancredi's place:

> Ei di fresco vigor la fronte e 'l vólto
> Riempie; e cosí allor ringiovenisce,
> Qual serpe fier che in nove spoglie avvolto
> D'oro fiammeggi, e 'n contra il sol si lisce.

[7. 71. 3-6]

8. Aguilera-Malta frequently uses what Gonzalo Sobejano calls the "El epíteto incoherente." See his study, *El epéteto en la lírica española* (Madrid: Gredos, 1956), pp. 468-70. This type of intensification ("ramos de víboras," in this case) serves to strengthen the relationship of men and nature and is a quality that is basic to Aguilera-Malta's style.

9. Demetrio Aguilera-Malta, *Lázaro. Caricaturas. Tres escenas y un prólogo*, in *Revista del Colegio Vicente Rocafuerte* (Guayaquil) 2, no. 3 (October 1941): 15. Future references to this work will be abbreviated (e.g., *Lázaro* 15).

10. *Aen.* 4. 173-90. Rumor is a product of Mother Earth and is sister to Enceladus and Coeus, giants who defied the Olympian gods. Note also the adjective "hissing" (v. 185), which implies a serpent characteristic. So too is Aguilera-Malta's "News Monster" part viper as it sweeps through Babelandia. The symbolic spread of misinformation exceeds all imaginative limits in an animated, zoomorphic complexity which combines bat and scorpion properties. The hairy aberration, a match for Virgil's Rumor, conveys the distortion of facts concerning the tortures supposedly suffered by General Pitecantropo at the hands of his kidnappers (*Secuestro* 102-103).

11. Cataloguing heroes and ships is another convention found in epic poetry. The enumeration of snakes can be found in Lucan's *Pharsalia* (9. 700-33) and *Paradise Lost* (10. 524-31).

12. See Bernard M. W. Knox's study of this topic, "The Serpent and the Flame: The Imagery of the Second Book of the *Aeneid*," in *Virgil: A Collection of Critical Essays*, ed. Steele Commager (Englewood Cliffs, N.J.: Prentice-Hall, 1966), pp. 124-42.

13. The belief that spirits or demons impregnated women is an ancient one and is noted in the magical texts of Babylonia of the Sassanian Era. See Cyrus H. Gordon, *Before the Bible* (New York: Harper & Row, 1962), p. 247. The Tin-Tines of Ecuadorian folklore seem to function in a comparable manner as did certain Indo-Iranian deities.

14. The mystical number parallels the seven sins and seven virtues discussed later in the novel. The Book of Revelation itself, which is much of an expressionistic interpretation of death and resurrection, is dominated by the same numeral.

15. *Beowulf*, tr. Lucien Dean Pearson; ed. Roland L. Collins (Bloomington:

Indiana University Press, 1965), p. 77. Future references to this work will be abbreviated (e.g., *Beo. 77*). For other sea-monsters, both "real" and legendary, see R. A. Marchant, *Beasts of Fact and Fable* (New York: Roy, 1962).

16. The shark metaphorically is the aquatic counterpart of the classical bull, which symbolized virility, strength, courage, and other generally masculine traits. In "El cholo que se castró" the young lover wishes he could have the same characteristics that would then grant him dominance over any man and would consequently permit him to terrorize and conquer at will *(L.Q.S.V. 225)*.

17. Arthur Gilchrist Brodeur notes the handicap of confronting the troll in her lair beneath the water and the additional seabeasts that assail Beowulf. See *The Art of "Beowulf"* (Berkeley-Los Angeles: University of California Press, 1959), p. 98.

18. The evil portent of Baligant's arrival from across the sea is intensified by his standard, which displays a dragon (*Roland* 3330).

19. Hesiod, *Theogony*, line 267, in *Hesiod*, tr. Richmond Lattimore (Ann Arbor: University of Michigan Press, 1968), p. 138.

20. Ibid., lines 180-85 (p. 134).

21. *Cantar de Mio Cid*, ed. Ramón Menéndez Pidal, 3 vols. (Madrid: Espasa-Calpe, 1956), 3, lines 2749-51. Future references to this work will be abbreviated (e.g., *Cid* 2749-51).

22. One of the rarer images in classical epics is the mosquito. Although the insect lacks the noble or mighty traits of other creatures, Homer sees fit to use it in exemplifying the tenacity and courage Athena grants Menelaus during his fight to claim Patroclus's body:

> She put strength into man's shoulders and knees,
>> inspiring
> in his breast the persistent daring of that mosquito
> who though it is driven hard away from a man's skin,
>> even
> so, for the taste of human blood, persists in biting
>> him.

[Il. 17. 569-72]

23. Milton believed in the theory that the air was the domain of spirits and demons, which also controlled aerial portents such as meteors. See notes in John Milton, *Paradise Lost*, ed. Merritt Hughes (New York: Odyssey Press, 1935), pp. 28, 320. The title "Prince of Air" (*P.L.* 10. 185) is as ominous as "Prince of Hell" or "Prince of Darkness," since it conjures up the mysterious and the unknown and is related to that distant realm where mortals have never been, excepting those few heroes who were granted the privilege of visiting Hades and returning to earth.

24. The father's death several years before also fired the superstitious imagination of the peasants, for his ghost was reported prowling about, terrorizing the inhabitants of the Virgin Island. Everyone believes that it is the ghost of Pablo's father—all except the civilized *patrón*.

25. Dante Alighieri, *Inferno*, 34. 37-51, in *La Divina Commedia*, ed. Dino Provenzal (Verona: A. Mondadori, 1938). Future references to this work will be abbreviated (e.g., *Inf.* 34. 37-51).

26. The image conveys arrogance and is very much like Milton's description of Satan in his serpent form as the seduction takes place:

> So spake the Enemy of Mankind, enclos'd
> In Serpent, Inmate bad, the toward *Eve*
> Address'd his way, not with indented wave,
> Prone on the ground, as since, but on his rear,
> Circular base of rising folds, that tow'r'd
> Fold above fold a surging Maze.

[P.L. 9. 494-99]

4
Sin in Epic Tradition

Treachery and Discord

Satan's consort, Sin, half-woman, half-serpent, whose canine appendages howl, yelp, and bark, threatening destruction of the soul, symbolizes the distortion and deformity of vice. The once-beautiful daughter of Lucifer[1] manifests, in her physical metamorphosis, the effects of corruption and its inherent ugliness. Dante also reserved his most repugnant materialization of sin for the offense he considered the worst—fraud. His zoomorphic creation, Geryon, assisting the poet and his master, Virgil, in their descent into the lower recesses of Hell, makes his appearance in a swimming-flying motion and presents himself in all his horror:

> La faccia sua era faccia d'uom giusto,
> > tanto benigna avea di fuor la pelle,
> > e d'un serpente tutto l'altro fusto.
> Duo branche avea pilose infin l'ascelle;
> > lo dosso e il petto e ambedue le coste
> > dipinte avea di nodi e di rotelle.

> [*Inf.* 17. 10-15]

As the prototype of Fraud, he represents, in his physiognomy, and particularly in his virulent scorpion's tail, the most antisocial crimes of hypocrisy, deceit, and treachery to which man is vulnerable. When Dante creates the ninth and last circle, Cocytus, he allocates the icy zones of Caina, Antenora, Ptolomea, and Judecca to the traitors to kin, country, or cause, hospitality, and lords or benefactors. The traitors are many and of all stations; and rarely is their offense of minor significance in the destiny of the hero or main characters.

In the *Chanson de Roland* Ganelon's treachery causes the death of Roland and his followers, among whom are the noble, devoted Twelve Peers and Archbishop Turpin. Although he denies that he is guilty of treason (3760), he has indeed betrayed his liege, Charlemagne.[1] The other medieval epic, *Poema del Cid*, is almost entirely structured on family ties, and strong ones too, for the Beni-Gómez clan, conspiring against Rodrigo Díaz de Vivar, is neither concerned with the future of Castile nor with the king, Alfonso VI. Successful in instigating the exile of the Cid, they later cause the hero further suffering through the marriage of the brothers, Fernando and Diego, to the Cid's daughters.

Epic poetry before and after the medieval period consistently offers examples of the faithless and treacherous who abandon allegiance to their kin or to their lords. In the *Odyssey* the servants are particularly flagrant violators of trust, as Eumaeus knows from his own abduction as a child from a noble family. An aristocratic background seems to imply greater moral concern and fidelity. Yet Odysseus, during his visit to the Land of the Dead, listens to Agamemnon and the treachery that resulted in his murder by his wife and queen, Clytemnestra, whose betrayal recalls for Odysseus the other notorious member of her sex, Helen (11. 436-39). Dido, who rebukes herself for breaking the oath she made before her husband's ashes (*Aen.* 4. 552), finds her own abandonment by Aeneas a treacherous act, and Adam too, in his hour of grief, reviles the Mother of Mankind for her "inward fraud" (*P.L.* 10. 871), while Satan, the "Traitor Angel" (*P.L.* 2. 689), whom Dante places in the center of Judecca for his betrayal of God, celebrates his success in accomplishing the Fall through deception: "Him by fraud I have seduc'd / From his Creator" (*P.L.* 10. 485-86).

Sin's first daughter, Discord, a creature "with a thousand various mouths" (*P.L.* 2. 967), performs a highly significant role in the destiny of the epic hero. Satan's legion of rebels was swayed by his schismatic plans and thus departed from the angelic realm. Well aware of the detrimental effect that disunity can have, Satan wisely counsels his followers:

> To union, and firm Faith, and firm accord,
> More than can be in Heav'n, we now return
> To claim our just inheritance of old.
>
> [*P.L.* 2. 36-38]

Dissension or civil strife is a major theme in many epics. The *Iliad* begins on that note of discord which creates the atmosphere that inspires the poet:

> . . .And the will of Zeus was accomplished
> since that time when first there stood in division of conflict
> Atreus' son the lord of men and brilliant Achilleus.
>
> [*Il.* 1. 5-7]

Friction and disunity reach the point where the Achaeans almost abandon their mission, to which eight years have already been dedicated. But Odysseus, quelling the last instigator, Thersites, who hypocritically defends Achilles and insults Agamemnon, reunites the assembly and restores unity (*Il.* 2. 211-69).[2]

In the *Aeneid* the founding of Rome is previewed by the dissension among the Italians, who are divided, some following Turnus, while others join the Trojan ranks. But

Jupiter too is surrounded by the same situation in his own Olympian realm:

"Great dwellers in the sky, why have you changed
      your minds,
and why do you contend with such discordant hearts?
I had forbidden Italy to fight with the Trojans;
why this dissension against my commands?"

[*Aen.* 10. 6-9]

It is a moment critical to the structure of the *Aeneid* when the people of Latium are aroused to disregard their king, Latinus, and his holy message that they should accept Aeneas as the future husband of Lavinia, for dissension and war will henceforth rage on until the end of the poem. The final frenzied confusion of disunity comes at the gates of Latium when Aeneas approaches them:

Strife arises among the frightened people; some want
to unlock the gates and open the city to the Trojans
and even drag the king himself to the battlements;

[*Aen.* 12. 583-85]

Gerusalemme Liberata, which found much inspiration in the *Aeneid*, contains numerous episodes of friction and dissension that primarily revolve around the plot and are based on the malevolent influence of the sorceress Armida. Her function, as proposed by Satan (Pluto) to the wizard Idraote, is to divide the Crusaders through deception and her feminine charms. Further complications and unrest arise in Book 5, when Gernando, the King of Norway's son, is stirred to insulting Rinaldo as they each consider succeeding the deceased King Dudone in the position of leadership. The incident is concluded with the death of Gernando at the hands of Rinaldo, who withdraws from the major scene of action, thereby affecting his army's mission much in the same way Achilles does the Achaean cause. But discord becomes open rebellion when Allecto stirs up another knight of the Italian forces who in a dream hears Rinaldo accuse Goffredo of his supposed death. Argillano awakens to rouse the Italians to mutiny under the influence of the Fury:

> Rota Aletto fra lor la destra armata,
> E co 'l foco il venen ne' petti mesce.
> Lo sdegno, la follía, la scelerata
> Sete del sangue ognor piú infuria e cresce;
> [*G.L.* 8. 72. 1-4]

The Duke, who would loathe being part of any bloodshed caused by civil strife ("la destra mia del civil sangue abborre," 8. 76. 4), finally succeeds in restoring peace to the camp. However, Goffredo continues facing moments of discord, including those caused by climatic conditions. But assisted by God, who hears his prayers, and the return of Rinaldo, the virtuous leader of the Crusaders finally delivers Jerusalem from bondage.

Lust: Sex, Glory, Power, and Gold

Tasso's implementation of discord as an evil which can destroy the holy purpose of the Christian mission uncovers basically the sins and weaknesses which convert the knights into vulnerable targets for Satan and his constituents. Each knight contributes to disunity because of some flaw in his moral structure. For Gernando it was pride, for Argillano, wrath, and for most of the other young Crusaders who succumb to the wiles of Armida, lust. Dante categorizes carnal desire among the milder vices in Circle 2, where it is less severely punished because the sin is motivated by passion, not by cold-blooded scheming, which characterizes the fraudulent in the lowest regions of Hell. But lust is often the driving force that expresses itself in dissension and violence, the essential motifs in epic poetry.

The role of lust in its purely sexual connotation cannot be given a subordinate position in the scale of offenses punished in the *Inferno*, for it was Satan who lay with his desirable daughter and begot a monstrous son, Death. The "odious offspring" (*P.L.* 2. 781), in turn lusting after his mother, fathered the howling dogs that breed in Sin's womb (2. 761-802). Thus Satan as the Arch-Sinner created immorality through his own lascivious behavior.

Concupiscence is what caused the destruction of Ilium, which was brought about by the offense committed by Paris,

> who insulted the goddesses when they came to him
>   in his courtyard
> and favoured her who supplied the lust that led
>   to disaster.
>
> [*Il.* 24. 29-30]

The end of Troy, in turn, brought Aeneas to Italy, where further violence and death occur. Not without cause does Dido regret her passion for Aeneas. His departure, which is interpreted as a rejection of her love, conjures up thoughts of violence not only toward herself, but for all the Trojans and for Aeneas's son, Ascanius, in particular (4. 600-602).

Fulfillment of carnal desires such as the artificial garden and Armida symbolize is the weakness exploited by the diabolic host that seeks the Crusaders' defeat. Attraction for the lovely sorceress leads many a knight astray and causes friction within the Christian camp. Tasso was fully aware of the conflict between divine love and profane love with all the complications involved: erotic distractions almost prevent the reconquest of Jerusalem—a feat that represents not only the salvation of the Holy City, but of the Crusaders' souls as well.[3]

Adam's fall often is attributed to uxoriousness, a weakness that implies an attachment to his consort based on her physical appeal, as Raphael observes:

For what admir'st thou, what transports thee so,
An outside?. . .

[*P.L.* 8. 567-68]

Adam is reprimanded for his overzealous interpretation of
Eve's fair qualities, and Raphael continues his instruction on
man as distinguished from beast:

. . .To heav'nly Love thou may'st ascend,
Not sunk in carnal pleasure, for which cause
Among the Beasts no Mate for thee was found.

[*P.L.* 8. 592-94]

When Adam chooses between immortality and Eve, the Fall
and Satan's increasing corruptive influence culminate in the
final act of erotic abandonment in the Garden, from which
they emerge ashamed, no longer innocent, and reflecting in
their faces "evident signs / of foul concupiscence" (9.
1077-78).

But lust in its broadest sense, involving an uncontrolled
passion, drive, or desire, is the cause of most of man's
suffering. Unfortunately, Adam does not heed Raphael and
ignores his advice on excess:

And govern well thy appetite, lest sin
Surprise thee, and her black attendant Death.

[*P.L.* 7. 546-47]

The First Couple's transgression is in keeping with the Greek
concept of sin, which is essentially one of intemperance, of
passion over reason.[4] Almost all epics, examined from this
point of view, will reveal the effect of lust, not only in its
carnal meaning, but in general dominance by an extreme
desire for something which takes precedence over any other
person or value. The gods call "wickedness" or "recklessness"[5] this primacy of self over social or divine law. The drive
for knowledge is a sin familiarly attributed to Odysseus, as

well as to Adam and Eve ("But Knowledge is as food, and needs no less / Her Temperance over Appetite," (*P.L.* 7. 126-27). Satan also, as a multifarious symbol of evil in general, was driven by ambition or pride, a sin which characterizes many epic heroes. The classical figures are no exception: Odysseus's own "recklessness," which costs him his booty and companions, stems from an irrepressible desire to let his name be known to the blind giant, who in turn prays to his father, Poseidon, to execute his vengeance. The compulsive determination to achieve glory or fame, then, can incur the disfavor of the gods when others stand to suffer for it.

Camões, who lived in the midst of Portugal's conquests of land and sea, knew all too well the immorality and destruction for which Dame Glory could be responsible:

"Dura inquietacão de alma e da vida,
Fonte de desemparos e adultérios,
Sagaz consumidora conhecida
De fazendas, de reinos e de impérios!
Chamam-te ilustre, chamam-te subida,
Sendo dina de infames vitupérios;
Chamam-te Fama e Glória soberana,
Nomes com quem se o povo néscio engana!"

[*Lus.* 4. 96]

National pride and personal glory, as Camões indicates, often conceal the baser appetites to be satisfied. Bloodlust had its own pleasures when fulfilled as the Homeric poems reveal, and rare was the warrior who did not value the economic profit which was more than tangentially related to the conquest at hand.

The passion for wealth indubitably has had its influence on the hero's destiny. The compulsion to accumulate it, the fear of losing it or having to share it, often stimulates the crimes which are the most antisocial and, therefore, the most reprehensible. Odysseus's men, even before their final sacrilegious act against Hyperion, already indicate their preoccupation with material gain beyond their chief's judgment when they conspire to open the bags which contain the winds instead of gold and silver as they thought.

The *Aeneid* also has its examples of misery and death brought about by lust for wealth. Dido's grief begins with the death of her husband. Her brother, Pygmalion, "blinded by love of gold" (1, 349), murders Sychaeus at the altar, and Aeneas during his wanderings hears a voice speaking in pain to him which is that of Priam's son Polydorous; sent with treasure to seek protection from a supposed ally of Troy, he was killed instead. Aeneas bemoans the fate of the murdered youth and the reason for the heinous act:

> . . .To what crimes men are driven
> by the cursèd lust for gold!
>
> [*Aen*. 3. 56-57]

Even great leaders and warriors meet their end by paying for sins committed for gold. The model king Beowulf, who had been close to death many times in his deliverance of the oppressed, encounters his final enemy through circumstances for which he was not responsible. Lust for gold drives the unknown thief to plunder the treasure hoarded by the dragon. The loss of the flagon stirs the beast to vengeance and Beowulf must go forth to challenge another monster in a contest which costs him his life. In the *Chanson de Roland*, Ganelon, who betrayed his liege, also admits his actions had economic roots (lines, 3758-59), and the Cid's peripatetic existence after his exile is based on a very real need to regain his material security. Disinherited when he leaves Alfonso's court, he successfully increases his assets and those of his men, and his prosperity becomes instrumental in his being restored to the king's favor. It is also ironic that this new economic status revitalizes the treachery of the Beni-Gómez clan and attracts the prospective husbands for the Campeador's daughters:

"Las nuevas del Cid   mucho van adelant,
demandemos sus fijas   pora con ellas casar;
creçremos en nuestra ondra   e iremos adelant."
[*Cid* 1881-83]

The Infantes of Carrión, unsated in their quest for wealth, while admitting the dowry received is so generous that they could hardly spend it all during their lifetime (2541-42), consider an additional crime. It is the murder of their host and friend of the Cid, Abengalbón, whose wealth draws their attention in the midst of their plans to assault and abandon the Cid's daughters (2659-63). It is no wonder that Milton called Mammon "the least erected spirit that fell from heav'n" (*P.L.* 1. 679-80) for it was he who inspired the ravaging of Mother Earth in search of gold. Milton's admonition in abhorrence of this drive rings simple and clear:

. . .Let none admire
That riches grow in Hell; that soil may best
Deserve the precious bane.
[*P.L.* 1. 690-92]

According to Clotilde Quindales, who begins a Circean crusade against the offenders of her sex, "the devil is in every man," (*7/7* 91). How much of a claim Satan has on the individual soul, however, depends on the type of sin committed by Aguilera-Malta's characters. Transgressions follow a pattern of categorization comparable to Dante's system, which distinguishes between the less flagrant violators of the code and the more treacherous oppressors of mankind. Lust, in its broadest connotation as an excessive desire for wealth, power, fame, or sexual fulfillment, motivates violence and destruction and dominates most of the thematic structure of his works.

The heroes of the discovery and exploration of the New World, whose wanderings and experiences were as fabulous as those of Aeneas or Odysseus, are propelled by a thirst for fame or fortune, or both, and frequently fall victims themselves to someone else's passions. Francisco de Orellana's story, particularly reminiscent of the trials and tribulations of the Ithacan king and his crew, is replete with adventures and tales about searching for the wonderland of El Dorado, the Land of the Cinnamon Tree, the Great River, and the legendary Amazons—all told against a background of the unpredictable course of nature and the less reliable behavior of men. The discovery and exploration of the New World occurred in an era that found treachery to be as diffuse and endemic as it was in Dante's; and the motive, when not based on fame or glory, was the passion for gold that drove the explorers to commit countless crimes against humanity. Not without reason did Luís de Camões condemn the effect of the precious metal on every aspect of social and moral behavior:

Este rende munidas fortalezas;
Faz tredores a falsos os amigos;
Este a mais nobres faz fazer vilezas,
E entrega capitães aos inimigos;
Este corrompe virginais purezas,
Sem temer de honra ou fama alguns perigos;
Este deprava às vezes as ciências,
Os juízos cegando e as consciências.

[*Lus.* 8. 98]

But the Spanish conquerors as well as the Portuguese whose lust drove them to crime occasionally were castigated as Balboa's men are when they fall into the hands of the Indian chief, Pocorosa:

Cuando tuvo a los prisioneros, desarmados, completamente a su merced, los encaró, rabioso:
—¿Quieren más oro?; ¡Ya van a tenerlo!
Ellos, espantados, vieron como el Cacique ordenaba fundir varios lingotes del metal precioso. Después rugió:

—¡Córtenles la boca y la lengua!
Y sobre la herida sangrante, les vertió oro derretido.
Mientras se esparcía el olor a metal candente en absurda
mezcla con carne quemada, siguió gritando:
—¡Hártense! ¡Hártense de oro!

[*Mar* 224]

For Aguilera-Malta the historical variant has altered
neither the passions of the powerful nor the tribulations of
the weak. The reprobates of the sixteenth century in military
or courtly garb find their modern counterparts in the
dictator, the *patrón,* the imperialist, and all the institutions
that foster the self-interested primacy of a few over the
welfare of the many, and particularly the privileged over the
underdog. Although sexual appetite in its incontinent drive
toward satisfaction can be destructive and even self-
annihilating, as bloodlust, for example, often is,[6] neither
passion meets with the condemnation that treachery does; for
the worst antisocial offenses are those deliberately defrauding
and betraying one's fellowman for personal profit.

Invariably, twentieth-century injustices to which Aguilera-
Malta's oppressed hero is subjected are motivated by the
drive for power represented generally in financial terms.[7] The
tyrant who victimizes his people is a grotesque image of
perversion which is rooted in a lust for wealth. The unscru-
pulous lawyer, Cercado, in the short play *Honorarios,*[8] lusts
sexually, but is essentially driven by a thirst for money; the
patrón, violating all codes of decency, rapes and seduces
Indian women, but he too is mainly concerned with his
fortune and in augmenting it through inhuman treatment of
the peasants under his domination. All wars and acts of
aggression stem from causes that are basically economic, and
when a foreign power intervenes in the internal affairs of a
nation, as in the case of Panama, the motive is rarely based
on any noble intention. Money as the root of many an evil
produces the havoc of profligacy in the anatomical exposé of

Panama and the famous canal. The journalistic novel *Canal Zone* demonstrates the nation's ailment, which fundamentally is caused by rapacity and its contaminating effect on all people.[9]

Man's true bestiality is revealed when sudden prosperity during the first phase of the canal's prominence converts Panama into a terrestrial Inferno in which sinner persecutes sinner and few go unpunished. Like Dante's Florence, the city presents a vast panorama of self-perpetuating vice where everyone is corruptible and all appetites are insatiable. In this anti-epic of waste, corruption, and sensual abandonment, Aguilera-Malta intertwines one round of offenders into the next, and none are spared. The land is ravaged by construction workers, many of whom die of disease. Those who prosper on exorbitant salaries are abused by increased inflation or are in turn exploited by places of diversion; the foreigners, tourists, and laborers are defrauded mercilessly and those who survive the period of affluence face an economic depression in continued castigation. As one character explains the effect of money on the Panamanians:

> "Lo que pasa es que los hombres se acostumbraron a ganar el dinero, casi sin trabajarlo. Los persiguió el dólar, en un abordaje inaudito. Aunque no quisieran, tuvieron que verlo llegar, en oleadas. Lo sintieron metérseles en el bolsillo. . . Y así—tan fácilmente como llegara—lo vieron marcharse. Esto en las clases bajas, que en las altas no lo trabajaron nunca y lo derrocharon más rápido que les viniera."
>
> [*C.Z.* 31-32]

The United States, as an intruder who profited from the engineering feat, even as a great power, is also a victim of maleficence. The fleet on maneuvers participates in the orgiastic rape of Panama, yet the foreign sailors fall prey to the wily and diabolic proprietors of bars, restaurants, casinos, and brothels. Technological progress has succeeded in reconstructing another Sodom and Gomorrah, and the soul of an entire nation wanders through the Malebolge with little hope for redemption.

The passion for money in Aguilera-Malta's works can range in portrayal from the grotesque to the pathetic. In *El secuestro del general* the Secretary of State's wife literally gorges herself with paper currency (pp. 169-71); while in *Lázaro* the impoverished teacher tragically suffers the torments of his conscience for renouncing his humanitarian ideals in exchange for a new security. His name is honored and his love requited after signing the apostatic document which celebrates the cult of Mammon:

> "¡No hay mejor sociedad ni mejor época que la nuestra! ¡Estamos en el Siglo de Oro, porques es el metal maravilloso que domina todo el orbe, porque es el máximo símbolo de nuestra civilización!"
>
> [*Lázaro* 19]

Lázaro has become a traitor to his ideals and to his other self. The pact with the demonic establishment he formerly opposed has its price: to live in his own Inferno forever aware of his spiritual and intellectual prostitution.

The theme of self-betrayal is carried into the atmosphere of a nightclub in *Dientes blancos*, another short play which is compact and intense in the presentation of racial and social oppositions. Three black musicians earn their livelihood entertaining a white audience. William plays the saxophone and laughs to drums rolled in robot-like fashion by Ernest.[10] Peter, the embittered member of the trio, reaches the critical point of his existence and begins to rebel by refusing to accept the abuse of the customers and by challenging his companions for resigning themselves to a destiny as grotesque entertainers of a scornful public. To work in what seems to be a more comfortable setting than is usual for the underdog, and to receive an occasional glass of champagne, the musicians pay for the luxury by degradation and by performing according to the stereotyped impression that the white public has of blacks—they are musically talented, fun-loving, and enjoy laughing.[11] The three, particularly the active buffoon, William, have denied their race: "¡Eres un traidor a ti y a tu raza!" says Peter,[12] and the response is hysterical laughter which in turn stimulates the inebriated audience and increases the tense polarization of black and white, diversion and misery.

The *cholo* too reaches moments of corruptibility. Banchón has prospered by exploiting his erstwhile companions who now patronize his bar and blame his unethical transformation to the malignant influence of money. "La plata desgracia a los hombres," comments Guayamabe (*L.Q.S.V.* 32). Banchón has trapped his friends into incurring debts and squandering the little they have. Once a partner in the daily pattern of simple living and fishing to support family needs, the *cholo* proprietor's wickedness is now aptly described in piscatory terms:

> Les estiró como redes de carne para acumular lisas de plata en el estero negro de su ambición. . . . .
> [*L.Q.S.V.* 30]

Crisóstomo Chalena, the most successful underdog of them all, is a composite symbol of the malefic self-interest since his lust for wealth is limitless. In a dialogue with himself he recalls how he offered his soul to Satan in exchange for prosperity:

> "Mandinga[13]; cómprame el alma. Te la vendo por lo que me des." No creíste que El pudiera responderte. Te engañabas. Ya él estaba allí. Contestando a tu llamada. Cuando acordaste, te rascaba la oreja izquierda con el rabo. "¡Acepto, Güevón"—Durante mucho tiempo sólo te dio ese nombre. Sólo más tarde te llamó Don Crisos. y después Crisóstomo—Repitió: "Acepto, Güevón. ¿Qué

quieres por ella?'' ''Plata. Mucha. Muchisísima plata. Uni-
camente muchisisisísima plata.'' Sonrió sonrisa de horno
bocanada en llamas. ''Tendrás la plata, Güevón. Serás el
más platudo de estos lados.''

[*7/7* 370-71]

He once more invokes Satan; this time he requests death for
his enemies and expresses the wish ironically through the
symbol of salvation:

Ya no quería plata. Quería cruces. Cruces. Cruces.
Quería sembrar de cruces todo el pueblo. Cruces sobre
las tumbas de los santoronteños. Muchas cruces. Que
obstruyeran el paso. Hasta perderse de vista, en la
lontananza. Muchas cruces. Aunque se quedara, otra vez,
pobre. ¿Otra vez, pobre? Bueno. No tan pobre. Pero
acabar, eso sí con los secuaces de Juvencio. Para ya no
tener quien se atravesara en su camino. Cruces,
Mandinga, muchas cruces. Sólo cruces.

[*7/7* 371]

Chalena is almost capable, *almost*, of relinquishing his pros-
perous status in order to accomplish the annihilation of his
opponents.

Betrayal of the Public Trust

For Dante, betrayal of the public trust was a deadly
offense, for the public interest was regarded as more sacred
than the private.[14] This, too, is the predominant evil which
persecutes the underdogs of Aguilera-Malta's works. Worse
than a pact with the Devil is a contrived agreement between
the individuals who control or possess the means for controlling the destiny of a tribe, a society, or a nation.
Motivating the acts of conspiring against the people
invariably is a desire for personal gain. Plato's separation of
economic power from the governing aristocracy in the ideal

state was based on his awareness of the material greed of politicians.[15] Homer also knew of the corruption that characterized officials who break faith with the public trust. His condemnation is found in a simile expressing Zeus's reaction against mortals

> . . .after they stir him to
> anger
> because in violent assembly they pass decrees that are
> crooked,
> and drive righteousness from among them and care
> nothing for what the gods think.
> [*Il.* 16. 386-88]

Aeneas, too, is reminded by Anchises of the punishment in store for the wicked whose crimes are such that they affect a nation's welfare. Those sinners find castigation in Tartarus, where Phlegyas warns:

> ". . .'Learn to do justice and not scorn the gods.'
> This one sold his country for gold to a powerful tyrant;
> another made laws and rescinded them—all for a price."
> [*Aen.* 6. 618-22]

But the Trojan leader hardly needs a reminder that he himself is the personification of a *pro bono publico* commitment. In secondary epic Virgil replaces the Homeric tradition of individualistic fulfillment or personal gain with the responsibility of the hero to the destiny of a group or nation. This social concern is what distinguishes Beowulf from Roland, or Goffredo from Achilles, and it is also the principle underlying Aguilera-Malta's denunciation of those public officials who reject what might be termed "Ciceronian" precepts for the commonweal, which are part of the spirit familiarly associated with the *Aeneid*.[16]

The Ecuadorian author's condemnation of corruption within the political structure of society is directed largely against those figures of power whose creation is based on the historical reality of Latin America. The dictator who rises from obscurity to control a country's destiny by military means is a well-known phenomenon, expounded upon by Aguilera-Malta in an early essay, *Leticia* (1932). Several years later, the author creates the shadow of such a ruler, never on stage, but who lurks in the background of *No bastan los átomos*. The fully developed dictatorial head of state, Holofernes Verbofilia, appears ultimately in *El secuestro del general* (1973) in skeletal form to represent totalitarianism as a calcified order, doomed to destruction by multiple treachery within the oligarchic ranks of self-interest.

Oligarchies are particularly susceptible to malversation and are prime material for anti-heroic characterization. In the scale of greater and lesser sinners which exists in the microcosm of *Siete lunas y siete serpientes,* the worst offenders are those who are supposedly serving the community but instead group together in a cohesive clique to oppress the villagers who depend on them. The real conspirators against the peasants are dominated by Crisóstomo Chalena, and, like the characters of Tasso's and other epics, they succumb to vice through some weakness of their own. Gaudencio, the new priest who joins the powers that control Santorontón, suffers from simony and easily yields to the perverted influence of money by parceling out heaven to the undeserving sinners. The town doctor and funeral director, the head of the rural police, and the civil authorities all align themselves with the truly satanic figure, Chalena, who eliminates those who hamper his plans to acquire more wealth. Candelario Mariscal is not so wicked as they are, for his sexual crimes and bloodlust are caused by some spiritually uncontrollable force; and they are openly expressed with no recourse to hypocrisy. Above all, he has no passion for money. He eventually capitulates to a military figure, Colonel Epifanio Moncada, who is supported officially by the state. His crimes represent massive perversions of the power structure that rules, and Candelario admittedly cannot match Moncada's politically approved, organized violence:

> "El único que es como yo—o como era yo hasta hace poco—asomó por fin, las narices. Y él está haciendo las cosas bien hechas. En grande. En forma legal y organizada. En un día entierra más gente que yo en un mes. No puedo atravesármele."
>
> [7/7. 130-31]

Another example of oligarchic tyranny driven by lust for power and wealth is found in *Infierno negro*, a play about racial persecution that combines the dignity of a ritualistic black chorus on one plane echoing the tragedy of oppression, while on another the author unfolds a caricature of unethical rulers whose performance is as grotesque or ludicrous as the oppressed people they dominate are noble.[17] In presenting the guilty, Aguilera-Malta ridicules them with pompous names: Creso Topo (Croesus Mole) is a banker complemented by Arácnido Mefítico (Mephitic Arachnid), the industrialist. Feto Eunuco (Fetus Eunuch), the public-relations specialist, adds his casuistic remarks, which are punctuated by the growling of the military chief, General Pimpampum.[18]

As greed is represented by the group controlling the fictitious city of Nylónpolis, virtue and reason are symbolized by the caged intellectual Ariel,[19] who observes the action and protests in vain. Technological advances of the modern age work to improve the lot of the businessman rather than the plight of the underprivileged masses. There is no limit to the use of the human mind for profiting from tragedy and the woes of mankind. Ariel warns the totalitarian council that their methods and diabolic schemes cannot continue oppressing the unfortunate. But righteous indignation only meets with specious rebuttals from Feto Eunuco, who admits the primacy of business over ethics, a sociopolitical condition especially prevalent in this atomic age:

FETO [*A Ariel*]: No olvides que vivimos en el siglo
  atómico. ¡Todo nos está permitido! El negocio
  es nuestro altar.

[*Infierno* 111]

The Creative Genius and Sin: Weapons of Destruction

Among the elite that govern and hold the public trust, the
man of science stands as a dominant figure who also can control the destiny of man. It is not without justification that
Virgil rewards those who "made life better with their skill
and inventions" (*Aen.* 6. 663) with eternal bliss in the Elysian
Fields. Nor was Dante unaware of the crimes that the artistic
or creative genius could perpetrate against humanity; for,
reserved for those fraudulent sinners is the last of the
Malebolge, the Tenth, before the descent into Cocytus, where
the treacherous are punished. There is indeed a place in Hell
for the criminals who have deceived the public as had the
falsifiers of currency and the pseudo-scientists who
manipulated their knowledge of alchemy and abandoned the
search for truth, a vocation that was less profitable than
duping the greedy who desired the conversion of base metals
into gold.

The inventive mind put to use for perverted ends existed as
early as human passions, and perhaps the most famous man
of science in Western mythology to lend his services to the
satisfaction of lust was Daedalus. Better known for his personal tragedy, when he and Icarus departed from Crete, the
inventor of the wings of wax also fashioned the wooden cow,
so that the Pasiphaë, the queen, could lie with the bull she
desired. Out of this unholy union the Minotaur was born,
and, as has often been the case when sin begets sin, Daedalus
continued his collaboration with evil by devising the labyrinth
which led sacrificial youths and maidens to the monster until
Theseus destroyed the beast.

The most sinful implementation of the creative intellect is undoubtedly the conception and design of devices and tools for the destruction of human beings. The epic battlefield, cluttered with victims who have succumbed to arrows, darts, swords, axes, and other familiar lethal weapons, often contains instruments that find inspiration in natural phenomena. As the spear recalls the lightning of Zeus and the thunderbolts that Christ in *Paradise Lost* uses to attack the defiant angels, the technological wonder which defeats the Trojan army is the product of the inventive genius who draws from nature and religion for the creation of an instrument of death. The event is described in Book 2 of the *Aeneid*, where Pergamum falls to the Greeks through the skillful craftsmanship of Epeus, the inventor of the Trojan Horse. Once again a beast of nature in abnormal form and function acts to challenge the hero's survival. The wooden structure frequently is referred to as a "monster" by Aeneas as he tells the story of Troy's downfall to Dido. The horse, as if coming to term, produces death-dealing progeny, clearly expressed in the lines: "The fatal engine climbs our walls pregnant with arms" (5. 237),[20] and "four times there came the clang of weapons from its womb" (5. 243). Finally, the destruction of Troy is assured when the "ill-omened monster" (5. 245) is delivered of its demons by Sinon:

> . . .A signal flashed from the flagship,
> and Sinon, shielded by the malignity of Heaven,
> stealthily unlocked the imprisoned Danaans
> from the horse's wooden womb. They joyfully emerge,
> disgorged by the monster's hollow cavern into the air.
> [*Aen*. 5. 256-60]

In *Gerusalemme Liberata* success or failure of the Crusaders' mission again depends on the construction of a mobile device whose properties are much like those of a monstrous animal and for whose creation the talents of a master craftsman are essential. Engines, rams, and towers were the popular war machinery of the medieval and Renaissance periods, and Tasso utilizes these instruments of destruction along with the conventional ones. The engine which finally succeeds in penetrating the walls of the Holy City is as magnificent a feat of engineering as the Trojan Horse. Designed by a famous Genoan architect, it is a combined battering ram and fortress-like structure, complex and awesome to the beholder. The offensive protruding battering ram, the protective animal hides, and the hundred wheels[21] which propel it forward at unusual speed transform the weapon into almost an aerial monster that has just glutted himself on the many men it now contains. Much like the Trojan Horse, the image conveyed is one of an animate object on the brink of parturition:

Per le facili vie destra, e corrente
Sovra ben cento sue volubil rote,
Gravida d'arme e gravida di gente,
Senza molta fatica ella gir pôte.

[*G.L.* 18. 45, 1-4]

Ismeno, the wizard, can hardly compete with the strange weapon that resembles a composite beast. His own invention, the balls of fire that have been successful in destroying other engines (Canto 13), no longer is effective.[22]

The most famous inventor of an instrument of annihilation was also the most reprobate. Satan, during a moment of creative inspiration, conceives of the weapon which is used in celestial civil warfare:

A triple-mounted row of Pillars laid
On Wheels (for like to Pillars most they seem'd
Or hollow'd bodies made of Oak or Fir
With branches lopt, in Wood or Mountain fell'd)
Brass, Iron, Stony mould, had not their mouths

With hideous orifice gap't on us wide,
Portending hollow truce.

[*P.L.* 6. 572-78]

The monstrosity is as destructive as it is bizarre:

. . .Immediate in a flame,
But soon obscur'd with smoke, all Heav'n appear'd
From those deep-throated Engines belcht, whose roar
Embowell'd with outrageous noise the Air
And all her entrails tore.

[*P.L.* 6. 584-88]

Nevertheless, the rebel angels cannot overcome the Lord's forces. The inspiration for the future, however, has been created along with the infernal machine, and Raphael predicts the terrestrial realization of the same weapon after Adam's time when some human inventor

. . .might devise
Like instrument to plague the Sons of men
For sin, on war and mutual slaughter bent.[23]

[*P.L.* 6. 504-506]

Modern weaponry, like Raphael's chance projection of internecine instruments yet to come, still recalls the composite monster animated by the Sorcerer for diabolic ends. Artillery as described by the twentieth-century writer is reminiscent of the awesome bestial entity whose "mouths with hideous orifices gap't on" the heavenly host:

Los rifle y los cañones relucientes asomarán sus bocas
antropófagas ante el asombro de las masas.

[*Madrid* 44]

For Aguilera-Malta, who recorded the holocaust of a civil war between men, artillery reflects the horror and brutality of all the classical and Renaissance aberrations that persecuted the hero. As Sin's pursuit of mankind is announced by the ominous hounds that are part of her, the "barking" of the anti-aircraft guns (*Madrid* 103, 117) is also Cerberean in allusion and infernal in effect. While machine-gun fire "devours" the innocent (p. 82), the monsters of the air, paralleling their Achaean antecedent in Troy, "spew" their contents over the city of Madrid (p. 102). The man-made alar beast ravages the earth with its lethal droppings and in turn creates by its devastation another image of gruesome and tragic proportions:

> Acá en San Jerónimo, hay los efectos de una bomba gigantesca. Parece la boca de un monstruo milenario. . . . Tierra que se abre en mueca trágica.
>
> [*Madrid* 138]

The tank also joins other zoomorphic weaponry to add to the Dantesque imagery of war, and it appears in metaphoric context as part of a ballad verse where it is referred to as an "apocalyptic anserine" creature (*España* 58), as well as compared to the thick-skinned pachyderm. In the drama, which concerns an atomic instrument of annihilation, Fausto, a soldier returning from war, recalls the crawling unit of artillery that reflects the insanity of internecine combat:

> "¿Pensaste alguna vez que los tanques dan la impresión de paquidermos enloquecidos caminando de rodillas?"[24]

Fausto, after taking part in the destruction of his fellowman, demonstrates the gradual loss of his own human sensitivity as he explains his role in the slaughter and his consequent assimilation of the ferrous, automatic properties that characterize present-day instruments of mass annihilation:

> FAUSTO: Ultimamente no he sido otra cosa que una máquina: una regadora de existencias automática.

ALBA: Te engañas.
FAUSTO: Tuve las entrañas metálicas.
ALBA: Repito que te engañas.
FAUSTO: Me alimenté de proyectiles.

[*Atomos* 39][25]

But it is Fausto's father, Arquímedes, who has committed the maximum sin, for he has invented a genocidal atomic weapon and sold his talents to tyranny. His wife, Ifigenia, explains the situation, which merits him no Elysian reward:

"Sabía lo que el Dictador ansiaba: que vendiera su ciencia no para el disfrute y dicha de la humanidad, sino para su desgracia, en beneficio de unos pocos. ¡No para la creación, sino para la destrucción! ¡No para la virtud, sino para el delito! ¡No para la vida, sino para la muerte!"

[*Atomos* 66]

Dovetailing the advanced nuclear instrument of annihilation is the simple and ancient weapon of destruction, the sword. The literary versatility of the implement in functioning as material for metaphoric expression and as part of the plot has an ancient trajectory which is essentially religious and sexual in significance. In its epic roots as an instrument used in the Near Eastern ritual which renewed the king's position as supreme ruler of his people, the sword was a symbol of both fertility and political power traditionally associated with seasonal change. Its combined representation of a sexual and war image,[26] the plunging of the sword and its extraction signified rebirth at the end of the year's cycle.

The heroes of myth and legend of European tradition also participated in comparable ceremonies of kingship. Theseus, reared in secrecy, had to extract the sword from under a stone before he could succeed Aegeus as king of Athens, and the tale of Arthur and Excalibur similarly repeats this ritual. In the literary world, although the steel weapon does not necessarily grant the warrior the right to rule, it does confirm superior prowess, a condition that implies virility. In most cases the hero is already a leader in his own right as Beowulf is when he receives Hrunting from Hrothgar, or the Cid when he earns Tizón and Colada in battle. In Tasso's epic the hero, Rinaldo, once he has repented his lust and sloth, vices which he enjoyed in Armida's garden, is granted the sword of the deceased warrior and prince of Denmark, Sveno, which corroborates his selection as leader of the knights against the paynims.

Literary tradition, however, seems to have lessened the pristine sexual significance of the violent weapon even though a warrior's prowess implies virility and overall excellence as a male. The sword in symbolic dichotomy is found again in the unsophisticated world of the Latin American peasant, functioning in a more primitive form as the machete, and it participates as companion to the underdog in his battle to earn his livelihood, and in acts related to his own honor and survival. In the works of Aguilera-Malta the most frequent usage of machete imagery is in connection with scenes of violence or sexual conquest. The young *cholo* Nicasio Yagual in the short story "El cholo que se castró," driven by lust, attacks his cousin, whose cry is a complex typological allusion: "Tal que un machetazo sonó un grito" (*L.Q.S.V.* 215). When her passion becomes his, the *chola*'s physical response to Nicasio's advances is then related to the same instrument ("La chola vibraba como un machete de carne," p. 216), which eventually functions as a weapon for killing her father. In *Don Goyo*, Cusumbo, once happy as an adolescent, finds manhood disillusioning, for he experiences sorrow and misery caused by the *patrón* who dominates his life and who must be obeyed because of the inherited debts of his father, which he joins to the ones he also incurs. Embittered by the harsh reality of interminable obligation, he finds little joy in work and no longer caresses his "loyal companion"—the machete—as he once did (*D.G.* 36). The *patrón* repays Cusumbo by seducing his wife, but one afternoon the *cholo* returns unexpectedly to his home and takes revenge on the pair. The vivid scene, which he can still remember after many years, is a mélange of color, pitiful exhortations, and the whirlwind[27] performance of the blade:

> Hasta aquí—despues de tantos años—recordaba perfectamente. Después, todo se borraba en una serie de imágines superpuestas, macabras, absurdas, deslocadas. A ratos, se veía como un remolino en la mano. Un remolino de acero que cortaba y cortaba sobre carne prieta y sobre carne blanca. Después, un diluvio de sangre, sobre el rostro, sobre el cuerpo todo. Gritos de angustia, de dolor, de súplica; insultos, imprecaciones, gemidos. Dos cuerpos que dejan de agitarse. La gran vacilación. Los antepasados, que brincan sobre su carne. Toda una raza que protesta.
>
> [*D.G.* 44-45]

Implacable as his epic predecessors were, Cusumbo is absorbed by the whirlwind force of his passion, which seeks revenge for honor lost—his own and that of a subjugated race which, for centuries, has been forced to accept the indignities of the conqueror.

Like any hero, the underdog is most comfortable and secure when his weapon is by his side. Yet for the untutored white man this symbol of sexual and political might is discomfiting. Néstor, the man facing his destruction on the Virgin Island, also is challenged with the same test that will confirm his right to "kingship" of the land he wants to dominate and the woman who represents the hope of rebirth, Esperanza. When he is drawn to her and she tells him of the type of man who can win her through conquest in machete fashion ("capaz de ganarme, si posible fuera, a machetazos," *Isla* 232), Néstor laughs nervously. The "sword" is not his instrument, he will never be the victor, and the equation of mastery of the implement with acceptance of his authority is something beyond his civilized comprehension.

Néstor's weapon, the pistol rather than the machete, leads to the death of Pablo Melgar's father, a virile and fearless man. The *patrón* is summoned to interrupt a duel between the *cholo* and his opponent. When Melgar disregards the order to stop, Néstor fires his gun, thereby killing the man who dared to defy him. The *cholo*'s son, however, becomes equally proficient with the machete when he abandons a life of servitude for a career of piracy. His passion for violence toward men and his uncontrollable lust for women are synthesized in his dominance of the blade. Although he never confronts Néstor directly, his male superiority is eventually established in the act of revenge for his father's death when he abducts Esperanza and the *patrón* loses himself in the maze of the jungle.

Pablo Melgar is a schematic prototype of Candelario Mariscal, the pirate-bandit of *Siete lunas y siete serpientes*, whose life of sex and violence is prompted by a blinding passion for war on men and women alike. Although he enjoys a variety of arms, and is even capable of creating his own spontaneously (he propels his victims to their homes by using trees as catapults, *7/7* 126-27), the Colonel is partial to his faithful companion, the machete, which is endowed with supernatural powers in much the same way that other famous swords of myth and legend were. Even in the hands of others, the instrument functions magically for the borrower, as Captain Canchona realizes, much to his surprise, when Candelario offers it to him, and it begins to move about with a will of its own:

Le tendió el machete. Al empuñarlo, Canchona tuvo una impresión desconocida. Entre el machete y él empezó a circular la misma sangre. Como si el arma tuviera vida y no fuese sino la prolongación de su brazo. Sin embargo, no le obedecía. Paradójicamente, parecía que poseyera voluntad propia. O que estuviera obedeciendo ajenas órdenes. Lo cierto es que empezó a remolinarle en vértigo. Miró a su jefe. Se diría que éste alumbraba con sus ojos pequeños una sonrisa irónica. Regresó la vista a los recientes adversarios. Estos se le echaron encima, dispuestos a liquidarlo. Vano empeño. El machete-remo. El machete-remolón. El machete-remolino. El machete-remolineante. El machete-remolinete. Remolino. Remolón. Remolineante. Remolinete. El machete.

[7/7 107]

The strange whirlwind of acrobatic steel appears again when Candelario brandishes his weapon to coerce the priest, Gaudencio, into agreeing to marry him and Dominga. Flying above the terrified clergyman, the machete strikes a precision blow on the tip of the simonist's slipper. As the hypocritical priest's fear increases in proportion to the machete strokes, a humming Candelario and his weapon ominously become multiplied and transfigured:

En su lugar había caimanes. Caimanes-coroneles. Muchos caimanes-coroneles. Dándole vueltas. En una serie de figuras superpuestas. Fundiéndose unas con otras. El machete tampoco era un machete. Eran decenas. Centenas de machetes. Golpeaban el suelo. Sacaban chispas. Al compás de la canción que las múltiples bocas habían vuelto a tararear.

[7/7 167]

Bloodlust and sexual lust merging in the phallic symbol of violence become the only means by which Candelario can achieve peace within himself; and the weapon's image of destruction joins its counterpart of procreative energy to secure the sanction of matrimony with Dominga, the girl who is suffering from her own physical desires.

The daughter of the wizard Bulu-Bulu performs, in a somnambulant state her primitive ritual of "seven moons and seven serpents" (Chapter 1)—a ceremony related as well to the same instrument of destruction. Her sexual frustration, expressed in a series of symbols, is also represented by the machete, which serves as a tool for burying her pretended seducer, a snake she must strangle each night. Through union with Dominga, the wielder of the magic machete, instrument of destruction and emblem of fertility, can expect his own rebirth (for he has been living with a dead mistress, Josefa Quindales), and the creation of many progeny to add to what is hoped will be a happy life.

Spanning the cultural and chronological gap that separates the rudimentary weapon, the machete, and the ultra modern devices of annihilation is easily accomplished in Aguilera-Malta's drama *Infierno negro*. The play provides a curious blend of primitive methods of destruction and the advanced industrial techniques which made mass production possible. The genocidal theory of the inventor, Hórridus Nabus, another traitor to mankind, is proposed to the oligarchy ruling Nylónpolis, who celebrate his brilliant proposition for solving the racial problem. Cannibalism is the basis of the master plan for the creation of a factory which will exterminate the black population and at the same time, fulfill the economic desires of the perverted leaders. The by-products of the fiendish operation will be sausages and prepared meats to be sold to the general public. The reaction of the council is as infernal as that of their antecedents in oppression and destruction—the rebel angels. The celebration of the ingenious weapon is found in *Paradise Lost* when Lucifer explains his conception of the cannon to his companions:

> Th' invention all admir'd, and each, how hee
> To be th' inventor miss'd, so easy it seem'd
> Once found, which yet unfound most would have thought
> Impossible:. . .

> [*P.L.* 6. 498-501]

Feto Eunuco, spokesman for the group, reflects comparable

envy of the monstrous idea by recalling historical precursors to the inventor of the sausage factory:

"Además el invento del muy respetable señor Hórridus Nabus no es ninguna novedad.
....
¿Recuerdas, por ejemplo, al leñador Grossman, que asesinaba en Berlin a las muchachas de provincia? Las contrataba como sirvientes y, después, las convertía en salchichas."

[*Infierno* 113]

The factory is uncannily successful, and the inventor, much to his dismay, is rewarded with a negligible percentage of the profits.

The components of nature again function in creating another instrument of subjugation and destruction when Hórridus invents a second device which he hopes will bring him the wealth he desires. The aerometer, a helmet-like apparatus created by him, will measure the amount of air consumed by a person and limit the most plentiful element of nature. The plan will convert the oligarchy into "administrators of air" (59), which will bring them a step closer to their sire, the "Prince of Air." The diabolic headgear controls the amount inhaled by each citizen; the quantity allotted will be contingent upon the council's evaluation of the individual's worth, and the price will be regulated according to consumption. The prospect of a moneymaking enterprise again delights the tyrants who govern Nylónpolis, while Ariel, the caged intellectual, protests to no avail. His admonitions are concluded with a lament for the man of talent who devoted his efforts to demonic inventions: "Tú, que pudiste hacer tanto bien con tu talento, ahora sólo inventas cosas para el mal" (*Infierno* 59).

Although the pernicious aerometer of Nylónpolis functions basically as a symbol of war against the downtrodden, it also can express unity among men; for despite theories of superiority, it is air, the most precious element of all, not gold, that sustains mankind and forges a common bond of necessity between the weak and the strong. The strange helmet, however, has further significance in its relationship to humanity and its ever-changing destiny. This symbol of violence, which is reminiscent of the warrior's headgear, is also capable of projecting man's generative impulses and dreams: it is the emblem of Don Quixote, defender of the weak and champion of justice, when he converts a barber's shaving basin into the marvelous Helmet of Mambrino; it is the mark of the astronaut's realized fantasy in outer space, and the sign of the oceanographer's aspirations for conquering the marine wonderland. All are related to discovery and the application of ideals, knowledge, or power for aiding mankind—values which Hórridus unfortunately rejects in his role as a creative genius in society.

Bondage: Physical, Spiritual, and Economic Tyranny

Infierno negro is the dramatization of the black people's plight in a modern world which has maintained many of its primeval characteristics of barbarism; for the efforts of the inventor to construct devices of torture or annihilation seem to be a far cry from civilization. The instruments of destruction, however, are inextricably woven with another invention of man—slavery—a system also devised for the economic benefit of the powerful. Sometimes a cause for war, more frequently the result of it, bondage, after its epic inception as the practical sucessor to the Trojan Horse, which destroyed Ilium, flourishes in subsequent centuries until the present, when, in modified but still recognizable form, it functions to continue persecuting the helpless. Sin, tyranny, and helotry are all part of evil as interpreted by the epicist in contrast to what is essentially a Christian heroic ideal.[28]

Bondage, and the deliverance from it, is the theme of *Gerusalemme Liberata*, which celebrates the holy feat accomplished by Goffredo, paragon of virtue and victor over all infernal opposition to his divinely inspired purpose (1. i). In addition to the actual slavery which exists within the walls of Jerusalem, the bondage theme is related to the sins of which the Christian knights might be culpable. A parallel between servitude and the quest for worldly fame is made in the etiological dream of Goffredo in which he views the Celestial City and the insignificant earth below. Goffredo regards man's terrestrial domain as a place of bondage when compared with the beauty of Heaven; and he marvels at the folly of the search for mundane glory:

> Ed ammiró che pur a l'ombre a i fumi
> La nostra folle umanità s'affise,
> Servo imperio cercando e muta fama,
> Né miri il ciel, ch'a sé n'invita e chiama.
>
> [*G.L.* 14. 11. 5-8]

Servitude has a third and moral or religious trajectory in the development of the vulnerable and passionate Rinaldo. When the knight yields to Armida's charms, he relinquishes his spiritual freedom by casting off his armor and capitulating to sloth and physical pleasure.

The richest and most interesting development of the bondage theme is found in *Paradise Lost*, where Milton poses the opposition of servitude and liberty and condemns the oppressive elements of evil that pursue man. But the presentation is more significantly a juxtaposition of antithetical values expressed in a language manipulated to convey a mockery of justice that is characteristic of Satan and his followers. Christ and Satan announce their roles as leaders in ironically reversed positions when the former speaks of enslavement:

I through the ample Air in Triumph high
Shall lead Hell Captive maugre Hell, and show
The powers of darkness bound. . . .

[*P.L.* 3. 254-56]

And Lucifer, in "virtuous" contradiction of Christ, has already preempted his function as Liberator of the Enslaved:

. . .I in one Night freed
From servitude inglorious well nigh half
Th' Angelic Name. . . .

[*P.L.* 9. 140-43]

Satan is doubly victorious and noble, for he has also "delivered" Sin and Death, now ready to join him to form an "unholy trinity"[29] for the persecution of man:

I come no enemy, but to set free
From out this dark and dismal house of pain,
Both him and thee. . . .

[*P.L.* 2. 822-24]

Once Satan reigns in Hell, he considers his status an improvement over subservience since he is now free and in a position of complete authority:

. . .Here at least
We shall be free; th' Almighty hath not built
Here for his envy, will not drive us hence:
Here we may reign secure, and in my choice
To reign is worth ambition, though in Hell:
Better to reign in Hell, than serve in Heav'n.

[*P.L.* 1. 258-63]

The majority of the defiant host, nevertheless, is not as pleased with the new abode, which is described in terms more suited to the dismal and tenebrous conditions of the subjugated, oppressed, and unenlightened rather than to the open, radiant environment associated with truth and liberty. For Moloch it is a "dark approbrious Den of shame" (*P.L.* 2. 58), and Beelzebub sees this residence in Hell as a state of "strictest bondage" (*P.L.* 2. 321). .After the Traitor Angel makes his conquest in the Garden of Eden, he is able to offer the devils the entire world for their enjoyment and perversions. As a result, he vents a more accurate, if not honest, description of his circumstances:

> I call ye and declare ye now, return'd
> Successful beyond hope, to lead ye forth
> Triumphant out of this infernal Pit.
> Abominable, accurst, the house of woe,
> And dungeon of our Tyrant. . . .
>
> [*P.L.* 10. 462-66]

But liberty, as opposed to bondage, is expressed by Milton in terms of free will, granted by the Lord to angels and men alike, to choose whether or not to fall. The concept is repeated by God (*P.L.* 3. 98-99), Raphael (*P.L.* 5. 525-57), and Adam (*P.L.* 9. 351-52). Reaffirmed by Michael, following the First Couple's disobedience, are the importance of reason and the consequences of pursuing instead the dictates of one's passions:

> Since thy original lapse, true Liberty
> Is lost, which always with right Reason dwells
> Twinn'd, and from her hath no dividual being:
> Reason in man obscur'd, or not obey'd,
> Immediately inordinate desires
> And upstart Passions catch the Government
> From Reason, and to servitude reduce
> Man till then free. . . .
>
> [*P.L.* 12. 83-90]

However, helotism in its political and social connotation is also present in Milton's epic when an affirmation of liberty in this respect is made by Adam:

He gave us only over Beast, Fish, Fowl
Dominion absolute; that right we hold
By his donation; but Man over men
He made not Lord: such title to himself
Reserving, human left from human free.

[*P.L.* 12. 67-71]

Despite Adam's shocked disapproval of the projected institutionalization of servitude, his scions will be the despots of history who perpetuate the enslavement of man until the present day. The Latin American writer is particularly sensitive to the apparent incompatibility of bondage and freedom; yet, ironically, from the interrelationship of master and slave evolved the biological and cultural amalgamation which defines the Hispanic nations to the south. It also is, however, a historical fact that the Spanish and Portuguese conquerors imposed the yoke of slavery upon the African and Indian elements in the New World, and the effects of abuse and degradation by no means have been entirely eradicated.

The theme of bondage permeates the works of Aguilera-Malta with the same intensity revealed in *Paradise Lost*. The presentation of slavery and its opposite, freedom, is developed in physical as well as spiritual contexts resulting from causes which are predominantly economic. All of the tyrannical figures created by the author are, like Satan, slaves to their passions, and their victims in every period with which he deals are generally helots in an organized system of servitude, oppressed through some fraudulent means that are calculated to enhance the personal gain of the tyrannical force concerned. The early conquerors and colonizers of the New World enslaved the Indians, who were regarded as "things" to be bought and sold like any other item. An impressive account of the natives' insignificance is found in Balboa's story in which the victims are used as stakes in games of chance among the Spaniards:

Los indios se habían convertido en mercancía mínima. Frecuentemente, en los ratos de ocio, los españoles los

jugaban, como cifras de apuesta. Una vez, el propio
Pedrarias, en una sola mano, perdió cinco esclavos.

[*Mar* 223]

The parallel between money and slavery is intensified by the
less than exemplary form of entertainment that occupies the
conquerors' (ironically) free movements ("ratos de ocio").

But the Indians were soon supplanted by African slaves,
who were more suited to the demands of physical exertion
which agricultural production required. Their odyssey across
the Atlantic to serve in the American colonies is re-created by
Aguilera-Malta, and the black captive's tragedy is recounted
in *Siete lunas y siete serpientes* as part of Bulu-Bulu's own
history. In a trance the medicine man relives his ancestors'
journey to the Americas and the story is told in a series of
rhythmic impressions:

Antes—ese antes canoso cuatrocentenario—él llegó en un
barco negrero. De cuadernas y tablas en muecas sono-
rosas. Negrero. De velas y mástiles con saliva de océano.
De casco ataviado con nácar vivo de bivalvas. Bulu-
Bulu entre esclavos—príncipes, guerreros, vírgenes,
artistas, artesanos, brujos—con cadena al cuello. Entre
muchos esclavos. La mitad la devoró la distancia. La
otra mitad, ¿estaba viva? Negrero. Bamboleo de las
velas. Carcajadas del viento. Dentelladas del sol abras-
ante. Las tripas resecas de hambre y de sed. Los cuerpos
vestidos con huellas de látigo. Negrero. Empujados.
Hundidos. Descendidos. Catarata de sangre y de lágrimas.
Negrero. ¿Cuántos soles y lunas, hacinados, prensados,
muriendo en la cárcel flotante de noches inmóviles?
¿Cuántas veces siete? Con el aro de hierro en el cuello.
Unidos por hondas cadenas de hierro y angustia. ¿Cuántos
soles y soles? ¿Cuántas lunas y lunas?

[*7/7* 280]

With the punctuating repetition of the word for slave ship
("negrero"), which reflects the movement of the vessel as it

travels through the waters and at the same time recalls the pervasive beat of Africa's music, the author achieves an effective interpretation of the persistent futility that accompanies the unchanging destiny of an enslaved people.

Infierno negro, the play which concentrates on the evils of racial prejudice and its potential effect on civilization, involves the complete annihilation of the individual, rather than the advocation of slavery. Feto, the genius of sophistry, proposes the extermination plan for the underdogs and those who oppose the scheme in terms of a "liberation" movement (*Infierno* 114-15). But African heritage and the historical background of black subjugation once more are combined in the pulsating exchange made by the Negro figures who function much in the same way as a Greek chorus, as they respond to the dialogue of the depraved white oligarchy. This time sexual enslavement is the tale of Caoba Mórbida (Morbid Mahogany), a young woman who symbolically portrays the attractive female, victim of all the violence which the women of her race have suffered over the centuries. The ritualistic interpretation of a masked chorus relates how Caoba passed from her noble station to common hands while in transit to the New World:

NEGRO I: Era princesa. Un negrero la adquirió por un pedazo de espejo roto.

NEGRO II: Vino atada hasta el litoral, arrastrada por los guías.

NEGRO III: Pieza muy buena. No le faltaba ni un diente y era más bonita que cualquier inglesa.

NEGRO IV: En la cubierta la desfloró el Capitán. En nagó, elevó la voz hacia Oxalá.

CAOBA: [*Implorante, las manos en alto*]. ¡Loado sea Oxalá, para simpre loado!

CORO: Empezó a arañarse, porque él no la oyó. ¿Navío funeral!

NEGRO I: Después, la herraron con un ancla, en las caderas.

[*Infierno* 83-84]

With no one to protect her but her African deities, Caoba continues experiencing abuse and violence on a plantation in the New World. Escape is in vain, for she is found and returned for further oppression.

Bondage in twentieth-century terms proceeds along a bifurcated course of economic subjugation which began with the conquest and colonization of Latin America. The first track is found in the prolongation of the original policies and institutions of Spain and in land arrangements which were comparable to a feudal system of bondage. The modern version of serfdom is a form of indentured servitude (*concertaje*), which is denounced in *Don Goyo* as evidenced by Cusumbo's enslavement on the mainland. Responsible for the debts of his deceased father, he works to reduce a never-ending series of exorbitant charges for the basic necessities of life. In addition, he accumulates his own debts and falls as well into the self-imposed bondage of alcohol, from which prospects for liberation become even bleaker. After killing the *patrón* and successfully fleeing to the islands, Cusumbo's lot improves, but the white businessman appears again as a threat to the *cholos'* freedom when of economic necessity they must accept minimal recompense for the mangrove wood they sell to him.

The *patrón* also looms forth in the play *Dientes blancos*, in which he faces the insolent retorts of the black musician, Peter. The drunken landowner, in response to Peter's daring revilement, calls for the implement with which the slave owner is traditionally associated—the whip:

"En mi hacienda siempre les doy látigo. ¿Puedes conseguirme un látigo? Pídele al dueño del cabaret. Tal vez él tenga un látigo."

[*Dientes* 45]

But the play is also an example of the second path that slavery takes in modern times. The contemporary helot, like his forebears, is doomed to perform the function of affording pleasure to the masters of society. As Caoba Mórbida indicates in the scene which summarizes her history, black women served to satisfy the sexual appetite of their oppressors; so too, the musicians, to the sensual delight of the customers in the nightclub, entertain them by reviving ancient African rhythms, which in turn stimulate the erotic passions of an inebriated audience. Stereotypification is in itself a variant of bondage, and the Negro performers, in order to continue in the employ of their cabaret "master," must comply with the preconceived notions of the public seeking amusement.[30]

Prostitution is another vocation that provides diversion and which frequently subjugates the underdog. Unlike the chained Caoba of *Infierno negro*, the female victim of oppression in *Canal Zone* appears to be more at liberty, but is in fact hopelessly trapped by the economic crisis of the country along with other women of African ancestry. At the mercy of landlords, shopkeepers, and government, there is some chance for survival by this means of livelihood. Pedro Coorsi, too, as a *chombo*[31] joins the ranks of those whose economic needs dictate sensual entertainment as the last recourse. Performing the role of a pander, he solicits, collects, and drives sailors to "Tommy's Place," where they meet women who will satisfy their lust and mitigate their loneliness. Under these conditions of servitude, the masters vary from customer to customer, and the motivation of the enslaved is purely financial. Tasso's condemnation of helotry based on carnal desire stands in dramatic opposition to the indifferent acquiescence of the Panamanian prostitute whose behavior is not ruled by passions but by economic necessity.

But Aguilera-Malta returns to the allegorical presentation of bondage and restores the Renaissance opposition of servitude and liberty as spiritual components of a society or the individual. The Platonic confrontation of reason and appetite in a modern play such as *Infierno negro* still retains

its original significance. Physically incarcerated is the figure
of Ariel, held captive by the oligarchy that rules Nylónpolis.
Although Ariel is a twentieth-century humanist who believes
in equality and the welfare of the public, he is at the same
time the symbol of the imprisoned intellect subjugated by the
uncontrolled passions that can dominate the human soul.
The governing tyrannical council represents sin in its various
forms: lust in terms of sensual pleasures, wealth, power, and
all the perverted drives that can enslave reason. When
regarded as a single unit, Nylónpolis demonstrates the psyche
out of balance with the rational powers (Ariel) made sub-
servient to appetite (the council). Ariel is an impassioned
symbol of reason, for even reason can be vehemently
expressive when frustrated in its attempts to contend with
barbarism. A believer in brotherhood, justice, and harmony,
he protests and condemns each step toward what could
eventually lead to mankind's total extirpation. Exasperated
at the oligarchy's fiendish logic, Ariel can only toss out a
prophetic warning:

> "¡No podrán seguir actuando impunemente! Sus días
> están contados. La rebelión está en marcha y los ahogará,
> como una marea incontenible.
>
> [*Infierno* 111]

Instruments of violence or systems of bondage are part of
the involvement with the constant theme of power in epic
poetry. Tyranny and injustice, for Milton, are anticipated
consequences of uncontrolled appetite as shown by Eve's
inabstinence—one of the many violations of God's Law
committed in the Garden of Eden. Sin basically, for
Demetrio Aguilera-Malta, continues the tradition of
Christian epicists, for also in his works can be found the
inordinate drive, passion, or lust which motivates the wicked
in their travesties against mankind. Immutably destructive in
purpose, sin can assume many poses and forms. Tasso's

representation of vice is an appealing one: Armida is irresistibly beautiful, and the corruptive influence of her charms is not easily detectable. For Milton, Sin is an ugly monstrosity conceived by Satan and deformed by his own lascivious desires. According to Dante's interpretation, evil, like Geryon, can reveal the body of a zoomorphic aberration, but may also bear the face of a "just man." Aguilera-Malta particularly condemns the fraudulent and treacherous aspects of sin and employs the techniques of bestial degradation to present those nefarious characters whose lust for either wealth or power relates them to their diabolic predecessors of epic fame.

But as Milton believed, according to his Platonic and theological convictions, despotic rule can be brought about by the individual himself. For man, following the footsteps of his Parents, must learn to cope with his own weaknesses and temptations. Endowed with intelligence superior to that of beasts, he must struggle to preserve the sovereignty of reason over desire. Without the primacy of the rational component of the soul, the hero, whether peasant or king, will fall victim to the same passions that caused the fall of Troy, the death of Beowulf, the tragedy of Roland, the ineluctable fate of Odysseus's crew, and worst of all, the loss of Paradise.

Notes

1. Ganelon, whose name was a byword for "traitor" in the Middle Ages, actually is guilty of compound treachery toward kin, for he was related to Roland, and he betrayed his lord, Charlemagne, along with his country and the Christian faith.

2. In view of this function of Odysseus in the *Iliad*, it is ironic that Dante places him among the fraudulent as a false counselor for convincing his crew to sail beyond the Pillars of Hercules (*Inf.* 26).

3. The allegorical presentation of lust as an evil obstacle represented by the beautiful woman was a popular medieval and Renaissance topic. Particularly

alluring are the nymphs who attempt to delay or prevent the rescue of Rinaldo by Carlo and Ubaldo (*G.L.* 15. 58-66).

4. Milton's concept of wickedness is basically Greek. See *Paradise Lost*, ed. Merritt Y. Hughes (New York: The Odyssey Press, 1935), note, p. 340.

5. The *Odyssey* begins by referring to the hero's companions who "were destroyed by their own wild recklessness" (1. 7). They too could not govern their appetite, both in its limited as well as its broader sense.

6. Epic heroes often suffer from this afflication, and some meet their end because of it. Turnus demonstrates this in the *Aeneid* (7. 461; 9. 760); and the youths Nisus and Euryalus in Book 9 are stirred by bloodlust when they silently enter the enemy camp and slaughter the soldiers while they are asleep. Euryalus is especially "carried away by his excessive lust for slaughter" (354), but they stay too long, and finally are apprehended and killed.

7. A summary of offenses committed by the sinners in Dante's *Inferno* indicates that most crimes stem from a desire for wealth: thieves, counterfeiters, usurers, panderers, simonists, etc., in the fraudulent category generally are punished for hypocritical and deceptive acts executed for their own financial benefit.

8. *Honorarios* was published along with *Dientes blancos* and *El tigre* in Demetrio Aguilera-Malta, *Trilogía ecuatoriana*, prol. Emmanuel Carballo (Mexico: Andrea, 1959). Aguilera-Malta frequently notest his evil characters' morality and its effect on the underdog by naming them accordingly. Cercado's name means "enclosure," and his victims are indeed hopelessly trapped.

9. An incisive study of this era is David McCullough's *The Path Between the Seas. The Creation of the Panama Canal* (New York: Simon and Schuster, 1977). In a review of the book Gaddis Smith keenly observes that "the opening of the canal and the outbreak of World War I occurred simultaneously. The one event marked the fulfillment of the nineteenth-century vision of man's dominion over nature. The second event marked the nightmare of man's failure in the twentieth century to use this dominion for peace." See *The New York Times Book Review*, June 19, 1977, p. 39.

10. In this drama, which has received considerable acclaim from critics, the author stresses the use of the percussion instruments. Their function recalls a comparable dramatic effect in *The Emperor Jones* and, according to Hernán Rodríguez Castelo, lends the play a "sabor o'neillano." See "Teatro ecuatoriano," in *Cuadernos Hispanoamericanos* 172 (April 1964): 105.

11. For a study of this concept in fuller detail see Lemuel Johnson's *The Devil, the Gargoyle, and the Buffoon: The Negro as Metaphor in Western Literature* (Port Washington, N.Y.: Kennikat Press, 1971).

12. In Aguilera-Malta, *Trilogía ecuatoriana*, p. 41. Future references to *Dientes blancos* will be taken from this edition and will be abbreviated (e.g., *Dientes* 41).

13. Aguilera-Malta's many names for Satan include Ese, El Mismísimo, Aquel Cuyo Nombre No Se Pronuncia, El Socio, El de los Siete Mil Cachos, El Traga-Almas, El Maligno, El Que Sabemos, El Coludo, Candanga, El Otro, El Malo, etc. The rich, earthy euphemisms are reminiscent of the lofty epithets Milton uses for Lucifer: The Tempter, the Adversary of God and Man, the Fiend, the Artificer of Fraud, the Arch-Enemy, the Antagonist of Heaven, the Prince of Hell, the First Grand Thief, etc.

14. John D. Sinclair, *The "Divine Comedy" of Dante Alighieri* (New York: Oxford University Press, 1959), 1 (*Inferno*): 417-18. The Florentine poet also places such sinners lower in Cocytus than those treacherous to kin.

15. W. K. C. Guthrie, *The Greek Philosophers: From Thales to Aristotle* (New York: Harper, 1960), pp. 111-12. Ironically, in the Republic the "masses" were to be the only class permitted to hold private wealth.

16. See Maurice McNamee, S. J., *Honor and the Epic Hero: A Study of the Shifting Concept of Magnanimity in Philosophy and Epic Poetry* (New York: Holt, Rinehart, and Winston, 1959), pp. 180ff. The author discusses the differences among the Greek, Roman, and Christian ideals of honor and magnanimity as related to epic tradition and philosophy.

17. In this context Friedrich Dürenmatt's remarks concerning political satire and the grotesque are most applicable: "Tyrants fear only one thing: a poet's mockery. For this reason, then, parody has crept into all literary genres, into the novel, the drama, into lyrical poetry. Much of painting, even of music, has been conquered by parody, and the grotesque has followed, often camouflaged, on the heels of parody: all of a sudden the grotesque is there." See Friedrich Dürrenmatt, *"Problems of the Theatre," An Essay, and "The Marriage of Mr. Mississippi," A Play*, tr. Gerhard Nellhaus (New York: Grove Press, 1964), p. 36.

18. Degradation by such epithets combining Latin terms and bestial allusion is in keeping with Dante's presentation of the barrators (Cantos 21, 22), which the Italian poet treats as "an extravagant farce." The names of his devils, who parallel Aguilera-Malta's offenders of humanity, are "as uncouth as their persons and conduct": Malacoda (Evil-tail), Barbariccia (Curlybeard), Cagnazzo (Low Hound), Draghignazzo (Vile Dragon), Ciriatto (Swineface), etc. See Sinclair, *The "Divine Comedy" of Dante Alighieri*, pp. 278-79. In both cases the atmosphere is overcast with a sense of mutual treachery should the occasion arise, for the devils, like the barrators, and the rulers of Nylónpolis or the oligarchy of Babelandia, are no more capable of keeping faith among themselves than they are with those who are in their charge.

19. Ariel is associated in Latin American literature with the spirit of enlightenment and served as the title of a famous essay by the writer and statesman José Enrique *Rodó,* who was equally concerned with the destiny of the Latin American republics.

20. See Bernard M. W. Knox, "The Serpent and the Flame," in *Virgil: A Collection of Critical Essays,* ed. Steele Commager (Englewood Cliffs, N.J.: Prentice-Hall, 1966), pp. 129-30. Mr. Knox explains the use of grotesque allusion when referring to the Trojan Horse's movements (i.e., "climbing"). The author also relates the chain of events expressed in serpent and fire symbolism to death and rebirth; however, he does not present the full cyclical sequence: the concept of birth as seen in the release of the Greeks from the horse, then death in the conflagration of Troy, and finally rebirth in Italy.

21. The image is somewhat of an artificial Typhoeus, offspring of Earth and Tartarus, the giant of one hundred heads who breathed fire.

22. Ismeno, too, can be considered a man of skill or science, but his Moslem affiliations and the evil purpose to which he devotes his talents (i.e., fighting against the Christians) determine his profession as that of a magician or sorcerer. Aguilera-

Malta's medicine man, Bulu-Bulu, however, although more pagan than Christian in his practices of African and Indian religious customs, is undeniably a virtuous wizard. Among the many functions he performs on the island of Balumba is that of accepting and often curing the hopelessly infirm in his open-air hospital.

23. "To create / Is greater than created to destroy," (*P.L.* 7. 606-607), is the Seraph's reflection of God's attitude; yet paradoxically, it is the "Great Creator" himself who applies his skill and inventive talents to fashion from clay the father of the race that will produce many men of genius perversely dedicated to the principles of destruction rather than creation.

24. *No bastan los átomos* and *Dientes blancos* (Quito: Casa de la Cultura Ecuatoriana, 1955), p. 39. Future references to this work and edition will appear in abbreviated form directly after the citation (e.g., *Atomos* 39).

25. The transformation of the soldier into a machine that kills (usually in anti-war literature) recalls Brecht's play *A Man's a Man,* where, during the concluding scene of "Final Metamorphosis," Galy Gay becomes a "Human Fighting Machine." See *"Baal," "A Man's a Man"* and *"The Elephant Calf." Early Plays by Bertolt Brecht,* adapted by Eric Bentley (New York: Grove Press, 1964) p. 192.

26. As part of the pre-Hellenic fertility rites, the plunging of the sword into stone was connected with the double functions of the early Indo-European divinities Indra, Area, and Mars as gods of fertility and war. See Gertrude R. Levy, *The Sword from the Rock* (London: Faber & Faber, 1953), p. 16.

27. The "whirlwind" motion of the machete is reminiscent of warriors described in the *Iliad* as each opponent fights for survival or vengeance—Nestor (11. 746) and Hector (12. 40)—and the spear of Aeneas also is compared to the same natural force in the *Aeneid* (12. 923). The fierceness of revenge is essentially the same in classical or modern context. For a more detailed study of this topic as it relates to Aguilera-Malta's works, see my article "El aire como materia literaria: la épica, la nueva narrativa, y Demetrio Aguilera-Malta," in *Nueva Narrativa Hispanoamericana* 4 (January-September 1974): 261-68.

28. The *Aeneid* has its moments of condemnation, particularly in view of the Trojan War's aftermath. Andromache meets Aeneas during his wanderings and relates her woes of "enduring the youthful insolence of Achilles' son, / bearing children in slavery" (3. 326-27); yet, rewarding the winner of a race with a female slave from Crete (5. 284) is the hero's token of esteem and passes uncommented. Anchises, however, more typically reflects Roman justice when, in the Lower World, he counsels the future leaders of the empire to "spare the subject nations" (6.853). The Greek attitude toward bondage is discussed by Gilbert Murray, who notes Homer's "half-puzzled tenderness" toward slaves. He concludes that the poet considered the institution a "terrible thing," although Homer does not call specifically for reform. For other Hellenic viewpoints on the topic see Mr. Murray's *The Rise of the Greek Epic* (New York: Oxford University Press, 1960), pp. 15-18.

29. The term is used by David Daiches in *Milton* (New York: Norton, 1966), p. 177.

30. This theme and other elements relating *Dientes blancos* to *Négritude* poetry of the French-speaking Caribbean and Africa are analyzed in my study "Hacia la *Négritude*: las ediciones *variorum* de *Dientes blancos*," in *Homenaje a Andrés*

Iduarte (Clear Creek, Ind.: The American Hispanist), pp. 285-300.
   31. *Chombo* is the term used to designate the black in Panama.

5
Justice:
The Iron and the Golden Scepters

And the rest of the men which were not killed by these plagues yet repented not of the works of their hands, that they should worship devils, and idols of gold, and silver, and brass, and stone, and of wood; which neither can see, nor hear, nor walk: ·

Neither repented they of their murders, nor of their sorceries, nor of their fornication, nor of their thefts.

[Revelation 10:20, 21]

Divine Retribution by Death, Loss, Metamorphosis

The traditional theme of sin is conjointly developed with that of expiation or retribution and eschatologically with the concept of salvation òr rebirth. St. John's Revelation is in essence an excoriation of evil and the consequences of mankind's falling prey to vice by committing acts offensive both to God and to all codes of ethical behavior. The execution of divine justice is as basic to the literature of classical times as it was to the patristic. Punishment on earth was the function of the dreaded Furies, the Erinyes or Eumenides, who pursued men generally for crimes that included violation of laws of hospitality, respect toward the aged and suppliants, and com-

178

mission of perjury or murder. They lived in Tartarus as well, along with other familiar "monsters" that brought woe to mankind and plagued the hero on earth:

> Before the Entrance Hall, and in the jaws of Orcus,
> Grief and Avenging Cares have made their dwelling place.
> There dwell pallid Disease, and melancholy Old Age,
> and Fear, and ill-advising Famine, and shameful Want,
> all horrid shapes to behold, and Death and Suffering,
> and Sleep, Death's brother, and all the guilty joys
>   of the Soul,
> and on the opposite threshold War, the bringer of Death,
> the iron chambers of the Furies, and mad Discord
> with bloody fillets that encircle her snaky locks.
>
> [*Aen.* 6. 273-81]

The gods, whose wrath is personified by Nemesis, participated in castigating the warriors and offenders of divine law. Apollo's plague is the response to the abduction of Chryseis and the subsequent refusal of her father's ransom by Agamemnon. Disrespect for Phoebus's priest, Chryses, whose age and condition as a suppliant compound the leader's sin, is punished by disease and death, which continue until Agamemnon returns the girl to her father (*Il.* 1). The offense to Hera made by Paris and the adultery of Helen are the causes of Troy's downfall but also the generative thematic source of the three great epics related to the events in Ilium. Odysseus merits Poseidon's acknowledgement of his son's prayer, when, after blinding Polyphemus, the Ithacan king incurs his additional enmity. He barely survives the vengeance of the god for tormenting the sightless giant while boasting and celebrating his own name. Excess, or recklessness, uncontrolled passion, or sin, is the cause of death of Odysseus's crew; despite forewarnings by Circe and Tiresias, the sacrilegious act performed on Hyperion's island decides their fate. But violation of the gods' precepts has its ethical and social significance as well. Homer's development of treachery and betrayal in terms of hospitality is at its fullest in the *Odyssey*, when the suitors' depravity contrasts with the exemplary behavior of Telemachus and his father during their visits to various royal households. Disrespect for the host is part of the moral issue and is an offense that merits both divine and human castigation. Odysseus explains the fate of the suitors as just punishment for what is essentially antisocial behavior:

> "These were destroyed by the doom of the gods and
>   their own hard actions,
> for these men paid no attention at all to any man on
>   earth
> who came their way, no matter if he were base or
>   noble.
> So by their own recklessness they found a shameful
>   death."
>
> [*Od.* 22. 413-17][1]

Divine retribution is frequently executed for acts of sacrilege committed by those who defy supernatural will when expressed by natural phenomena traditionally considered as oracles or totemically involved in the culture of a pagan or primitive society. The chronological gap between the classical epic characters and the contemporary island dwellers of Aguilera-Malta's works does not reveal any significant difference in what transpires when the deities of the earth are offended. Don Goyo, whose relationship with the mangroves of the island is a determining factor in the destiny of the people he leads, receives the portentous message that the foreign white invader will destroy the simple peace that the *cholos* have had for generations. The aging patriarch hears the prophecy from a voice which comes to him from the oldest tree in the swamp:

"Los Blancos dejarán las islas solitarias. . . .Os arran-

carán a vosotros mismos. . . .Vuestros hombres, como
harapos de carne, un día se arrojarán sobre el océano.''

[*D.G.* 79]

Latinus, king of the Laurentians, another venerable
spiritual and political leader who finds himself during a time
of crisis in a comparable position to that of Don Goyo, also
has communicated in the sacred grove with the gods of
nature:

Suddenly a voice came from the depth of the forest:
"Do not seek to join your daughter in Latin wedlock,
and put no trust, my son, in bridal-chambers prepared:
for foreign sons shall come, whose blood will exalt
  our name
up to the very stars.''

[*Aen.* 7. 95-99]

The message of Faunus places the king in the position of confronting his people to determine another course of action
than that of marrying his daughter, Lavinia, to Turnus. Don
Goyo too relates the new decision concerning a "foreigner,"
and his followers temporarily acquiesce and begin fishing,
abandoning their former occupation as woodcutters. After
meeting with little success and no profit, the *cholos* return to
tell Don Goyo that they must resume their original trade and
restore their business relationship with the white man. The
will of the oracle is about to be challenged as they ominously
approach their leader to tell him of their decision:

Todos—hombres y mujeres—lo rodearon. Poco a poco,
fueron acercándose en silencio, sin musitar una sílaba,
con los ojos bajos, temblorosos, como una descomunal
atarraya humana. Don Goyo—que se encontraba sentado
en un cajón de kerosén vacío—se levantó.

[*D.G.* 124]

The humble dwelling of Don Goyo, who is reminiscent of

another Italian king, Evander in the *Aeneid*, is contrasted
with a palace, Latinus's abode, yet it is paradoxically
dignified by the silent presence of the Indians. The royal
premises are approached, however, by a mob of people
vociferously protesting and asserting their desires:

> And all of them, despite the oracles and omens,
> perversely throng, and clamor for an evil war.
> They gather in noisy crowds about Latinus' palace.
> And he resists them, like an immovable cliff by the
>   sea
> which, though the waves come crashing with their
>   mighty roar,
> stands unmoved in its bulk above the hollowing billows;
> the rocks and foamy waters seethe in useless rage;
> the seaweed, hurled against its side, is sent swirling
>   back.
>
> [*Aen.* 7. 583-90]

Latinus and Don Goyo stand firm in their belief of their
own spiritual advisers, and they refuse to contradict the
portent conveyed by the powers of nature. Each responds to
his followers with nonaction and withdrawal from any
further responsibilities of leadership. The two men are helpless in altering the course of events, and they express a
prophetic warning to the people who have challenged the pro-
nouncement of nature's divinities. Latinus looks at the crowd
gathered and predicts the punishment awaiting them for their
sin:

> "And you, my poor children, will pay the price with
>   blood
> for sacrilege. You, Turnus, guilt and punishment
> remain for you, and you shall pray to the gods, but
>   too late.
> My rest is near at hand, for I am on the threshold
> of life; all I lose is a happy death." He spoke no
>   more,

but shut himself in his palace and dropped the reins
  state.

[Aen. 7. 595-600]

Don Goyo extends his judgment of impending castigation for
the *cholos* who defied the will of the great mangrove. The
white man's domination of the once free, just, and simple
society is at hand:

—Ustedes no sirven para nada. . . .El Blanco los mandará
siempre. . . .Y algún día no podrá vivir nadie por estos
lados. Y entonces se acordarán del viejo don Goyo. . . .
Corten mangle. . . .Hagan lo que les dé la gana.

[D.G. 125-26]

Evil times are indeed on their way, for the peace and
harmony of the islands and the land of the Latins will be
destroyed as part of the castigation for disobeying the spirits
of nature. The descendants of Saturn, according to Latinus,
are "just men, not by compulsion or law, / but of our own
free will we hold to the ways of God" (*Aen.* 7. 203-204).
Although the Italian race will eventually blend with the Trojans to produce the Roman Empire, it will be brought about
through the devastation of the land and the death of many
innocent people in a war which could have been averted had
the oracle of Faunus been accepted. For the people led by
Don Goyo, their castigation is, first, the death of their tribal
leader, and then war; but their war will be basically
economic, and their bondage to the white man will begin with
his domination of the islands where the *cholos* once lived in
the Saturnian tranquility of isolation from the mainland and
the forces of civilization.

Sacrilege and sin as transgressions of the laws of a supreme
being become predominant factors in the plot of the
Christian epic. The classical aegis is exchanged for God's
sword of justice and iron or golden scepter, which will
execute reward or punishment. So, too, in the narration of

heroic deeds accompanying the fervent spread of Christianity in the New World, divine retribution relentlessly pursues the sinner for his crimes. Francisco de Orellana, the quixotic discoverer of the Amazon River, sets sail from Spain without the authorization of the Crown. Compounding the illegality of the departure, Orellana commits a crime which will incur the enmity of his God and parallel the sin that caused the destruction of Odysseus's crew. With scant provisions for the seven-month journey, the explorer sanctions an attack by his men upon a band of shepherds guarding their cattle. The conclusion of the adventure is one which leaves some of the shepherds wounded or dead, but the ships sufficiently supplied with livestock.

The crimes against his king and countrymen continue, and the next adventure is one of piracy. Attacking a Spanish ship, Orellana and his crew force the vessel to surrender arms and supplies which are essential for their crossing. The act of felony compounds his crimes, which will soon be punished. The first manifestation of retributive justice continues to parallel epic tradition in the form of castigation, almost of divine order, and the superstitious reaction of the men, who fall victim to a plague which spreads rapidly, claiming lives:

> —Es un castigo de Dios.
> —Sí. Por haber tracionado al Rey.
> —Por atacar a los pastores.
> —Por atacar el barco.
> —Estamos malditos.
> —Moriremos todos.
>
> [*Quijote* 233-34]

The punishment like that meted out by Apollo for Agamemnon's sin of abducting the priest's daughter, Chryseis, is not so easily suspended. The girl is returned in the *Iliad* (1. 442ff.), but Orellana's crew must continue accepting the consequences for their offenses. They have gone beyond the point of redemption. Dissension begins to mount, the situation grows worse, and fear of death by contagion affects the unafflicted men by stimulating their bestial desires and the urge to satisfy their sexual appetites.[2] Somehow Orellana manages to control them and to protect the women who are traveling on board.

The next form of retribution takes place when the water supply diminishes and thirst becomes unbearable. The men gamble among themselves, wagering their ration of the precious liquid. The more water lost in the game, the more determined each one is to recuperate his portion, and the scheme eventually erupts into a frenzied desire for vengeance against the sailor who seems to have all the luck. His own demonic taunts almost cost him his life, but Orellana again holds the crew in check, and they withdraw to await the day when the water supply is entirely exhausted. When the moment arrives and the men are informed, Orellana has the same problem as Goffredo, in *Gerusalemme Liberata*, does in quelling rebellion amongst his soldiers, who suffer from drought, heat, and a merciless sun in the vastness of the desert. The complaints and accusations are realistically human in each camp as the men look upon their respective leaders and assume that their lot is better than their own. The French knights discuss Goffredo with intense resentment:

> Or mira d'uom, ch'ha il titolo di pio,
> Providenza pietosa, animo umano:
> La salute de' suoi porre in oblío,
> Per conservarsi onor dannoso e vano;
> E veggendo a noi secchi i fonti e 'l rio,
> Per sé l'acque condur fin dal Giordano,
> E, fra pochi sedendo a mensa lieta,
> Mescolar l'onde fresche al vin di Creta.
>
> [*G.L.* 13. 67]

And the Spanish crew on Orellana's ships reacts in an equally bitter fashion:

—¡Se acabó el agua!
—¡Se acabó el agua!
Reaccionaron. Como si despertaran, se abalanzaron contra él.
—¡Mentira!
—La tiene guardada.
—La guardó para él. . .
—¡Y para su mujer!

[*Quijote* 244]

The only difference between the Crusaders and the Spaniards is the geographic control imposed upon the latter group. To abandon their leader on the high seas is a physical impossibility; whereas, many of the knights desert Goffredo in *Gerusalemme Liberata.* But in spite of the sins committed by the members of each expedition, God does alleviate their sufferings and restore sanity through rain. In both the verse form of Tasso's style and Aguilera-Malta's narrative prose, the response of harmonious participation in a kind of joyous rebirth and baptismal rite is dramatically communicated:

> Cosí gridando, la cadente piova
> Che la destra del Ciel pietosa versa,
> Lieti salutan questi: a ciascun giova
> La chioma averne, non che il manto, aspersa:
> Chi bee ne'vetri, e chi ne gli elmi a prova;
> Chi tien la man ne la fresca onda immersa,
> Chi se ne spruzza il vólto, e chi le tempie;
> Chi, scaltro, a miglior uso i vasi n'empie.

[*G.L.* 13. 77]

And in *El Quijote de El Dorado:*

Sin poderse contener, abrieron las bocas, cara al cielo, tratando de recoger lo más que podían del maravilloso liquido. Cada gota era como un puñado de vida que les entrara a circular en todo el cuerpo. Pronto las gotas fueron más frecuentes y abundantes. Poco después, la lluvia arreció. Siguieron con las bocas abiertas, recogiendo

mayores cantidades de ese don del cielo. Al propio tiempo, trataban de que sus cuerpos se empaparan, como si cada uno de sus poros también tuviera sed.
Todos los hombres y las mujeres de los barcos habían salido a las cubiertas. Se mezclaron. Disfrutaron hasta saciarse de ese imprevisto regalo de la naturaleza.

[Quijote 246]

Following the storm at sea, Orellana and his companions manage to reach the Amazon again, but his success is short-lived. The captain dies in the New World jungle and his hopes for redeeming himself in the eyes of his king perish along with him.

As the hero and characters in epic tradition become less divine, justice and its administration are assumed as responsibilities of men in a world becoming more complex, where societies establish legal and judicial systems to maintain order. But the presence of divine will is pervasive in those Christian epics which involve as thematic material war against Mohammed's followers. As surrogate to a supernatural being, Charlemagne, leading his warriors, enters battle to execute the destruction of Islam in God's name:

"Carles ad dreit vers la gent *paienie*:
Deus nus ad mis à l' plus verai juïse."

[Roland 3367-68]

Divinely inspired judgment of who has sinned and who is virtuous is also extended to contests among Christians for settling personal disputes. The outcome, begun in a court trial, is terminated in the confrontation of opposing factions, one of which will prove that the Lord's approval will be seen in the winner. When Thierry fights Pinabel, who challenges the claim of Ganelon's treachery, he exclaims: "Deus facet hoi entre nus dous le dreit!" (*Roland* 3898).

The same pattern of deciding justice is found in the *Poema del Cid*, where the juridical organization is complex in the administration of justice. The Cid demands retribution for the wrong done him by the Infantes of Carrión, who have beaten and abandoned his daughters. A decidedly weak king, Alfonso VI, who exiled the hero, redeemed him, and also arranged the disastrous marriage, frequently is adamant about seeing to it that there be no inequity committed:

> . . .i es el rey don Alfons,
> por querer el derecho   e *ningun* tuerto non.
>
> [*Cid* 3548-49]

Representatives of the Cid opposing the sons-in-law, Diego and Fernando, overcome them in battle and the case is resolved justly. The daughters' dowry is returned, the swords Tizón and Colada as well, and the Cid's honor restored. The violators of the social and moral code will deservedly suffer shame, dishonor, and the loss of wealth acquired through marriage to the hero's daughters.

The fullest treatment of justice on various levels, both human and divine, exists in *Paradise Lost*, along with the severest punishment of the offenders for disobeying the law. For the worst sinners, Hell is their castigation:

> Such a place Eternal Justice had prepar'd
> For those rebellious, here their Prison ordained
> In utter darkness. . . .
>
> [*P.L.* 1. 70-72]

Violation of one law—not to eat the fruit of either tree in the Garden—results in a series of "losses" as retribution for disobedience; Adam and Eve lose their innocence, their earthly Paradise, their happiness and immortality. For the fallen angels, God is an inexorable judge. Sin comments sarcastically on the Lord's wrath, "which he calls Justice" (*P.L.* 2. 733), and Abdiel confirms the relentless castigation of Satan and his followers with no hope for salvation. He tells the Adversary:

> . . .Those indulgent Laws
> Will not be now voutsaf'd, other Decrees
> Against thee are gone forth without recall;
> That Golden Sceptre which thou didst reject
> Is now an Iron Rod to bruise and break
> Thy disobedience. . . .

[*P.L.* 5. 883-88]

Satan's continued moral decline and forthcoming persecution of mankind are reflected in the gradual loss of his majestic state and in the process of transformation that is frequently brutish in nature. The technique of metamorphosis culled from the classical tradition, where offenders of the gods encounter punishment and mythological fame through conversion into topomorphic or zoomorphic entities,[3] is the heritage of Christian poets such as Dante, Camões, and Milton. Camões frequently alluded to characters of Greek or Roman mythology, but he creates his own transformed entity in the horror that appears as a phantom to perform a short but complex role in the poem. Adamastor's function, much like that of the devils in Dante's Hell, where landscape too participates in tormenting the sinners,[4] is one of causing misery and death to those who have transgressed. Before revealing the reason for his metamorphosis, eternally condemned as a topographical monster in the abusive confines of the Cape of Storms, around which the Portuguese sailed, he forecasts destruction for those who dared to exceed the limits set by the Pillars of Hercules:

> . . ."Ó gente ousado, mais que quantas
> No mundo cometeram grandes coisas:
> Tu, que por guerras cruas, tais e tantas,
> E por trabalhos vãos nunca repousas,
> Pois os vedados términos quebrantas."

[*Lus.* 5. 41. 1-5]

Hubris, lust for profit, knowledge, and fame, and the holocaust of war, a concomitant evil, shall earn the nation divine enmity:

> "Ouve os danos de mi que apercebidos
> Estão a teu sobejo atrevimento,
> Por todo o largo mar e pola terra
> Que inda hás de sojugar com dura guerra."
>
> [*Lus.* 5. 42. 5-8]

The sequence of punishment by physical change reaches its climax in *Paradise Lost*, when the poet resorts to the famous serpent transformation of the devils after Satan returns to Pandemonium to report the success of his mission in Eden. The Prince of Hell, in huge dragon form, contrasts with the equally virulent, but lesser ophidian disciples, and Milton specifies his technique as one of condign retribution for their evil thoughts and deeds:

> They felt themselves now changing; down their arms,
> Down fell both Spear and Shield, down they as fast,
> And the dire hiss renew'd, and the dire form
> Catcht by Contagion, like in punishment,
> As in thir crime. . . .
>
> [*P.L.* 10. 541-45]

Adhering to the thematic, vertical structure of ascent and descent, Milton compounds just castigation by adding sudden hunger and thirst to their affliction, and the metamorphosed demons crawl up trees to partake of the tempting fruit, which is turned to ashes instead. (*P.L.* 565-72).[5]

In *Gerusalemme Liberata* zoomorphosis as punishment is a type of Circean bondage,[6] and it occurs as part of an episode which also determines the destiny of Goffredo's men, who have deviated from the path of virtue by following Armida. One of the knights, returning to camp, relates to Goffredo the transformation into fish which the sorceress, reading from her magic book, executes:

"Legge la maga; ed io pensiero e voglia
Sento mutar, mutar vita ed albergo.
(Strana virtú!) novo pensier m'involgia:
Salto ne l'acqua, e mi vi tuffo e immergo.
Non so come ogni gamba entro s'accoglia.
Come l'un braccio e l'altro entri nel tergo;
M'accorcio e stringo; e su la pelle cresce
Squamoso il cuoio; e d'uome son fatto un pesce."

[*G.L.* 10. 66]

Although the beautiful witch restores them from their ichthyomorphic state, she promises to change her captives at will into whatever she pleases if they do not renounce their faith. They do not accede to her wishes and are eventually saved by Rinaldo. However, the knights have been punished for succumbing to the temptation of physical pleasures which Armida represents, and temporary zoomorphosis is sufficiently awesome to revive their dedication to the holy cause of liberating Jerusalem.

The transformation of the knights into fish is particularly significant in view of the poet's aversion to contaminating the divine image with the bestial form. The reaction to Indian deities whose "abominable" representations are encountered by the Portuguese in an exotic temple is one of utter shock, if not revulsion:

Ali estão das deidades as figuras
Esculpidas em pau e em pedra fria,
Vários de gestos, vários de pinturas,
A segundo o Demónio lhe fingia.
Vêem-se as abomináveis esculturas
Qual a Quimera em mebros se varia;
Os cristãos olhos, a ver Deus usados
Em forma humana, estão maravilhados.

[*Lus.* 7. 47]

Milton, like Camões, expresses the same viewpoint of abhorrence for distorting deities that are assigned zoo-morphic properties:

A crew who under Names of old Renown,
Osiris, Isis, Orus and their Train
With monstrous shapes and sorceries abus'd
Fanatic Egypt and her Priests, to seek
Thir wand'ring Gods disguis'd in brutish forms
Rather than human. . . .

[*P.L.* 1. 477-82]

Thus the association of the human with the divine image or belief in euhemerism is a corroboration of the nobility of man, and any zoomorphic means of retributive justice is more spiritually painful and demeaning. The convention of subhumanization or "subcelestialization" is a popular device for the Christian poets who use the technique as Dante does in Canto 25 for castigating the thieves or as Milton does when he marks the fallen angels as well as Satan's progeny, Sin and Death. The procedure is consistent with the basic anthropocentric concern of those authors, whose humanism was the inspiration without which great epics could not have been created.

Poetic Justice in Demetrio Aguilera-Malta: The Trial, Zoomorphosis, and Subhumanization

The punishment of the guilty for transgressions of human and divine law is as imaginatively varied as the crimes themselves in epic tradition. The forms of requital include death, physical and emotional torment, as well as topomorphic or zoomorphic persecution. Divine retribution can indeed be severe, especially when interpreted by poets such as Dante, whose own iron rod serves as a warning of God's implacable wrath:

Oh potenza di Dio, quant'è severa,
che cotai colpi per vendetta croscia!

[*Inf.* 24. 119-20]

There is no question that the ghastly preview of tyranny and injustice vividly displayed for Adam by Michael is a reality for the poet today as well as in Milton's time. The writers of the twentieth century who inherited the apocalyptic visions of the past and have experienced the holocaust of war in modern times could easily consider the iniquities of their society as a confirmation of the English epicist's projection of moral decay: "Thus will this latter, as the former World / Still tend from bad to worse" (*P.L.* 12. 105-106). As sensitive to injustice as Dante or Milton were, the contemporary author responds in a similarly exhortative manner, both exposing the dearth of righteousness and retaliating with the familiar punitive measures of epic tradition.

Demetrio Aguilera-Malta, present-day observer of human ills, acts as his literary predecessors did when they raised the sword of justice like the Supreme Poet to smite the offenders of divine will. When legal and judicial machinery is found wanting, the creative mind establishes its own court of justice, where the poet's decision reigns uncontested. Many are the cases of faulty or corrupt social and political systems in the novels of the conquest in which Vasco Núñez de Balboa and Francisco de Orellana, for example, suffer the inequities parceled out by bureaucratic red tape or diabolic interpreters of the law, and the adverse elements of time and space which prevent application of jurisprudence. In the play *Honorarios* the lawyer Cercado is a contemporary model of legal perversion, and the administrative authorities of Santorontón in *Siete lunas y siete serpientes* are patterned after the many oligarchical structures that govern with no concern for the principles of justice.

But proper execution of justice in juridical circumstances does occur in the play *Infierno negro*, whose plot is unfolded on two planes of action—one, Nylónpolis, where Hórridus Nabus and the oligarchy are shown in flashbacks planning and realizing the persecution of the underdogs, and the other, Necrópolis, where a posthumous trial for the inventor is conducted in the City of the Dead. Here the court of law is controlled by the very victims sacrificed to promote the social and financial ends of the degenerate leaders. At the mercy of those for whose massacre he was responsible, Hórridus, propped up in his coffin, listens to his accusers presenting the indictment. His concern, ironically, is for justice and proper legal counsel:

> HORRIDUS: Por lo menos tendré un defensor blanco, ¿verdad?
> NIEVE: Tu defensor será negro.
> HORRIDUS: ¡Protesto! Me quejaré a los máximos poderes. ¿Por qué mis jueces, mis acusadores, mis testigos y mi defensor deben ser negros?
> NIEVE: En los juicios de ultratumba por delitos raciales se ha decidido que los culpables sean juzgados por las razas que ellos agredieron.
>
> [*Infierno* 47]

The system of poetic justice has been set into motion with social reality transposed as inspiration, and the accused made aware of the inevitable judgment that will be rendered. In spite of an attempt to defend him made by Caoba Mórbida, the spirit of African bondage whose own tale summarizes the history of Negro suffering, Hórridus is found guilty, and the punishment fits his crime. He is condemned eternally to be a "Wandering Black Jew" (p. 133), destined to follow the path of those he persecuted in a living Black Hell:

> NEGRO I: . . .¡Al infierno negro!
> CORO: ¿A nuestro infierno?
> NEGRO I: Sí. ¡Que sea negro por los siglos de los siglos!
> CORO: ¡Negro por los siglos de los siglos! Sí, señor!
> ....
> NEGRO I: ¡Que sufra una y mil veces, como todos nosotros cuando nos desenraizaron para esclavizarnos y lanzarnos al perpetuo exilio!

CORO: ¡Sí, señor!

. . . . -

NEGRO I: ¡Y que en las selvas urbanas de acero y
            cemento sea despreciado, perseguido, mar-
            ginado, escarnecido y condenado al hambre
            de pan, de saber y de justicia. . .¡por sus
            propios hermanos blancos!

                                    [*Infierno* 132-34]

Retributive justice in the works of Aguilera-Malta when
placed in the hands of the individual hero seeking recompense
for offenses he has suffered, generally is talionic in essence
and often is violent. The *cholo* Cusumbo, who has been dis-
honored by his wife and the *patrón*, kills them both, flees,
and is not apprehended. Pablo Melgar, orphaned when
Néstor kills his father, abducts the wounded fiancée of the
white landowner; Crisóstomo Chalena, abused and emascu-
lated by his depraved parent, plots and successfully executes
his progenitor's doom at sea; Clotilde Quindales, a victim of
rape, wanders about imagining she castrates lustful men;
Banchón, the *cholo* who has abandoned poverty and thrives
on his former companions' patronage, loses his source of
affluence through destruction of his property—an act perpetrated by his friends. Andrea, the *cholo* who dismissed her
sweetheart for another, faces daily physical punishment at
the hands of her husband and additional verbal castigation by
the nonviolent Melquíades. Nicasio Yagual, who spends his
youth violating women, meets his end by castrating himself;
and the demonic sergeant who terrorizes the peasants of the
Cuban hamlet commits suicide at the climax of his madness.
Many are the examples of retribution in the panorama of
heroes and anti-heroes that Aguilera-Malta has created; but
the predominant technique for punishing the guilty is based
on another device of Miltonic precedence and Platonic
influence:

There wanted yet the Master work, the end

Of all yet done; a Creature who not prone
And Brute as other Creatures, but endu'd
With Sanctity of Reason, might erect
His Stature, and upright with Front serene
Govern the rest, self-knowing, and from thence
Magnanimous to correspond with Heav'n.

[*P.L.* 7. 505-511]

Created in God's image, man was a symbol of divine origin, distinct from the beast and reflecting his essential nobility in the upright posture he was granted.[7] The technique which Aguilera-Malta uses is not simply one of degradation by bestial reference often employed by the writer as castigation for the sinner in this world or the next. It is rather a method which could more aptly be termed "subhumanization" or "dehumanization," in order to show the deterioration of the soul by external physical changes. In the degeneration of the human form the sinner evidences his remoteness from the divine image and, most important of all, his alienation from humanity, an almost self-imposed exile which originally stems from his antisocial behavior, which has been injurious to his fellowman.

Zoomorphic castigation in name and physical appearance prevails in *El secuestro del general.* The Congress is comprised of chameleon senators; Cerdo Rigoletto, a government official, is porcine, while Equino Cascable with viperous and horselike properties is saddled and ridden by the gorilla-general Jonás Pitecantropo. The latter suffers his own bestial conversion but occasionally becomes more anthropomorphic when he demonstrates some compassion for humanity. However, the most innovative form of punishment is reserved for the skeleton-dictator of Babelandia, Holofernes Verbofilia. Symbol of an ossified tradition that has dominated many Latin American nations since independence, he must retire alone to a coffer each night, collapsing his bare bones like an accordion. He is additionally dehumanized in lacking the organs of speech, another characteristic that distinguishes man from beast. Verbofilia, as his name indicates, is a somewhat sentient entity with a passion for the word, which ironically echoes Creation (*Logos*). But in order to speak to the public a cassette must be inserted in his thorax. This contact assures him of his power, and to deprive him of the capacity to orate is tantamount to, if not worse than, death:

> Tal vez, lo único que no podría soportar sería que le impidiesen pronunciar discursos. Eso representaría el mayor castigo que pudieran infringirle. . . .Sin discursos no podría seguir viviendo. Sería como arrancarle el corazón.
>
> [*Secuestro* 143]

In addition to using the technique of punishment by appellation, as Dante does in the *Inferno* for his devils and sinners, Aguilera-Malta also employs zoomorphic transformation. When metamorphosis takes place, however, it usually exists on an expressionistic plane and in surrealistic circumstances. Candelario Mariscal himself and the villagers project the protean mutations that range from cayman to bat, while Crisóstomo Chalena bears the markings in color, shape, and sound of a frog. The oligarchy of *Siete lunas y siete serpeintes* is duly castigated by the author when they are converted into the five-headed crocodile and three-headed serpent emerging from the sea.

The Apple and Elixirs:
Chemical and Biological Punishment

Retributive justice follows another course, however, than direct bestial metaphorization or transmutation of the sinner. The effect is physical, spiritual, and even social in the degenerative process which reduces the divine to mortal and the human to a baser state. The instrument which is the degrading element gives the illusion of superiority only to reverse its effect and promote behavior that is either antisocial or self-demeaning.

Adam and Eve are the first to experience the disastrous results of succumbing to the strange, intoxicating substance which initially raises them to sublime heights only to end in generating a series of vulgar, animalistic changes, ironically reducing them to a level far different from their anticipated apotheosis. The contradictory effects of the fruit are not unlike those of any inebriating substance. Temerity is strengthened, frivolity increased, and abandonment encouraged. All powers of reason are narcotized by the mysterious apple; the rational is numbed, and the sensual stimulation is immediate:

> As with new Wine intoxicated both
> They swim in mirth, and fancy that they feel
> Divinity within them breeding wings
> Wherewith to scorn the Earth: but that false Fruit
> Far other operation first display'd,
> Carnal desire inflaming, hee on *Eve*
> Began to cast lascivious Eyes, she him
> As wantonly repaid; in Lust they burn.
>
> [*P.L.* 9. 1008-1015]

The entire evolution of sin in sequential order begins with the feeling of soaring above the Earth accompanied by an attitude of contempt for it, and the punishment for inabstinence is manifested in a continued pattern of uncontrollable passion followed by the torments of restless sleep (*P.L.* 10. 1046-52). As the decline of human dignity continues, the First Bacchantes, in a new mortal state of shame, execute their own castigation by mutual recrimination, which is totally human in expression, but which removes them even farther from the deified condition they expected while responding to the serpent's elixir.

Milton's transgressors, whose experience with the Edenic intoxicant caused their own physical penalty of death, preview man's tragic circumstances and self-degradation during his search for the sublime and the illusory. Decline, humiliation, and physical change as retribution for partaking of the magic potion is a technique which is frequently used by Aguilera-Malta in his works. Both good and evil elements of society succumb to the temptation of transcending reality and increasing their sense of power by indulging in alcoholic stimulants. The thrill of soaring to divine heights as a result of intoxication is the experience of Pedro Coorsi's father, who deludes himself into believing that he is greater than any epic hero of renown:

> Se enredaba en su garganta la emoción de haber vivido esa epopeya. Se sentía él—un capitán de dragas—más héroe que su Aquiles legendario.
>
> [*C.Z.* 12-13]

The illusion produced by alcoholic and economic inebriation soon reverses to conclude his ascent to epic greatness and he plunges to his doom by flinging himself into the sea.

Lázaro, the unfortunate schoolmaster, also succumbs to the potion which will make him sustain a caricature in pantomimed suffering and hysteria, a vulgar descent from the pomposity of his rational statement on abstinence when he is offered the first drink:

> "¡El licor es la perdición del hombre!. . .El licor es la peligrosa pendiente."
>
> [*Lázaro* 10]

He is interrupted by the diabolic pair of brothers and their sister, who performs her Eve-like role in seducing Lázaro into accepting the cup which will indeed lead him, like Adam before him, to perdition. The image of sublime lyricism is overcome by grimaces, incoherence, dozing, hiccoughs, and spastic movements as he frantically searches for his hat so that he may depart before the final act of self-destruction.

Lázaro projects a pathetic figure living the precarious illusion of a strong and courageous lover who is experiencing a miracle: "¡El amor y el alcohol que han hecho un milagro!" (*Lázaro* 15). This phase of abnormal, erratic gesticulations and expressions which deform the essential nobility of the idealist will soon be replaced by true degradation once he has signed the document denouncing his former self, and he will begin the castigation of a living Hell for the miscellany of crimes committed against his own spiritual values.

The less noble revelers of *Dientes blancos*, who lack any of the sensitivty that plagued Lázaro in his love of humanity, merit rapid chastisement for their depraved behavior. The anonymous *patrón* and his mistress are marked by epithets which are emblems of their incontinence, "Ebrio" and "Ebria," and the interplay of absurd justice is exhibited when the clumsy, inarticulate entity calls for his version of the scepter, a whip, to punish the tormented black musician. The bibulous customer displays his brutish grotesqueness while his female companion adds to his deterioration by casting aspersions on his masculinity for not reacting to Peter's insults: "¿No eres hombre? ¿No vas a hacerte justicia por ti mismo?" (*Dientes* 44). The entire effect of the couple's appearance is one of intended, caricatured distortion heightened by their drunken state, which makes ambulation difficult, verbal articulation ludicrous, and restoration of their supposedly human dignity hardly possible.

The affluent white man's alcoholic excess also touches those who are dependent on him. As Adam and Eve transmit the sin to their descendants, the *patrón* works to corrupt the *cholos*, who are unaware of the long-term punishment they will be forced to endure as a result of their accepting the libations[8] of Don Merelo, who will transport them to the Cursed Island of Néstor. The liquor, which acts as an anodyne, removes reality—past, present, and future—in as approximate a parallel between a desensitized being and the forthcoming picture of amorphous, subhuman matter that

Aguilera-Malta describes when the *cholos* reach the total eclipse of intoxication:

Se va llenando la tienda.
La luz de la lámpara ilumina débilmente la escena. Unos pocos cholos siguen bebiendo. La mayor parte ya no puede hacerlo. Están aplastados. En montones absurdos. Roncando estrepitosamente. Mascullando frases incomprensibles. Revolcándose sobre el piso bamboleante de la tienda. O sobre la tierra salitrosa de afuera. Todo en un hacinamiento horrible de harapos humanos.
    Los que siguen de pie, los que todavía pueden ver, hablan a gritos. Se abrazan y se golpean, llevando siempre la copa en la diestra. Bufandas oscuras les envuelven las cabezas. Manchas rojas y negras les decoran todo cuanto miran.
    Les parece que ya estuvieran embarcados y que los sangoloteara el vaivén de las aguas marinas.

[*Isla* 342]

The melee of ultrahuman sounds, disjointed movements, distorted vision, and the piles of raglike entities that vaguely resemble the human form reduce the *cholos* to a level prepared for them by the fraudulent perpetrators of their tragedy. But distorting man's form through exaggeration or mutilation is part of the technique which reaches the most imaginatively horrible proportions in the *Inferno*, where Dante populates his topographical prison with lepers, criminals with severed heads, split bodies, etc.; and the variation of this approach to condign punishment is also part of Aguilera-Malta's procedure for executing justice. The effect is to produce a less-than-human entity generally marked in his aberrated condition for crimes against divine will, his fellowman, or even himself.

In *Infierno negro* the genius of oratory, who is as casuistic in his rhetoric as Satan, is punished for his hypocrisy and general depraved thinking in a dual fashion, indicated in the two parts of his name, which signify his abnormal structure:

Feto Eunuco. As a "Hellish Abortion," which is what Ariel calls him (*Infierno* 110), Feto is designated as an amorphous mass of living tissue, but not really human. Further debasement is included in the reference to his mutilated masculinity, which marks his asexuality and thus represents neither male nor female of any species. He is therefore depicted as both sub-bestial and subhuman, for he is totally incapable of propagating any living organism. He can only perpetuate hatred and corruption.

The human form displaying itself as a sign of castigation has its extreme manifestations as giants, on the one hand, and dwarfs, on the other. The deformed figure appears in the works of Aguilera-Malta as retribution for aristocratic inbreeding, which bears as a sign the absence of the wholesome robustness traditionally associated with the people who cultivate the land. Admiration for the working class is evident in the novel ¡*Madrid!*, in which paradoxically the giant image is used to demonstrate the magnificence of the common people, their vast resources for courage, and their growth in spiritual stature during their fight for the principles of freedom. Like Antaeus, their strength stems from their contact with the earth. The perversion of diminutive caliber is subhuman physically as well as spiritually. The blue-blooded element of the Count in the novel, through years of "ill-mated marriages,"[9] produces the stunted aberration of soul and mind, which is reflected in his actions. His "product" is even more unholy, for he has engendered an idiot son, Carlitos. The punishment is nature's biological recompense by taking revenge on those whose life is essentially fruitless and is hedonistically spent, and whose contempt for the peasants who till the soil is castigated:

La naturaleza se vengaba en los eternos gozadores. En los que despreciaban el trabajo por considerarlo indigno menester.

[*Madrid* 29]

The son is less than human, a monstrosity that can neither reason nor function as the upright creature of divine origin:

> Tiene un aspecto ultrahumano. Los ojos desorbitados exploran mundos ignotos. A ratos, tiembla. Habla un lenguaje ininteligible. Y lanza un alarido clamoroso que estremece todo el vecindario.
>
> [*Madrid* 38]

Stigmatized for his pride, the Count is additionally guilty of indifference to his son's welfare and that of those who serve him. He escapes with his wife from their home in the capital as the siege of Madrid becomes imminent, leaving Carlitos locked in a room in the charge of Carmen, the maid, who is unaware of the events taking place. As hunger begins to rage in the abnormal creature, the idiot seeks some means to satisfy his natural craving for food. With nothing available in his midst, he looks to his own body to quell the pangs of approaching famine:

> Cierra los ojos.
> Y acerca esa mano a su boca anhelante.
> Un alarido de dolor y placer latiguean en el ambiente.
> El idiota lleva su mano ensangrentada.
> Pero come. Come frenéticamente.
>
> [*Madrid* 75]

The treachery brought about by politics and the conditions of war which result in such a scene of deprivation recall a comparable one in Dante's *Inferno* (Canto 33), where another count, Ugolino, watches his children slowly dying of starvation and bites his own "hands in grief" (33. 58). Sharply paralleling, yet contrasting the Spanish count, Ugolino's punishment also involves transmission of his sin to his own children. The contrast, however, lies in the very human response of the father to the children's plight, his own vengeance as he gnaws at the Archbishop's head, and the callous indifference of the father of Carlitos and those like him whose sins are complicated by their "insensibility to the welfare of their offspring."[10]

In the descending scale of dehumanization, the plane of vegetal castigation is reached in the episode of Dante's encounter with the victims of self-violence—the suicides—reduced to plants for their crime (*Inf.* 13). It also has application in *Infierno negro* with the name of Hórridus Nabus (Horrid Turnip) for a man whose duty should have been that of dedicating himself to aiding humanity, not destroying it. For the destruction of the human body, just as violently torn by the machines of his sausage factory as the souls of the suicides in the *Inferno*, he is given not merely a subhuman, but sub-bestial (even subterrestrial) name, that of a legume. His inhuman traits are marked by the strange appellation. His companion in antisocial behavior also bears his condign punishment while yet with the living: the military figure, a vestige of the *miles gloriosus* prototype, growls like a quadruped of sorts, but has less than an organic name—General Pimpampum—onomatopoeic reference to the clamoring ancient rite of beating the war drum while echoing at the same time the din of gunfire.

In presenting the decline of human behavior from the divine image of God which was projected in man, the writer of today, having recourse to current aspects of science and technology, can effect physical or spiritual punishment consistent with the evils of the present age. The play *No bastan los átomos*, oriented toward nuclear and biochemical subject matter, contains passages in which the scientist's son, Fausto, transformed as a result of his war experiences and his father's death, reveals his gradual dehumanization. His behavior is that of a Frankenstein monster—a composite of animal violence, yet dependent upon expression which is scientific, atomic, and at times inorganic in content. Fausto's path of sin begins with the rape of his sweetheart, Alba. Although his barbarism is one of lascivious appearance, his explanation is cold-blooded, beginning with a denial of his love for the woman. The only love that can exist between a man and a woman is that "biochemical phenomenon of human copulation which can be reduced to simple formulae" (*Atomos* 74). When he proposes the sex act, his statement contains the essence of self-extinction:

"Nos volveremos elementales, como el hidrógeno y el oxígeno en la fusión, que los torna agua. Obedeceremos a las supremas leyes de la energética, de la transformación incontenible de la materia.

[*Atomos* 75-76]

When Fausto discovers his father's formula and a sample capsule which can destroy any enemy, the process is still explained in terms of dehumanization. Instead of annihilating the opponent in bloody massacre, as Candelario Mariscal would, he says, "Lo descompondré en los átomos que lo integran!" (*Atomos* 93). His punishment, however, as his mother plans it, will be the ideal case of poetic retribution. The proposed atomic bombing of the island, which will retain the dead Arquímedes, Fausto, and the Dictator, will result in a return to the form from which they all evolved. As Ifigenia states:

"No quedará ni un sér vivo, ni una piedra sobre otra. Será como si esta isla no hubiera existido nunca. Los científicos que están al servicio del Dictador, éste, y su séquito volverán a ser energía, anónimas formas elementales de la materia."

[*Atomos* 97]

But the manifestation of punishment by dehumanization, which is demonstrated by stage effects that transform human attributes into lifeless expressions for the crime planned against his fellowman, centers about the scientific cave—the laboratory. Arquímedes, whose silhouette is projected against the glass partition, is merely a Platonic shadow of what he once was—he is no longer human, in fact, he is dead. After his body is discovered by Fausto, the son takes the scientist's place in the same position, continuing the course his father has prepared for him. By Act 3, after his violation of Alba, Fausto's inorganic deterioration is reflected in the tone of his complexion, which is described as "metallic" (*Atomos* 79), and physical metamorphosis as castigation is sustained until the moment of his redemption.

Hell and the Mind

Which way I fly is Hell; myself am Hell.

[*P.L.* 4. 75]

One of the most unbearable castigations that man faces is the torment of conflict within the mind that subjects the sinner to skepticism about his values or actions and their consequences. The more complex the transgression, the deeper the spiritual suffering that he induces in a process of mental self-flagellation. Many are the crimes of Lucifer that prompt the above statement after his Fall; the most nefarious are pride and ambition, which begin the chain of events that ultimately corrupt Adam and Eve, who also succumb to sinning for a number of motives.

The white man of *La isla virgen* is not, any more than Satan, merely the antagonistic symbol of evil confronting the innocent. Néstor's condign punishment terminates in a physical death which has been preceded by worse conditions accumulated for travesties and violations that he has committed against human beings and, above all, against the natural environment.[11] As a result, he suffers the torments that transport him to a personal Hell composed of failure and vacillating emotions, all of which are characteristic of Satan's crimes and subsequent dilemma. Néstor continues his own descent into the realm of the worst offenders of God's law when he thinks of his European heritage, which is "nobler" than that of the anonymous peasant, whom he regards with a certain amount of disdain: "Soy descendiente de los colonizadores españoles" (*Isla* 68), he says to himself, recalling those ancestors who were equally daring and ambitious in displaying their own aspiration to godhead and immortality. His desire for power and sense of omnipotence are partially summarized in the statement which also rings familiar among those guilty of hubris: "Mi voluntad es la ley, la única ley" (*Isla* 87), which is countered by an internal debate as to whether or not he had the right to kill a man, Melgar, the *cholo* who did not consider Néstor's will as the supreme law:

"Pero se trata de la vida de un hombre. ¿La vida de un hombre? Se trata de mi seguridad y de mi obra futura. ¡Pero es la vida de un hombre! ¿Un hombre? ¿Es que un cholo de éstos es un hombre?

[*Isla* 87]

Néstor's scorn for the peasant, the man of the soil, has justification in the Arch-Sinner's attitude when contempt for God's creation, literally "of the soil," is expressed as he plans his campaign on the "happy Isle": "A Creature form'd of Earth and him endow, / Exalted from so base original" (*P.L.* 9. 149-50); or as Tasso's Devil remarks in *Gerusalemme Liberata*: "l'uom vile e di vil fango in terra nato" (*G.L.* 4. 10. 8).

When Néstor is not consumed by doubt, he is persecuted during his lifetime by other fantasies as well, although they are not part of the animistic superstitions of Indians. He does not respond with paralyzing fear to the wandering spirits of dead men, but he spends restless feverish nights obsessed with the thought that the living Esperanza, his hope for the future, may be a figment of his imagination or a perverted illusion created by the Island in retaliation:

> Tal vez ni existe Esperanza. Quizás él no ha ido nunca donde don Merelo. Todo es una ficción que le ha creado la vengativa San Pancracio. Ella es la única cierta, la única auténtica. ¡Esa mujer encantadora, no es más que un sueño!
>
> [*Isla* 247]

The eternal contradiction that confuses mankind of illusion versus reality plagues Néstor as it does the Christian knights of Tasso's epic, and as it does many a windmill fighter. Néstor continues tormenting himself by granting reality to the island as a living creature, a woman, who is determined to execute his castigation:

> Su Enemiga implacable lo ha creado para atormentarlo, para gozar en su suplicio, para ver si le infiere una nueva derrota.
>
> [*Isla* 247]

The "Enemy" is like the "Adversary," like Armida as well—agents of evil that can convert the illusory temporarily into substance in order to grant the imagination a moment of pleasure and hope which will fade according to the condition of man's spiritual balance.

> The mind is its own place, and in itself
> Can make a Heav'n of Hell, a Hell of Heav'n.
>
> [*P.L.* 1. 254-55]

The satanic pattern of transgression and crime and the consequence of personal Hell as punishment are not exclusively characteristic of rebel angels or sophisticated inhabitants of societies that seem to be more tained with a sense of immortality as Néstor's background indicates. The peasant too has his weaknesses and is as vulnerable to sin and self-torment as any other human or divine being. His course of behavior in subduing internal suffering also can be a continuation of crime to alleviate the pain:

> For only in destroying I find ease
> To my relentless thoughts. . .
>
> [*P.L.* 9. 129-30]

Like Satan, Candelario Mariscal in *Siete lunas y siete serpentes* seeks relief through a constant campaign of destruction which makes no distinction among victims and serves to assure his reputation as the offspring of the Fiend. Candelario's impulse toward violence reaches the most perverse level when he desires to annihilate an entire city. The macabre thought delights him and terrifies his companion, Canchona:

> "Algún día voy a darme el gusto de convertir una ciudad en cementerio, Canchona. ¿Te imaginas lo que sería dejarlos a todos en pura calavera, riendo para siempre? ¡Ya lo verás, Canchona!"
>
> [*Isla* 125]

But Candelario Mariscal meets his just punishment for his violence, which began the night he killed Josefa's parents and raped her sister. His personal Hell is a nightly orgy with the ghost of the girl he desired, and sexual annihilation or impotence projects itself as condign repayment for his deeds. His private anguish is increased on the eve of his marriage to Dominga—a union which may be destroyed by the appearance of his ephemeral mistress. The man who created hell for so many others considers the future and resembles his

Mentor, who suffers the pangs of misery which carry with them eternal punishment:

> The Hell within him, for within him Hell
> He brings, and round about him, nor from Hell
> One step no more than from himself can fly
> By change of place: Now conscience wakes despair
> That slumber'd, wakes the bitter memory
> Of what he was, what is, and what must be
> Worse; of worse deeds worse sufferings must ensue.
> [*P.L.* 4. 20-26]

Like the Fallen Angel whose soliloquy begins with his sight of the sun and whose conscience temporarily subjugates his pride, the retired Colonel sits meditating on a hill which overlooks the village of Santorontón. As his disdain for those he has terrorized begins to wane, doubt enters to add to his affliction. The dialogue between Candelario and his unsympathetic conscience, filled with earthy colloquialisms, appropriately contrasts the grandiloquence of his Inspirer:

> ¿Te das cuenta lo que es vivir amarrado para siempre a una difunta? ¿Tener que revolver su chirimoya sin descanso? ¿Y esta noche? ¿Tendrás su visita en esta noche? Quizá lo sabe todo. Los muertos nada ignoran. A lo mejor ya viene sobre el viento a restregarte la entrepiernas. Tratará de concentrar todas sus ganas. De sacarte hasta lo último del jugo que te queda. Así mañana no le harás ni una sola a la Dominga. ¿O la difunta no quedará contenta ni con eso? ¿No querrá helarme los güevos, con sus besos de tumba, como en otras ocasiones? ¿Me dejará la picha seca cascarón de culebra acabada de mudar? ¿Todo será por gusto? ¿Las cosas volverán a ser como antes?
>
> [*7/7* 357]

As sin can be multifaceted, so too castigation is easily complicated. In addition to doubt, despair, and any number of emotional responses that reflect Satan's inner punishment, the question of embarrassment and shame accompanies the pride which caused his fall:

> . . .And that word
> *Disdain* forbids me, and my dread of shame
> Among the spirits beneath, whom I seduc'd
> With other promises and other vaunts
> Than to submit, boasting I could subdue
> Th' Omnipotent, Ay me, they little know
> How dearly I abide that boast so vain,
> Under what torments inwardly I groan.
>
> [*P.L.* 4. 81-88]

The future son-in-law of Bulu-Bulu fears the same effect of disgracing himself and the wizard if his wedding night proves him impotent ("Si así fuera, desgraciaré al Brujo Bulu-Bulu," 7/7 357). To be made the laughingstock of the people who feared and respected him at the same time is the thought that plagues the awesome Candelario Mariscal, whose virility and prowess were synthesized in his implacable machete. Loss of sexual power for his immorality is not so different from Adam's loss of social or political power for his transgression.

Candelario Mariscal looks upon his nightly Tartarean punishment as a case of evil propagating evil rather than an example of God's divine retribution. But the Colonel, retired now from a life of violence, is, in spite of his conjectures and fears, not the son of Lucifer. For by recounting his deeds and misdeeds of wickedness to Bulu-Bulu as a means of seeking guidance in ridding himself of the symbol of his crimes—the ghost of Josefa Quindales—he has actually played the role of a sinner facing his confessor. The possibility of redemption is real, and a new future is projected in his forthcoming marriage to Dominga. The strange combining sources of salvation—Bulu-Bulu the wizard, who has already performed the rite of fertility for his daughter, who should conceive on her wedding night, and the Wooden Christ, who counsels Cándido to restore the exile to his favor again—all portend success. Above all, the human love of Dominga, which flowers from compassion, holds the same promise for salvation as does the reconciliation of Adam and Eve:

The World was all before them, where to choose
Their place of rest, and Providence their guide:
They hand in hand with wand'ring steps and slow,
Through *Eden* took thir solitary way.

[*P.L.* 12. 646-49]

Notes

1. The despicable performance of the suitors is summarized by Richmond Lattimore's comment: "Not even an Olympian god is so prejudiced as to take their part." See Mr. Lattimore's introduction to The *"Odyssey" of Homer* (New York: Harper & Row, 1968), p. 17.

2. This is the reversed order of the situation in the *Iliad*. Agamemnon's lust precedes the plague, while Orellana's men are stimulated rather perversely in the midst of disease and death.

3. Classical mythology, as Ovid's *Metamorphoses* reveals, shows a preponderance of vengeful and unjust punishment dealt out by the gods. Although Lycaon, king of Arcadia, is changed into a wolf for his wickedness, his daughter, Callisto, is transformed into a bear because of Hera's jealousy, and Circe converts the nymph Scylla into a monster in retaliation for Glaucus's rejection of the sorceress. Particularly tragic is the tale of Dryope, who offends the nymph Lotus through sheer error and is summarily transformed into a tree.

4. See James G. Bergin, "Hell: Topography and Demography," in *Essays on Dante*, ed. Mark Musa (Bloomington: Indiana University Press, 1964), pp. 76-93.

5. The technique of degrading the devils in this manner of poetic justice is called by A. J. A. Waldock a "cartoon" device, which is utilized to trick the vainglorious "Big Bad Wolf" at the height of his success, where by some practical joke he deservedly falls to misfortune or grief. This scene is the nadir of the devils' condition in view of their irretrievable loss of a formerly majestic state. See A. J. A. Waldock's *"Paradise Lost" and Its Critics* (New York: Cambridge University Press, 1961), pp. 65-96.

6. The parallel is made by John Charles Nelson in his introduction to Edward Fairfax's translation of *Gerusalemme Liberata* (New York: Capricorn Books, 1963), p. xxix.

7. The various sources of this concept since Plato are given in John Milton, *Paradise Lost,* intro. and notes by Merritt Y. Hughes (New York: Odyssey Press, 1935), notes, pp. 238, 374.

8. They are indeed "libations" in the true sense of the word since the Indians are actually being sacrificed to the greed of their exploiters.

9. Milton confirms the unwholesomeness of the blend, though in reference to the giants, yet it is still applicable to the dwarfish entity:

> . . .These are the products
> Of those ill-mated Marriages thou saw'st;
> Where good and bad were matcht, who of themselves
> Abhor to join; and by imprudence mixt,
> Produce prodigious Births of body or mind.

[P.L. 11. 683-87]

10. This is another of the many offenses of which Adam and Eve are guilty. See Milton, *Paradise Lost*, note, p. 82.

11. E. M. W. Tillyard discusses the events in Eden and presents an argument applicable to Néstor's own tragedy. The First Couple ventured to transcend certain natural limitations, and their disobedience is a case of "disregarding the facts of existence, going against the nature of things, or refusing to come to terms with the conditions of one's environment." He adds: "And it is just because a large part of the Fall's meaning stands for something so simple and so fundamental as this that the heart of *Paradise Lost* can never be superannuated." See "The Crisis of *Paradise Lost*," in *Milton: "Paradise Lost": A Collection of Critical Essays*, ed. Louis L. Martz (Englewood Cliffs, N.J.: Prentice-Hall, 1966), p. 167.

6
Survival and Rebirth

The severest castigation that man can receive is to be for-saken by the deities he has revered and be left to himself along with the evil he has perpetrated. The threat of complete destruction is included by Michael in his historical prophecy of humanity's first annihilation:

> . . .till God at last
> Wearied with their iniquities, withdraw
> His presence from among them, and avert
> His holy Eyes; resolving from thenceforth
> To leave them to their own polluted ways.
>
> [*P.L.* 12. 106-110]

The concept of divine withdrawal, when again Satan shall reign supreme during the final days before the Conflagration, is not purely a Christian form of extending man's suffering. The early Greeks, who regarded justice and virtue as synonymous, anticipated comparable alienation of mankind for disregarding the moral code which sustains harmony and permits survival:

> And at last Nemesis and Aidos, Decency and Respect, shrouding
> their bright forms in pale mantles, shall go from the wide-wayed
> earth back on their way to Olympos, forsaking the whole race

of mortal men, and all that will be left by then to
    mankind
will be wretched pain. And there shall be no defense
    against evil.[1]

Yet despite the ominous forecast of total extinction,
whether it be made by the ancient pagan or modern Christian
poet, there remains the ultimate concern for the hero's survival and the continued cyclical motion of his course from
death to rebirth. The spiritual or physical eclipse is only
temporary, and the return to Paradise or the Isle of Love,
where harmony and peace once coexisted with bountiful
nature, is possible. The resurrective force is there and will
eventually appear

               . . .to dissolve
Satan with his perverted World, then raise
From the conflagrant mass, purg'd and refin'd,
New Heav'ns, new Earth, Ages of endless date
Founded in righteousness and peace and love,
To bring forth fruits of Joy and eternal Bliss.
                          [*P.L.* 12. 546-51]

Being restored, however, to providential favor involves
essentially a continuation of trials and suffering, with moral
edification occurring as part of the hero's endurance and
transformation.

The Social Code:
Deeds, Sacrifice, and Physical Salvation

Michael, the "Enlight'ner" of Adam's "darkness" (*P.L.*
12. 271),[2] gives the sinner instruction and information which
promise redemption, but the final guidelines are set in a
catalogue of ethical principles that will prove, if adhered to,
the true basis for mankind's salvation:

. . .only add
Deeds to thy knowledge answerable, add Faith,
Add Virtue, Patience, Temperance, add Love
By name to come call'd Charity, the soul
Of all the rest: then wilt thou not be loath
To leave this Paradise, but shalt possess
A paradise within thee, happier far.

[*P.L.* 12. 581-87]

The performance of "deeds" which may be termed the "social requisites" will take Adam out of his isolation; and action based on new heroic ideals, as well as restrictive or controlled behavior—inaction—will become part of a series of trials that can lead to the re-creation of Paradise. The accomplishment of such "deeds" finds expression in another traditionally religious precept that relates man to his gods and promotes regeneration, sacrifice, which may be a comparatively automatic and effortless act, or a commitment demanding the spiritual strength of a martyr.

Sacrifice as a religious element is constant in the evolution of epic poetry and it plays a significant role in both primitive as well as modern societies. Of all offerings, the easiest to make is that which is impersonal, bullocks, grain, wine, etc., and even the oblation of another human being can be an equally facile contribution. In the *Odyssey*, in addition to the usual consecratory donations to the gods, Homer presents the sacrificial problem through Circe, who informs the Ithacan king that six men will be seized by Scylla in order for the remainder of the crew to survive (*Od.* 12. 109-110). The *Aeneid* also contains several acts of offering as well as human sacrifice as propitiatory and ritualistic practice. Mention is made of Iphigenia, whose sacrifice initiated the successful journey of the Achaeans to Ilium (*Aen.* 2. 116-18); the appeasement of Aeneas's own anger is achieved when he commands the execution of four youths in recompense for the death of Evander's son, Pallas (*Aen.* 10. 517-20), and Neptune in Book 5 is satisfied by the drowning of the famous pilot Palinurus in the sea as assurance of the Trojans' safe arrival (*Aen.* 5. 814-15).

However, the death of Palinurus is, for Aeneas, only one of several personal losses that range from companions to members of his own family. Thus sacrifice in Virgil's epic develops beyond the purely religious level and becomes one of self-denial—a theme associated with the fulfillment of the hero's social and political goal, which is the founding of a new Troy. The imposed obligation of suffering for the commonweal is a painful one that reaches its climax of pathetic reluctance in Book 4, when Dido and Carthage must be abandoned for Pergamum's rebirth. Mercury reminds Aeneas of his responsibility for which his entire life's course is set:

"What are you planning? Why are you wasting your time
    in Carthage?
If you are not aroused with desire for such glory,
if for your own sake you will not shoulder the burden,
you should at least have a care for growing Ascanius,
and for his legacy—Italy and the Roman Empire."
[*Aen.* 4. 271-75]

"Sighing deeply, and much shaken by his love" (*Aen.* 4. 395), the personal sacrifice is further intensified for the Trojan hero when he must take leave of a bitterly grieved Dido. The tragedy of Dido's suicide is in essence a sacrifice on the altar of love, and Aeneas will feel deep remorse again when he encounters her shade in the nether world, where she does not deign to speak to him. After the death of the Sidonian queen, human sacrifice continues and the maximum contribution will be made to War as Aeneas attempts to fulfill the destiny of Troy. Juno's desire for vengeance also must be sated, and it is she who proposes the manner: "They shall pay with their people's lives for uniting the races" (*Aen.* 7. 317).

The theme of self-deprivation for the welfare of others or for the benefit of a religious or social cause becomes the sacrifice of one's own life within the development of the Christian epic. Duty, culminating in death and the annihilation of the individual, is as frequent as the classical offering of other humans or animals. Beowulf exemplifies the devoted, well-loved, and aging king who challenges the dragon to save his people.[3] This ideal of selfless martyrdom reaches its acme in *Paradise Lost*, when the divine figure will offer himself because, as Michael tells Adam, "some blood more precious must be paid for Man" (*P.L.* 12. 293). But the precursor to Milton anticipates a new concept of heroic virtue in *Gerusalemme Liberata*, an epic which is structured almost entirely on the correlatives salvation/sacrifice. Immortality or glory is synonymous with action related directly to the precepts of Christianity and to the deliverance of the Holy City. Yielding one's life for this purpose is to assure the salvation of the soul.

Tasso's interpretation of the sacrificial theme is dispersed throughout his poem. In Canto 3 Dudone is buried with the pomp and ceremony befitting a martyr; but in Canto 2 the actual confrontation of Islam and Christianity begins with a contrast of planned slaughter and proposed self-sacrifice. As evil is represented in the threat of massacre that King Aladino extends to his Christian population within the Holy City, virtue appears spontaneously when the maiden Sofronia offers herself as the supposed thief whom the Moslem ruler has sought and will punish. The virgin, hoping to save the guiltless masses, accepts the tyrant's wrath and castigation for herself alone:

> Sol di me stessa io consapevol fui
> Solo consigliera, e sola esecutrice.
> Dunque in te sola ripigliò colui,
> Caderà l'ira mia vendicatrice.
> Diss'ella: E guisto; esser a me conviene,
> Se fui sola a l'onor, sola a la pene.
>
> [*G.L.* 2. 23. 3-8]

Sofronia's remarks are those typical of a martyr, and her

chosen course is a determined one which will not be altogether lonely, for she permits Olindo, the youth who has loved her quietly, to join her as she faces immolation on the pyre. Although he does not associate fires and bonds with divine love, but rather with human passion ("Altre fiamme, altri node Amor promise" *G.L.* 2. 34. 1), he is content to accept this form of union.[4]

For the contemporary dramatist who creates martyrs in a sometimes equally exotic setting as that found in Tasso's epic, the female expiatory victim can be modeled after the Sofronia image or may become an ectype of Saint Joan. Historical variants notwithstanding, what results is the same mystical or religious impression conveyed by the heroic offering of one's life for the appeasement of a higher authority or for the redemption of another person. In Aguilera-Malta's play *Honorarios*, the only figures who appear on stage verbally develop other characters who are never physically present, but whose destinies are part of a family unit controlled by the lawyer Cercado, malevolent symbol of political and economic power. The mother (simply called "La Vieja") pleads with him to exonerate her imprisoned son Diego from false charges. The consequences of his incarceration have produced a situation of human deprivation and misery which can only be alleviated by consecrating Emérita, the old woman's daughter, as an "honorarium" for Cercado's efforts to liberate Diego. Juana, wife of Diego, is only too willing to give her sister-in-law as the price for saving herself and her children from starvation. But the young virgin reacts to her proposed fate with the total commitment reflected in the image of light and radiance associated with sainthood or martyrdom:

VIEJA: . . .Ese día le brillaban los ojos, como si estuviera dispuesta al sacrificio.[5]

Like Sonfronia, Emérita too feels the call of "glory" that

determines the sacrifice of one's being for the salvation of others.[6]

Paca Solana, on the other hand, is a militant heroine who dedicates herself to tripartite redemption in *España leal*. The sacrifice for saving country, humanity, and her father is charged with a resurrective current which is presented in the same effulgent imagery that surrounds Tasso's Christian maid, Sofronia:

> Mi Madrid se encuentra herido
> y lo voy a defender. . . .
> Soles me incendian el alma,
> soles de triunfo y de fe.
>
> [*España* 6]

Paca's commitment, totally messianic and mystical, bears the dynamic markings of her historical and literary antecedents. While her companion listens and loves her silently as Olindo does Sofronia, and is willing also to share the same tragic destiny, Paca explains her call to duty in familiarly passionate terms:

> "Pero muchas noches me he despertado sobresaltada. Escuchando voces extrañas en mi oído. Con un deseo loco de lanzarme a la calle. . . .E impedir con mi vida que nos lo quiten todo. . . .Por doquiera miro sangre inocente, derramada para salvar la humanidad. A veces he creído reconocer mi propia sangre y entonces, he sentido una responsabilidad extraña. De mártir, de heroína."
>
> [*España* 29]

With the death of the Spanish warrior-maiden, one of her wishes is fulfilled when her father joins his daughter's comrades in their fight against the enemy forces. Paca Solana's sacrifice has not been in vain.

When Aguilera-Malta combines pagan and Christian concepts of salvation within the vast background of tropical jungle and majestic mountains, sacrifice is still a prominent recourse in his style. In the novel *Siete lunas y siete serpientes*, where the characters seeking salvation make no distinction between pagan and Christian versions of expiation, it is Bulu-Bulu, the classic medicine man, whose Indian and African sorcery begins the redemption of Candelario Mariscal. By means of primitive rituals for exorcising the demoniacally possessed, it is the black warlock whose heritage gives hope to the retired villain:

> —Para eso tienes tus remedios y tus prácticas ¿no?
> —No sólo eso. Tengo mis oraciones. Mis aliados. Mis conversas con los santos blancos y negros.—Porque ha de saber usted que desde que llegamos del otro lado del mar, nos hemos aconchabado con los santos blancos—.
> [*7/7* 152]

Bulu-Bulu's eclecticism does not preclude the acceptance of "white saints" within his conglomeration of redemptive measures, but he adds among his remedial techniques the sometimes efficacious sacrificial ceremony which his forefathers bequeathed to him: "Y mis sacrificios. De animales. En algunos casos, hasta de gente" (*7/7* 152). For the moment at least, the medicine man is unaware that the human sacrifice which he may be considering is that of his daughter, Dominga, a willing victim, whose spiritual strength could permit her own survival and even restore Candelario through the regenerative power of love.

Love of cause, country, and individual is what distinguishes the heroines of martyrdom created or re-created by Demetrio Aguilera-Malta. Manuela Sáenz is a historical example of total involvement with the independence of Gran Colombia[7] and complete dedication to the man who represented freedom for the nations under Spanish domination. Her passionate devotion to Simón Bolívar recognized no limit in personal sacrifice, whether it meant forsaking comfort, reputation, or life. She considered his role of prime importance and her own significance during the critical moments of Latin American history as negligible when compared with the ideals that the Liberator symbolized:

> ¿Qué importa ser o no ser una figure de primer plano? Lo importante es que triunfen los patriotas. Y que él, que los conduce, pueda hacerlo con la ayuda de todos. Por eso ayudándolo, cumplimos un deber. Prestándole nuestras energías nuestra fe, nuestro sacrificio, ¡realizará mejor su obra!
>
> [*Caballeresa* 137]

Simón Bolívar's propitiatory character stimulates both idealization and persecution in the relentless pursuit of a course toward immortality. Intermittently regarded as a messiah during his lifetime, he writes a final message to the Colombian people confirming the dream he never quite substantiated of unifying the liberated territory and the price he paid for his commitment: "He sido sacrificado a mis perseguidores; me han traído al borde de la tumba; yo les perdono" (*Caballeresa* 407).

The most complex development of salvation by means of sacrifice is found in the drama *No bastan los átomos*, in which both method and purpose become syncretized in a cyclical pattern of death and resurrection. The soldier Fausto returns from organized carnage and destruction to his father's island, where Alba awaits him to begin a new life. But this rebirth is contingent upon two conditions which are essentially related to sacrifice and death. The drama begins with the potential shipwreck of Fausto hoped for by his mother, who fears his spiritual contamination by Arquímedes. Ifigenia establishes a bond between herself and her classical predecessor but seeks a reversal in her function in determining the hero's destiny. Rather than pacify the sea, as in the case of Agamemnon's offering of his daughter, the mother calls upon it to rebel and destroy Fausto in order to prevent the inevitable encounter between father and son.

IFIGENIA: Tal vez no encuentre ni una embarcación que lo conduzca hasta aquí.

ALBA: [*Esbozando una sonrisa, para dulcificar la situación*] Tú lo conoces. En tal caso, vendría a nado.

IFIGENIA: [*Continúa sin prestarle atención. Con exaltación creciente*] O puede que la embarcación sufra una avería.

ALBA: ¿Qué dices?

IFIGENIA: O que fuertes vientos embravezcan el mar.

ALBA: [*Repitiendo. Sin comprender*] ¿Embravezcan?. . .¿El mar?. . .

IFIGENIA: O que no llegue a atravesar el cinturón de arrecifes que hay en la bahía.

[*Atomos* 14][8]

However, with the successful crossing of Fausto, Ifigenia realizes, despite her apprehensions, that Fausto is "safe" for the time being. The holocaust of war as well as her unfulfilled wish for his death seem to have achieved his rebirth. The price, nevertheless, has been a human life—that of the scientist, whose silhouetted figure still exercises an influence over all the characters. Sacrifice has begun the cycle of redemption, but death continues reaching out to Fausto and effects his spiritual decline when he responds to the loss of his father with barbarous acts, which in turn lead to his own psychic demise. His performance of two "rites" indicates the darkening of his soul by sacrificing the symbols of enlightenment and spiritual illumination in an attempt to appease himself. The first is a verbal burning of the library's masterpieces during a flameless auto-da-fé ceremony; the second is his cold-blooded, calculated rape of Alba, his personal light and the hope of redemption. At this moment humanity becomes Ifigenia's concern. It no longer is a matter of saving Fausto, whose madness may begin to seek a third sacrificial victim—this time perhaps the world. The rape of Alba, according to Ifigenia, will work as a positive force and emblem of courage in the renewal of the young woman herself, and the mother predicates again those heroic ideals familiar to Christian epic tradition which demand inevitably the sacrifice of what is most cherished:

> "Tú reharás tu vida. Quizás hasta tengas un hijo. Un hijo que exhibirás como una viva bandera de carne, conseguida en esta dolorosa victoria. Una victoria que nos cuesta tantos muertos queridos. Yo por mi parte, necesito seguir predicando el amor, la fe, la esperanza; la paz, la justicia y la solidaridad entre los hombres."
>
> [*Atomos* 98]

The dichotomy of life and death is finally reconciled when Ifigenia decides what her son's destiny will be: "Sólo la muerte puede salvarlo" (*Atomos* 96). Although the plan of action is to abandon Fausto on the island which will be destroyed by bombing, he is indeed saved by and from death when his mother listens to his confession, after he has experienced the light of redemption. Fausto repents, and Ifigenia remains on the island to permit the couple's escape while executing her own doom along with those who deserve to perish. In achieving this Cadmean victory, her self-offering will complete the series of sacrifices upon which, on the one hand, Fausto's regeneration depends and, on the other, the salvation of mankind in view of the genocidal weapon that was her son's inheritance.

> . . .*only add*
> *Deeds to thy knowledge answerable.* . .

Self-sacrifice and the welfare of others, as the play *No bastan los átomos* reveals, are generally correlatives in epic tradition. Exemplary acts which serve to rescue the helpless from imminent danger are not merely devices created by the author to heighten the tension of the moment or to enhance the already noble character of the hero. There is something that transcends the desire for fame which fosters deeds that preserve either the hero's own life or that of others. The sparing of a virtuous character's life prompts a mental sigh from us: we would indeed prefer Beowulf live to a ripe old age like Charlemagne. It is also difficult to disagree with the shade of Achilles, who tells Odysseus of the tragedy of death and the joy of being alive, and it is a relief to know that Sofronia and her companion are released from the pyre. Despite the Christian medieval and Renaissance writers' emphasis on the eternal salvation of the soul, which is the meed of the righteous individual, somatic preservation is by no means undermined. The modern poet is also as concerned with all the natural and unnatural phenomena that threaten the hero with physical extinction.

But the author's intention from Homer on is not to have his protagonist spared merely for the sake of material survival. Both Odysseus and Aeneas in their misfortunes on land and sea are continuously menaced by annihilating forces. Intimately bound, however, to these episodes is the spiritual effect that results, and it is not just a fulfillment of their destiny which is of interest. Aeneas experiences a constant moral strengthening and revitalization which he needs to complete the role he has been called upon to perform. He has matured psychologically and bemoans his fate far less by the time he reaches Latium. His Ithacan predecessor finds, through all the threats to his corporeal state, a gradual humbling and increased reverence for the supernal powers. Above all, there is the ethical transformation or involvement which will take place by the end of *Paradise Lost*, for the final point of departure will be the code of behavior and attitudes that will apply to a mortal being's relationship with his fellowman. During his earthly existence Adam, or Everyman, must perform those "deeds" of simple caliber rather than the great feats of epic renown to permit survival of the social unit, be it family, nation, or the entire world. Finally, with the possibility of eternal perdition it will be that code of behavior, not only patience and martyrdom, the ethical interaction of men, which will determine spiritual salvation.

Physical survival is of great importance to the twentieth-century writer. The hero's material condition in contemporary Ecuadorian fiction is of primary interest, and his collective image—the common man, the Indian, the Negro, or the proletariat—is frequently besieged by political and economic monsters. Added to the potential devastation by those forces are the attacks of the natural elements that promise extermination by flood, earthquake, famine, and disease. Demetrio Aguilera-Malta, however, continues the trend which stimulated the revolutionary literature of denunciation and protest and unites it to the spiritual aspects of salvation which preoccupied the epic poets of Renaissance and medieval fame.

The blend of moral and physical values is evident in Aguilera-Malta's previous works, but it reaches a climax in *Siete lunas y siete serpientes*, where "deeds," as they pertain to conserving the mortal frame, are interwoven with those which involve the salvation of the soul. The two themes are tightly interwoven and assume the importance of rescue endeavors frequently associated with chivalric literature of the romance.[9] The microcosm of Santorontón and its insular neighbors exhibits a concatenation of alternating acts of salvation executed by individuals, animals, and divine or preternatural figures. The first episode occurs between the life-size crucifix, which has been stolen by pirates, and Cándido, who is called to the ship on the pretext of performing a sacrament. For his services the priest is given the cross and its occupant as a gift; the only problem is to survive the sea, into which both are tossed by the sadistic captain. Cándido remains afloat, however, through the magical and practical "life-saving" support offered by his companion:

—¡Súbete en la Cruz, igual que yo!
Con ágil movimiento, el Hijo de María, se desprendió

del Madero. Se acostó sobre éste. Con pies y manos, empezó a impulsarlo. Cándido lo imitó.

[7/7 34]

The element changes from water to fire in the substance of the regenerative spirit when, in a later situation after years have passed, Cándido enters his burning church, set afire by a drunken Candelario, to rescue the wooden savior. Surrounded by flames while removing the crucifix from the altar, the priest saves his friend, now marked by the scars of another passion. Christ's gratitude is countered by Cándido's sarcastic retort about his comrade's inability to demonstrate his famous reputation for protecting the innocent and the needy and, as the priest would have hoped, his hutlike temple as well. But salvation has its limits, and in this instance, the line has been drawn by a higher authority.

The theme of physical salvation continues in the next conflagration, when the mountain is set ablaze by the henchmen of Crisóstomo Chalena. The beasts, which have suffered from thirst along with the villagers, make an attempt to descend into Santorontón to seek out the containers of precious liquid guarded by the oligarchy. As all the creatures begin to panic to escape the flames, they reach the village only to be met by stones, machetes, and guns which the people use to kill those heading for the coveted supply of water. Juvencio Balda, Cándido, and his Christ fight to put an end to the "zoocidal madness" (7/7 210), for the monkeys, most daring of all creatures, are shot as they try to escape the mountain fire. Unimpressed by Cándido's crucifix, Chalena and his band continue the simian massacre until a threat to the priest's life is interrupted by the appearance of another unlikely savior:

—¡Un momento!
Alzaron la vista. Un estremecimiento de terror sacudió a la mayoría. En lo alto de un montículo. De pie.

Cruzado de brazos. Estaba el Coronel Candelario
Marsical. Parecía haber crecido. Una extraña sonrisa,
casi demoníaca, plegaba sus labios. Los ojos le echaban
chispas. Siguió hablando tranquilamente:
—Quien le toque un pelo a mi Padrino. . . .¡puede
darse por difunto!

[7/7 213]

The dramatic entrance of Candelario Mariscal is suddenly
overshadowed by the first storm of the long-awaited rainy
season, and the beasts as well as the villagers are calmed. But
additional work must be done to help the wounded animals
Clotilde, Juvencio, and Cándido begin to share the responsi
bility of caring for the injured anthropoids; in the chain of
reciprocal salvation the apes are being returned a favor
Tended by Clotilde and the other humans, they were pre
viously instrumental in the physical survival of the unfor
tunate adolescent who lost herself in the mountains and in her
own fantasy. As the warrior-maidens of epic tradition and
classical mythology did before her, she too spent part of her
life in solitude, wandering through the only environment that
afforded her protection from man—the beast which had
caused her misery. The animals of the jungle and mountains
sustained her and spared her any further attack. Clotilde
Quindales recalls very little of that night which was filled with
the Cayman's violence, but she is convinced that the monkeys
were responsible for saving her from any repetition of that
fantasmagoric episode:

Los monos la salvaron. De eso casi estaba segura. Los
monos. ¿Impidieron que la montara el tigre? ¿Se la
arrebataron al caimán? ¿La defendieron de los Tin-
Tines? ¿La protegieron de las serpientes?

[7/7 271]

Juvencio Balda, another victim of violence, is indebted to
the monkeys as well for his life. On the verge of total

annihilation, he is saved by his fellow primates from another attack by Chalena and his henchmen and carried to the girl who will restore his physical and spiritual health. Juvencio's case exemplifies the intimate relationship of psychic and substantial survival. In the peripatetic style and development of salutary events, the two rescued by the apes are joined by Cándido and his companion in a scene which is circumscribed by the theme of spiritual redemption. The interdependence of both aspects of salvation is crystallized when the tyrants appear at Cándido's door to arrest their wounded victim, Juvencio. The young priest, Gaudencio, pompously reminds the older clergyman that his function is to concern himself with spiritual matters only:

> —Nosotros somos religiosos. Y nuestro deber es sólo salvar las almas de los infieles.
> Alzó los ojos al cielo, beatífico. Cándido entrecerró los párpados.
> —Eso es lo que estoy haciendo, Padre Gaudencio. Nada más que el alma del doctor Juvencio Balda todavía está bastante pegada al cuerpo. Y me parece que nadie— mucho menos nosotros—tenemos el derecho de despegarla antes de tiempo.
>
> [7/7 116]

But Cándido's defense of Juvencio is in vain; nor are Clotilde's efforts of any avail. The odds are too great in favor of superior brute force. It is indeed time for the priest's friend to perform a miracle and save his comrades. When the attackers have gone, the burned Christ returns to his cross, from which he chides a reviving Cándido, who is unaware that the wooden figure has finally interceded in human affairs. Indebted to the divine image for their corporeal preservation, Clotilde, Juvencio, and the priest, like the rest of the inhabitants of Santorontón, must now look to themselves for the source of salvation in this world or the next.

The adventure that takes place will combine the three concepts of performing deeds, sacrifice, and the crucial drive to sustain a mortal existence. It will also revive the Felix Culpa motif—the Miltonic topic of evil turned to good—in the regeneration of those who participate in the action.

Ecumenism, Harmony, and Love

Perhaps the greatest feat that man or beast can accomplish is the modification of natural inclinations and control of passions. With the threat of imminent extinction because of Chalena's control of the water supply, the peasants of Santo-rontón unite and devise a plan whose realization will have the aura of epic greatness. An ecumenical spirit among human beings and animals—that harmony which once existed in Eden and was destroyed—begins to permeate collective activity in the building of a depository for water:

> Una especie de fiebre colectiva estaba sacudiendo a ese mundo vegetal-animal. Todos trabajaban. Los árboles caían y caían, talados por los hombres. Estos, quitaban las ramazones. Cortaban las más gruesas. Las que pudieran servir para estacas o travesanos. En seguida, los monos se trepaban a los troncos para limpiarlos. Los despojaban de hojas, flores, frutos o enredaderas. A veces, ellos mismos transportaban los trozos de madera hacia donde se unían los cerros. Otras ocasiones, no lo hacían. Habían aparecido, venidos, quién sabe de dónde, centenares de murciélagos. Eran éstos quienes cumplían el encargo.
>
> [7/7 302]

More phenomenal than the feat itself is the cooperation of bats, vipers, jaguars, and other one-time enemies of man in a miracle of zoological compatibility. The beasts formerly associated with death or destruction find their redemptive measure in the pace set by close fellowship among human beings. The animal kingdom, which either opposed human values or reflected by poetic allusion the baser character of man, now joins him in a task of mutual ennoblement, and the barrier of individual differences or appetites gives way to a drive toward something of greater priority than self-indulgence—the battle against a common foe that threatens their existence. Man has not only learned from the natural environment, but has united with its inhabitants to produce a weapon for survival which will, if not destroy, temporarily paralyze the satanic forces menacing them.

War or evil ironically is a cohesive factor in epic tradition which reconciles Adam and Eve in their fight against the enemy who caused dissension between the two. The proposition is made by the victim of her selfish motives in a plea for harmony (*P.L.* 10. 923-26). Satan himself, who instigated strife but established noteworthy harmony among his own constituents, expresses the essence of man's inability to form the bonds of comradeship even when death is imminent:

O shame to men! Devil with Devil damn'd
Firm concord holds, men only disagree
Of Creatures rational, though under hope
Of heavenly Grace; and God proclaiming peace,
Yet live in hatred, enmity and strife
Among themselves, and levy cruel wars,
Wasting the Earth, each other to destroy!
As if (which might induce us to accord)
Man had not hellish foes anow besides,
That day and night for his destruction wait.

[*P.L.* 2. 496-505]

For Camões the "hellish foes" were the followers of Islam and the powerful Ottoman Empire, which had subjugated the Christian nations. His condemnation of divisiveness among the European exponents of his faith caused by the Reformation and political intrigues is evident in the *Lusíadas*, where he denounces their disunity, which contrasts paradoxically the martial accord that characterizes the Moslem enemy:

> O míseros Cristãos, pola ventura
> Sois os dentes de Cadmo desparzidos,
> Que uns aos outros se dão a morte dura,
> Sendos todos de um ventre produzidos?
> Não vedes a divina sepultura
> Possuída de cães, que sempre unidos
> Vos vêm tomar a vossa antiga terra,
> Fazendo-se famosos pela guerra?
>
> [*Lus.* 7.9]

Ecumenism does exist, however, among men of different ideologies and backgrounds when armies are united to oppose a common adversary. The Saracens, themselves a combination of various Near Eastern and African groups, face Charlemagne's forces, which are composed of Bretons, Normans, Germans, Danes, and Franks (*Roland* 3026-95), while Goffredo, in the poetization of the First Crusade to deliver the Holy Land from bondage, commands a miscellany of European troops (*G.L.* 1. 37-64). As eternal as friction and enmity are, periodic fellowship surges in the cyclical pattern of human existence.

But common humanity becomes even more evident when pain and suffering, the normal conditions of internecine activity, levels opposing hosts and unites the dead and the mourners. This macabre fellowship, defined by the heroine of *No bastan los átomos* as "carnicería como espectáculo ecuménico" (*Atomos* 42), experiences little change during the course of civilization, for the tragedy of war is the same for all victims and their families who survive them:

> The rest—an undistinguishable heap of corpses—
> they burn, uncounted and unhonored; on every side
> the fields are aflame with the fierce rivalry of fires.

The third Dawn had taken the chilly shadows from Heaven
when sadly they piled high the ashes and mingled bones
from the embers, and heaped a mound of warm earth
    above them.
Within the walls and in the city of rich Latinus
is the greatest noise and longest lamentation.
The mothers and wretched daughters-in-law, and loving
    hearts
of sisters, and children bereft of their fathers,
all curse the cruel war and Turnus' marriage too.
[Aen. 11. 207-217]

There are occasions also when even opposing armies, at the
moment of impending death, are linked together in brotherhood, and a spirit of comradeship suddenly appears. Fond
memories of peace and goodwill are restored as Diomedes, in
the midst of carnage, asks Glaucus of the Trojan army his
name and origin. Reviving the friendship of their grand-
fathers, Diomedes confronts a man who is now an enemy,
and exclaims:

"But let us exchange our armour, so that these others
    may know,
how we claim to be guests and friends from the days of
    our fathers."
So they spoke, and both springing down from behind
    their horses
gripped each other's hands and exchanged the promise of
    friendship.
[Il. 6. 230-33]

Homeric verisimilitude becomes narrated history in Aguilera-
Malta's account of a similar suspension of hostility and
tentative amicability before bloodshed and death are
resumed. It is the general of the Spanish royalist army who
suggests permitting social exchange between friends and
relatives as a prelude to the battle of Ayacucho:

—Señores: Hay en vuestro ejército, como en el nuestro,

oficiales que luchan en bandos opuestos y que están
ligados por lazos de familia o íntima amistad. ¿No
sería posible, antes de que nos descalabremos mutuamente,
charlar un poco y despedirnos?
Los oficiales patriotas aceptaron la propuesta. Y, por unos
instantes, ese rincón del Valle de Ayacucho pareció un
sitio de reunión de amigos fraternales que se dispusieran
a celebrar alguna fiesta.

[*Caballeresa* 267][10]

It is an interlude such as this, when enmity is transformed
into conviviality only to be quickly reversed by political
exigencies, that makes the circumstances even more tragic.
But war and persecution threatening destruction or bondage
leave an indelible imprint on social, personal, and literary
memory. It is constantly revived, as epic tradition tells us,
and corroborated by the efforts of man to return to harmony
and peace or Paradise through negotiation, alliance, or
isolation.

The collective recall of Bulu-Bulu, black medicine man of
Balumba and Africa, of this century and many others since
the beginning of time, resurrects the past when his ancestors
fled from a slave ship to found a colony in the middle of a
jungle—the Emerald Kingdom, established by and for those
fugitives who summoned others successfully escaping from
their conquerors:

Fue un pedazo del mundo pretérito incrustado en el
mundo futuro. Los negros que en otras regiones cercanas
seguían esclavos fueron integrándose al Reino Esmeralda.
Los que iban huyendo. Los que eran castrados por haber
huído. Los que simplemente oyeron del sitio donde aún
se era libre. Todos. Todos. Todos se fueron fundiendo—
con sangre y con suenos—en el pueblo del Reino Esperanza.

[*7/7* 283]

On this island within an island there is unity, liberty, justice, and a spirit of regeneration—all of the productive currents emanating from a Utopian sanctuary away from the iniquities of the white man, close to the aboriginal red brother who could guide the maroon in adjusting to a new environment.

But the cause which merges dissimilar cultures is not always one of preservation and escape from tyranny. There are those motives inspiring epic feats which contribute to the progress of civilization. The atmosphere surrounding such achievements is generally charged with vital ecumenism and harmonious activity, resulting from the intermingling of different peoples involved in the construction of the Panama Canal:

El Canal daba para todos. Venían, de los sitios más lejanos, hombres y mujeres, como atraídos por un imán. Los barcos llegaban repletos con los nuevos contingentes de trabajadores y todos conseguían ocupación. El Canal aparecía como una ubre gigantesca de millones de tetas, para calmar el hambre de las multitudes. En las calles se empezaron a hablar todos los idiomas. Circuló el dinero de los más diversos países. Nadie tuvo desconfianza. Nadie vivió mal. Sonaba, desde lejos, con la estridencia de lo inaudito, la llamada de esta tierra de promisión.

[C.Z. 14]

A form of palpitating energy characterizes joint endeavors and existed in the sixteenth century, when Seville functioned much in the same manner as the New World crossroads. As part of the setting for the novel *El Quijote de El Dorado*, the Spanish city functions vibrantly and productively while its transient heroes prepare for the epic of conquest and exploration:

Una especie de fiebre circulante trascendía de todos los lugares. A medida que se aproximaban, advertían el *cocktail* cosmopolita de las razas, las religiones y las ideas.

Flotaba, eso sí, en el ambiente la dinámica imagen de las tierras conquistadas.

[*Quijote* 121]

The harmony defining such industrial fellowship reaches phenomenal proportions in the founding of new nations or new empires, but it is the same force that creates a Panama Canal or a crudely fashioned reservoir in a peasant village. This social ideal, predominant in epic tradition, is based on a concept of balance and organization, which negates the disorder or chaos circumscribing the physical conditions of war. It is part of an ideal drawing man closer to man, closer to his Creator, and farther from the brute and monster that destroy.[11]

To establish or restore order is part of the hero's role and the inspiration of many an epicist. As an opposition to disorder, it is this constructive instinct which motivates many a protagonist. It is what defines Aeneas and makes Odysseus's return to his home even more crucial, and it is what brings Beowulf to Heorot. The restoration of harmony is perhaps one of the most influential drives which underlie the writings of the great poets who witnessed the chaos of political, religious, and social upheaval. For Milton, order finds its source in the divine image who appoints his son to structure the universe out of the amorphous mass called Chaos.[12] But the hero of organization and harmony can be completely human, perhaps even a reformed sinner, for in Santorontón, hamlet of literary fancy where "things are beginning to be invented" (*7/7* 317), the notorious retired champion of anti-heroic feats, Candelario Mariscal, will establish order from chaos and structure a cohesive, balanced society out of the havoc to which he contributed:

"Hay que dejarlo que se case. Tal vez, esto le haga bien. Y quiera que mejoren las cosas en su pueblo. Aquí es el único que puede poner orden. El único."

[*7/7* 369]

In the case of Man, however, in order to create social harmony he must first acquire a comparable internal, psychic condition. The concept of spiritual balance which inspired the Archangel Michael's final message to Adam will yield both the just society and the "inner paradise" sought by heroes of all ages. It is a type of "ecumenism" created between passion and reason, the Platonic ideal, which will redeem humanity after the Fall and inspire the formation of a moral social unit composed of virtuous people whose spiritual components are in tune.

Add Virtue, Patience, Temperance

Balance between appetite and reason properly conditions the soul and is precisely what must be cultivated by the exiles of Eden, for the absence of such temperance—"excess" or "recklessness," according to the Greeks—is "sin" and it merits castigation of the sort that Achilles and Odysseus suffer. An ideal of major philosophical import in Plato's time, *Sôphrosynê*, has its roots in the tradition of earlier Hellenic attitudes regarding morality. Defined by Gilbert Murray in relation to those principles familiarly associated with the new, socially responsible hero seeking salvation, it is

> that special virtue which the early Greeks are always praising, and failure in which is so regretfully condemned, the elusive word which we feebly translate by "Temperance," *Sôphrosynê*. . . .It is something like Temperance, Gentleness, Mercy; sometimes Innocence, never mere Caution: a tempering of dominant emotions by gentler thought. . . .The man or woman who is *sôphrôn* walks among the beauties and perils of the world, feeling the love, joy, anger, and the rest; and through all he has that in his mind which saves.—Whom does it save? Not him only, but, as we should say, the whole situation. It saves the imminent evil from coming to be.[13]

Oddly enough, it is not only this virtue but its primitive,

emotional corollary, *Aidôs* (the opposite of Hubris), which occurs again in modern context as part of the social and religious concern. Without these two qualities, the just individual is indefinable, nonexistent. With them, he can create order and tranquility and the Utopian state or its paradisiacal equivalent. Particularly related to behavior toward the indigent and the helpless, *Aidôs* sustains a bond between the early Hellenes and all crusaders of social reform according to its meaning:

> It is the counterpart of what we, in our modern and scientific prose, call a "sense of responsibility" or the like; the feeling roused more or less in most people by the existence of great misery in our wealthy societies. To the Greek poet it was not scientific, and it was not prose. It was an emotion, the keener because it was felt by a peculiarly sensitive people; an emotion of shame and awe, and perhaps something like guilt, in meeting the eyes of the oppressed of the earth.[14]

Homer's contemporary, Hesiod, dramatizes the importance of such an emotion in man's behavior when he describes the goddess Aidos and her departure from the mortal world. (See page 214-15). A principle of conduct which was not intellectual in basis, *Aidôs* held great significance ironically in a society that was "wild and ill-governed,"[15] and it played a relatively small role in the later ethics of Plato and Aristotle. Yet the ideal assumes again, along with *Sôphrosynê*, a prime function in the doctrines of Christianity and as the ethological material of the Renaissance poet who restores the vitality of an ancient moral code:

> . . .*Add Love*
> *By name to come call'd Charity, the Soul*
> *Of all the rest.*[16]

Rather than the passion or weakness, also called by the

same name, which causes Adam's fall and that of many an
epic figure, love should transcend desire and manifest more
than compatibility or tolerance. The purely sensual emotion
is negated by Tasso when he juxtaposes the wayward,
romantic youths of *Gerusalemme Liberata* and Goffredo,
symbol of rational love and image of the Christian heroic
ideal. When Guelfo pleads for Rinaldo's return, the democratic liege acquiesces and recalls Armida's lover from exile:

> Come esser può, dicea, che grazia[17] i' neghi
> Che da voi si dimanda e si desia?
> Ceda il rigore; e sia ragione e legge
> Ciò che 'l consenso universale elegge.
>
> [*G.L.* 14. 25. 5-8]

So, too, Adam has modified his original emotions to include
mercy and thus begins his ascent by forgiving the cause of his
downfall and restoring Eve to his favor:

> But rise, let us no more contend, nor blame
> Each other, blam'd enough elsewhere, but strive
> In offices of Love, how we may light'n
> Each other's burden in our share of woe.
>
> [*P.L.* 10. 958-61]

Charity, which tempers justice with mercy, and not merely
pities, but forgives, is the virtue that saves Adam and
characterizes Goffredo. It can also be found in those poems
whose protagonists, often semidivine themselves, seem to be
less inclined toward selfless action. Despite the evident ego-
centricity of a wrathful Achilles, there is that quality which
redeems the leader of the Myrmidons when Priam comes to
beg for Hector's body. The intractable chief responds in a
manner that easily elicits a parallel between the ancient
emotion of *Aidôs* and the charity of Milton's faith:

He rose from his chair, and took the old man by the

> hand, and set him
> on his feet again, in pity for the grey head and the
>   grey beard.

[*Il.* 24. 515-16]

L. A. Post refers to this scene, which depicts a compassionate Achilles as he is confronted by an aged suppliant. He discusses the virtues demonstrated by Homer in his epics and stylistically equates the Hellenic with the Pauline ideal:

> Homer made strong the sense of common humanity and made weak the lust to kill merely because killing and destruction are glorious. The *Iliad* preaches glory, loyalty to a loved one, and last of all, pity; but the greatest of these is pity.[18]

Love, which has its excessive manifestation in the sensual delights provided by Armida in her garden, also has its divine, limitless counterpart which reaches beyond normal commiseration and joins the sinner in his mortal world. The Son of God, whether created by Milton or Aguilera-Malta, projects the same aura of love which is filled with compassion and is expressed in a time of crisis:

> . . .then pitying how they stood
> Before him naked to the air, that now
> Must suffer change, disdain'd not to begin
> Thenceforth the form of servant to assume,
> As when he wash'd his servants' feet, so now
> As Father of his Family he clad
> Their nakedness with Skins of Beasts.

[*P.L.* 10. 211-17]

So too Cándido, in his critical hour, when he must leave the hovel that was his temple and home to a younger priest, Gaudencio, experiences a similar response from the wooden savior, who lowers himself from his cross to console the aging exile:

Dos manos lo levantaban suavemente. Dos brazos le rodearon el cuello. Oyó una voz cuya ternura inefable le taladró las vértebras.

[*7/7* 199]

The "mild Judge" and "Intercessor" of *Paradise Lost* (10. 96) is still a model of charity in *Siete lunas y siete serpientes*, for he forgives the arrogant Gaudencio his insults and pomposity and the pain he has caused Cándido. Christ's magnanimity also permits a defense of Candelario Mariscal, the old clergyman's godson, who appears to be well on his way to an Infernal end:

—Bien sabes que mi ahijado. . . .Digo ese Coronel. . . . es un criminal. Además, quemó la iglesia. Y hasta ¡a ti mismo!
—¿Olvidas que perdoné a los que me crucificaron?

[*7/7* 190]

The lesson of mercy is a difficult one for Cándido to relearn, but he too, like Adam, must cast aside bitterness and reproach toward the cause of his unhappiness in order to begin his own salvation.

Like their progenitors, the mortals of Santorontón must sacrifice individual passions—wrath, pride, greed, and lust—in order to begin the process of rebirth. Although lustful passion was the early undoing of Candelario, he is, however, also capable of a sustained filial love as he thinks about the possibility of Cándido's being his real father:

No. No creo que mi padrino sea mi padre. Aunque lo quiero como si lo fuera. Es la única luz que tengo adentro.

[*7/7* 359]

Devotion to another human being casts the only redemptive light which exists in the retired Colonel's darkness, and it is love too which offers itself as the force leading to his salvation. Dominga, on the eve of her wedding, is not disquieted by the doubts plaguing her mother, who fears Candelario could be impotent. Nor is Dominga shaken by the possibility that he may be the Devil's son. Above all, the bride expresses her faith, particularly in her chosen mate's own (if only occasional) concern for others, which is present despite Candelario's normally antisocial behavior:

> "Trataría de ayudarlo. ¿No puede salvarse? ¿Tiene que estar fregado para siempre, sin ninguna esperanza? Además, hay gente con la cual es bueno. Con su Padrino, el Padre Cándido, por ejemplo. Y—queriéndolo o no— al doctor Balda lo ha ayudado varias veces."
>
> [7/7 247]

Dominga's charity is extended as well to those who have offended her. Offspring of a medicine man and issue of a pagan-Christian blend, the girl has been victimized by the same prejudice which persecuted and ostracized her mother. On the threshold of a new life, she is ready to forget the past and eager to forgive her enemies.

Aguilera-Malta reserves a comparable role of charity for another female character also symbolically associated with the archetypal redemptive figure. In *El secuestro del general* María the virgin-widow who has joined the guerrillas opposing the military dictatorship of Babelandia expresses her ideals in terms similar to Dominga's. She, too, has been persecuted by the villagers, who have tried to prevent her union with Fúlgido. But in a magical setting where condors carry off the future liberators of Babelandia, stranger miracles can occur. In her conversations with a millenary Saint Peter, María must remind the cynical fisherman of the basic precepts of Christianity. He questions, ironically, her association with the rebel forces, and María responds, like Dominga, who sees in the man she has chosen a projection of all humanity:

Fúlgido no es solamente Fúlgido. . . . Fúlgido es, también, la Humanidad. En él ama—igualmente—a los demás. Todos los seres humanos son dignos de amor. ¿Aun los chupasangre-ajena? Todos tienen derecho a salvación. Pero, según María, ella debe estar con los que más necesitan de su amor.

[*Secuestro* 214]

María echoes Dominga, who, in her noble innocence, can enlighten others and give hope to the apparently damned. Charged with the vital spirit of love, courage, and determination, Candelario's bride has overcome many a serpent and is capable of redeeming the sinner. Naïve, yet instinctively sensitive to justice and morality, she is one of the most significant participants in the scheme of resurrection which Aguilera-Malta carves out of a primitive society. It is here in a simple peasant world where human passions and frustrations are shown to maintain that universality of truth despite variants of time, space, and culture:

Human brotherhood acquires a palpable significance when we find our image of it confirmed in the poorest of tribes, and when that tribe offers us an experience which, when joined with many hundreds of others, has a lesson to teach us. That lesson may even come to us with a millenary freshness; for, knowing as we do that for thousands of years past mankind has done nothing but repeat itself, we shall attain that noble cast of thought which, transcending all that has been done and redone, assigns as the starting-point of our reflections that indefinable grandeur which is the mark of true beginnings.[19]

The Abandonment of Scepters:
From Symbiosis to Symphysis; Consubstantiation and Regeneration

Whether the common bond of fellowship and its revitalizing effect upon humanity is seen through the eyes of the poet, the philosopher, or the anthropologist, the approach to salvation often is effected through a type of "biological ecumenism." The product of love between pagan and Christian, as well as Negro and Indian, Dominga, whose name represents the Day of Resurrection, carries within her the seeds of irreversible harmony, of reconciled social, ethnic, and religious oppositions. Through human love and the progenic evidence resulting from union between the erstwhile villain, Candelario Mariscal, and the *chola* (hoped to be accomplished by Bulu-Bulu's fertility rites and his wife's prayers), a new generation will emerge to vitalize the couple as well as the village of Santorontón.

E. M. W. Tillyard has noted that the theme of the Fall and the theme of regeneration are inextricably interwoven in *Paradise Lost*.[20] Stated in other terms, Milton's epic demonstrates the cyclical pattern of life, death, and rebirth with particular emphasis on the resurrective conclusion found also in other great poems, such as the *Aeneid* and *Gerusalemme Liberata*. In all, almost invariably, a solution to the permanence of death is based on love and harmony between forces in conflict and specifically in a blending of characters in substance or spirit which will perpetuate or assure their immortality.

In *Gerusalemme Liberata* the relationship of Rinaldo to Goffredo is interdependent and essentially unified ("tu sei capo, ei mano / Di questo campo" *G.L.* 14. 13. 6-7). It is a synergetic association which must be maintained if salvation is to be achieved. Despite the conflict of reason (Goffredo) and passion (Rinaldo), the opposition is eventually resolved to the point of fusion as prophesied in a dream by the dead knight, Ugone. He speaks to the Duke of the merging which will take place in the future to produce a generation of excellence:

Sarà il tuo sangue al suo commisto. e deve
Progenie uscirne glorïosa e chiara.

[G.L. 14. 19. 3-4]

More intriguing is the assumption that virtue and its
corrupter will blend to yield the line destined to achieve great
fame for the House of Este as Ugone predicts. The likelihood
is that Rinaldo's downfall, Armida, will be the source of his
glory through her acceptance of his faith and a sanctified
union between the two. Tasso presents the conversion of the
dame[21] in a dramatic exchange between the former diabolic
sorceress and Rinaldo, whose compassion and newly
acquired rationality succeed in transforming Armida into a
human being, willing to accept the past as error and the
future as truth. Once spiritually enlightened and out of her
darkness, Armida will join Rinaldo in creating an illustrious
future through their descendants.

But the House of Este's glory is less impressive when compared with that of the Roman Empire, which also shall be
realized through the amalgamation of formerly antithetical
forces. The results of such a racial fusion, as Jupiter foretells,
will bring about not only peace between Trojans and Latins,
but will produce as well an especially pious nation:

> ". . .the Trojans shall disappear,
> and mingle with the Latin race. Sacred laws and rites
> I shall add, and make them all Latins with one
>   language.
> From them will come a race of mixed Italian blood
> which you shall see surpassing men and gods in piety."

[Aen. 12. 835-39]

The generative pattern initiated by Venus, Goddess of Love
and mother of Aeneas, culminates in the Roman Empire,
during which time through conquest and colonization the

merging of races becomes historical reality. But the messianic projection of the reign of Augustus, "child of a god, who will re-establish the Golden Age" (*Aen*. 7. 792-93), recurs by the same method of fusion in *Paradise Lost*. In Milton's epic, however, the substantial and spiritual blend assumes the function, not merely of restoring a dying nation and producing an empire, but of redeeming humanity itself and creating a Golden Age for all of mankind in the Millenium.

Union of matter and spirit as an expression of love is divine in origin. And Adam's own creation, which is the product of conjoint activity between natural and divine elements, also is the physical source of Eve's existence:

> . . .To give thee being I lent
> Out of my side to thee, nearest my heart
> Substantial Life. . . .
>
> [*P.L*. 4. 483-85]

Just as spiritual essences intermingle, and man and woman unite, the Divine Power will merge with human through the procreative process. Adam celebrates his rebirth seen in the generations to come, his descendants, among whom will be the Second Eve:

> . . .Virgin Mother, Hail,
> High in the love of Heav'n, yet from my Loins
> Thou shalt proceed, and from thy Womb the Son
> Of God most High; So God with man unites.
>
> [*P.L*. 12. 379-82]

But man, as his works admit, is capable of creating evil as well as good:

> . . .Doubt not but that sin
> Will reign among them, as of thee begot.
>
> [*P.L*. 12. 285-86]

And propagative activity becomes the source of destruction just as it can yield redemption:

> Then when lust hath conceived, it
> bringeth forth sin: and sin when it is finished,
> bringeth forth death.
>
> [James 1:15]

Death, however, produces nothing except the annihilation of mankind, for his role in consubstantiation is a completely edacious one according to Adam's interpretation to Eve:

> If care of our descent perplex us most,
> Which must be born to certain woe, devour'd
> By Death at last, and miserable it is
> To be to others cause of misery,
> Our own begotten, and of our Loins to bring
> Into this cursed World a woeful Race,
> That after wretched Life must be at last
> Food for so foul a Monster, in thy power
> It lies, yet ere Conception to prevent
> The Race unblest, to bring yet unbegot.
> Childless though art, Childless remain: so Death
> Shall be deceiv'd his glut, and with us two
> Be forc'd to satisfy his Rav'nous Maw.
>
> [*P.L.* 10. 979-91]

Communion, or the ritual of ingesting matter and/or spirit often for the purpose of regeneration, is another method of achieving fusion; however, the destruction of human life in the process not only repels Adam but defines Death as a monster as well. For the epic hero who is not shocked by the behavior of a bestial entity like Scylla, to witness a quasi-human creature in the act of consuming his fellow beings is particularly repugnant, as Odysseus knows from his experience with the Cyclops. Polyphemus (or the Laestry-gonians) becomes less than human himself and therefore less divine; for the fare of the gods was nectar and ambrosia, and in Eden our First Parents partook only of the fruits of their garden.

Cannibalism has its symbolic application in modern societies when tyrants—political and social monsters—are often characterized in anthropophagous terms. But actual consumption does occur in *Infierno negro*, when extermination of a race is planned as ethics and morals give way to greed. Hórridus Nabus, the diabolic genius of the drama, inspired by his Miltonic prototype, who also saved his rebellious companions from bondage in Empyrean, redeems Nylónpolis by the successful implementation of his ideas. With Illumination (Ariel) now incarcerated, man's baser instincts and passions rule while the city is purified—a feat made possible by the mechanized transformation of the black underdog into a palatable item.

Communion is only one of several ritualistic or religious devices developed in the play. Like any savior, the "messiah" or Nylónpolis must experience his sojourn on earth, peripatetically marking his stations and suffering mortal pain before final apotheosis. His judges and jury posthumously plan a trip (*in perpetuo*) through the factory he created where the stages of his conversion are transitional points of industrial processing:

NEGRO IV: Que las trituradoras lo preparen para los molinos. . .

NEGRO III: Que las bandas sin fin lo conduzcan a los gabinetes donde se preparan las mezclas. . .

NEGRO II: Que después se le empaque y se le envíe para ser ingerido por alguno de sus congéneres. . .

NEGRO IV: Que viaje a través de los tubos digestivos de estos. . .

NEGRO III: Que termine este periplo volviendo a sus formas naturales. . .

NEGRO IV: Y que regrese a la Fábrica a cumplir, otra vez, todo el proceso. . .

CAOBA: . . . ¡Qué final apoteótico! ¿no?

[*Infierno*, 130-31]

If brotherhood cannot approach the phase of symbiosis in a society which persecutes and destroys the defenseless, unity of racial oppositions is accomplished ironically through a form of miscegenation brought about by converting human beings into alimentation:

NEGRO I: [*Furioso*]. . .¿Y no te conmovías cuando nos hacían las redadas?, ¿cuando gritábamos desesperados, con rabia impotente?, ¿cuando seguíamos todo el proceso macabro, hasta, por último, convertirnos en producto industrializado, con envoltura de plástico, para ir a alegrar los intestinos de algún hermano blanco?

[*Infierno* 121]

When the cannibalistic tyrant is not sated by the victims sacrificed to appease his passions, he may turn his voracity upon himself. Crisóstomo Chalena, exemplary malefactor of *Siete lunas y siete serpientes*, is also the model of autophagic behavior. Not only do his efforts prove fruitless in cultivating a rosebush, but his greed for money has destroyed any reproductive powers. The only issue he can create is hatred for humanity and countless schemes for his neighbor's annihilation:

Gelatinoso, triste y adhesivo. Salía del petate. Se enredaba en un sartal de maldiciones. Maldecía y maldecía. La hora en que nació. La hora en que eligió a Santorontón para vivir. La hora en que regresó Candelario Mariscal. La hora en que apareció por allí Juvencio Balda. La hora en que se salvaron del incendio Cándido y su Cristo.

Maldiciones. Puras maldiciones. En perenne autofagia alimentóse sólo con su bilis.

[*7/7* 370]

The selfish, consumptive method of melding, rather than harmonious intermingling of spirit and matter is directly related to death, sin, and distortions of the natural order, be they monsters or ghosts. Aguilera-Malta molds the phantom of Josefa Quindales out of Candelario's acts of violence and their cumulative effect on his conscience. Mating with her ghost can only yield ashes—his own:

Nada la calmaría. Nada la enfriaría. Estaba hecha de candela. ¿Y si se quemaba? ¡Cuidado, Candelario! ¡Te puedes hacer carbón! ¿Cómo podrás, así, cumplirle a la Dominga? ¿Cómo te presentarías en la iglesia? Quemado. Negro. Crespo. Carbón.

[*7/7* 363]

Like the purely erotic sentiments of Rinaldo for his mistress, an enflamed Dido for the Trojan leader, Calypso for Odysseus, the results, if not annihilating, are illusory, barren, and anodynous; they hardly serve to immortalize the hero.

Sin, however, also absorbs by the very shadow it casts—a reflection of itself and the propagation of evil. The threat to Candelario's resurrection is the nocturnal visit of a shade which has been projected by a darkened soul:

. . .Thou my Shade
Inseparable must with mee along:
For Death from Sin no power can separate.

[*P.L.* 10. 249-51]

And evil with the destruction of mankind as the motive can extend itself as a silhouetted figure menacing its victim with absorption through triple coalescence:

"Hijo mío. Cuando vuelvas, se acabaron mis secretos para ti. Este Laboratorio será tan tuyo como mío. ¡Porque tú serás como yo mismo!"

[*Atomos* 53]

The son, his father's shadow, and the laboratory in which death is generated almost merge, but Fausto's eclipse is not total, for the vital force which his mother, Ifigenia, contributed during his own creation can participate again in his redemption.

The paradox of oneness which combines both destructive and regenerative power is resolved by Milton when he juxtaposes Adam and Christ in their relationship to mankind:

As in him perish all men, so in thee
As from a second root shall be restor'd.

[*P.L.* 3. 287-88]

And that same indissoluble union between individuals is expressed by Eve during the critical moments which will decide the course of their action and consequently their destiny. Upon the fate of one depends the other's:

Our State cannot be sever'd, we are one,
One Flesh; to lose thee were to lose myself.

[*P.L.* 9. 955-59]

Whether in the Garden of Eden or in the village of Santorontón, the sense of inviolable cohesion between people who love one another is essentially unchanged, as Juvencio Balda affirms:

Clotilde era un tatuaje en sus sentidos y en su mente. Vértice de sus sueños y esperanzas. Tendría que convencerla. Los dos eran sólo uno. Cuernos de la misma Luna. Alas de la misma tijereta.

[*7/7* 366]

In similar thoughts the namesake of the second Eve also repeats the vitalizing essence of unity between two people, relating life with love and evil with death as she thinks of Fúlgido:

> Ni siquiera saber dónde termino yo y dónde comienza él. Quiero vivir en él. Y que él viva, también, en mí. Es lo justo. Lo humano, natural y verdadero. Lo demás es pura sombra, injusticia y falsedad. Fundidos somos vida. Separados, muerte.
>
> [*Secuestro* 139]

The couples in Aguilera-Malta's fiction are not the only ones who find redemption or regeneration in psychic syncretism or in the physical sign of their reproductive energies. The phenomenon is evident in the major literary epics, where harmony and peace are achieved by way of merging races and individuals. So, too, Latin America's history, the inspiration for the *Episodios americanos*, reveals the blend of divergent religions and races eventually combined to produce a New World. The holocaust of war notwithstanding, fusion between the aboriginal element and the conqueror has been accomplished. Through the technique of historical prophecy, Balboa, whose love for the Indian princess demonstrates ideal symbiosis between the native and the invader, predicts an optimistic future based on racial coalescence:

> —Algún día esto cambiará, Anayansi; algún día nos querremos todos, y sabremos comprendernos mejor. No se podrá distinguir dónde comienza la sangre de ellos y dónde termina la nuestra. Así ha sido siempre.
>
> [*Mar* 112]

But the fact of cultural amalgamation produced another generative current perpetuating the spirit that defines the Hispanic nations to the south. The blending of indigenous and Spanish elements has also been the inspiration of the "Grupo de Guayaquil" and other regional writers of Ecuador, whose new fiction was dynamic and whose influence has left its mark on the narrative of today. Jorge Icaza, an exponent of that period, explains the synthesis and its innovative effects upon their style:

Fue un surgir y un insurgir de un estilo nuevo impuesto por una realidad nueva, por un contenido humano, propio, que renacía desde los mitos y desde los símbolos de piedra y barro del antepasado indígena, por un lado, y desde la sangre aventurera y ecuménica de los conquistadores por otro.[22]

The apocalyptic force which the Spanish conqueror represented for the Indian also is the ethnological link that connects generation with generation; for, despite continued social and political differences, mother country and colonies are spiritually inseparable. The chaos of war cannot reverse the inevitable course of destiny, as Aeneas and Adam well know, and it is the function of the etiological vision to give meaning to the hero's tumultuous existence. Whether on a Latin American hilltop, in Hades, or in a dream, rebirth and immortality are shown to stem from a type of psychic or physical fusion. It is that knowledge which may sustain or revitalize, but at least console the disillusioned and the dying, who in their tragic hour cast aside futility as a response to seek a better motive for their suffering. Such is the case of the moribund soldier who hears the voice of an illuminated image which overshadows the lofty Andes and the battlefield of Ayacucho:

—No te preocupes, hijo mío. En Ayacucho no hay vencedores ni vencidos. España nunca será derrotada en América. Nos quedaremos para siempre en estas tierras. Son parte de nosotros mismos. Nuestra sangre, nuestro idioma, nuestras costumbres, nuestra cultura, nuestros

ideales y nuestra fe son comunes con los de los hombres
que aquí nacieron. El holocausto de tantas vidas es
fermental para la fusión. Por los siglos de los siglos,
la grandeza y el progreso de estos pueblos nos pertenecerán así como los nuestros pertenecerán a ellos. Nos
unen lazos que nada ni niadie podrá romper jamás.

[*Caballeresa* 272]

The prediction of the imposing venerable figure who
resembles Bartolomé de las Casas is as old and as new as the
human condition. The forecast is the same for the heroes and
heroines created in epic tradition and in those works where
violence abounds and is brought on by dissension and man's
travesties against his fellow beings. However, the redemptive
power of human love, a love that can cause the downfall of
Our Parents, surges again to obscure the past and its bitter
memories. Through the unity that creates life—a new experience for Adam and Eve during their exile, when they will
salve their wounds of remorse, like Aeneas and Lavinia,
Rinaldo and Armida, Fausto and Alba, Fúlgido and María,
Candelario and Dominga, and the numerous other couples of
literary tradition—the generative and revitalizing process
continues. It is the concept of fusion—human, natural,
divine—that contains the essence of salvation and
resurrection. Despite the threat of total annihilation, which is
periodic and timeless, the poet envisions a return to the Isle of
Love in Paradise, where harmony and peace once reigned
supreme, and where the implementation of justice will no
longer be a concern because the Law can indeed be fulfilled
by love:

> The world shall burn, and from her ashes spring
> New Heav'n and Earth, wherein the just shall dwell
> And after all thir tribulations long
> See golden days, fruitful of golden deeds,
> With Joy and Love triumphing, and fair Truth.
> Then thou thy regal Sceptre shalt lay by,

For regal Sceptre then no more shall need,
God shall be All in All. . . .

[*P.L.* 3. 334-41]

Notes

1. Hesiod, *The Works and Days*, vv. 197-201, in *Hesiod: "The Works and Days," "Theogony," "The Shield of Herakles,"* tr. Richmond Lattimore (Ann Arbor: University of Mich. Press, 1968).

2. From Homer to Milton and in the tertiary phase of epic tradition the instructive function of certain characters is crucial to the wayward or wandering hero. Whether the misguided be Candelario or Rinaldo, spiritual salvation or physical survival depends largely on the path as indicated by the illuminating guide without whom the sinner is eternally lost:

Nel mezzo del cammin di nostra vita
mi ritrovai per una selva oscura
che la diritta via era smarrita.

[*Inf.* 1. 1-3]

3. The entire episode saves the Geats but is considered a "vain sacrifice," for their eventual conquest by the Svear can be found as an underlying note of tragedy. See Arthur Gilchrist Brodeur, *The Art of "Beowulf"* (Berkeley-Los Angeles: University of California Press, 1959), p. 76.

4. C. M. Bowra notes this "conflict between passion and piety and the sudden twist by which passion is sanctified," *From Virgil to Milton* (London: Macmillan, 1967), p. 176. It should be added, however, that Sofronia's propitiatory act is closely related to the concept of resurrection. Although at the last moment the victims are saved from being burned alive, they have experienced death by its very proximity, after which in sanctified matrimony they will begin a "new" life together.

5. In Demetrio Aguilera-Malta, *Trilogia ecuatoriana. Teatro breve,* prologue by Emmanuel Carballo (Mexico: Andrea, 1959), p. 28.

6. Carlos Solórzano notes this attitude, which he explains in the following manner: "La sorpresa del espectador llega al máximo cuando la joven se entrega no sólo sin protesta sino sintiéndose muy honrada de entregarse al hombre que dirige los destinos del pueblo." *Teatro latinoamericano en el siglo XX* (Mexico: Pormaca, 1964), p. 112. This relationship of martyr to "prime mover" is equally exhilarating for the victim and shocking to the audience whether the drama takes place in a small Ecuadorian village or in Jerusalem, where Sofronia faces King Aladino.

7. Manuela's patriotism won her the distinction which inspired the title of the novel: *La caballeresa del sol.* The honor of belonging to the Order of the Knights of the Sun was bestowed upon her by General San Martín.

8. Iphigenia of classical fame and Ifigenia in this modern play are both related

to the behavior of the natural environment, which in turn affects the chain of events leading to death and destruction. In the first instance, Troy's end will result, and in *No bastan los átomos*, there is Fausto's spiritual demise, Alba's rape, and the physical death of his father and mother.

9. Although this study does not deal specifically with the chivalric epic or the romance narrative, the influence of such works as Ariosto's *Orlando Furioso* on Tasso's epic is significant, particularly since he proved to be a master of integration. Fantastic and romantic elements were combined with the religious and patriotic seriousness of *Gerusalemme Liberata*. Tasso, Milton, Virgil, and all outstanding epicists are great for their capacity to reconcile what appear to be incompatible ideas and style, as well as to innovate. It was precisely the blending of the *Iliad* and the *Odyssey* which created the *Aeneid* and why, form notwithstanding, the epic spirit still survives.

10. The problem of understanding and harmony among the inhabitants of Latin America is a basic preoccupation with Aguilera-Malta. Particularly in the *Episodios americanos*, a sense of common heritage accompanies the narration of war and strife, and serves as a background for the deeds of Balboa, Orellana, and Bolívar. What the author achieves in these novels is a union of opposing factions through historical perspective. He explains his intention in a letter which is part of a review by Saúl Sibirsky in *Revista Iberoamericana* 32, no. 61 (January-June 1966): 176-79.

11. The concept of relating monsters, chaos, and evil is synthesized by J. R. R. Tolkien when he explains Grendel's function as one of hostility toward humanity and particularly its "frail efforts at order and art upon earth." See *"Beowulf": The Monsters and the Critics, Proceedings of the British Academy*, vol. 22 (London: Humphrey Milford Amen House, E.C., 1936), p. 38.

12. Order and harmony are also part of the concept of bliss, which parallel nature's reaction in this newly created state. Marjorie Nicolson notes "the pervasive sense of happiness and gladness of all parts of Nature as they emerge from Chaos." *John Milton: A Reader's Guide to His Poetry* (New York: The Noonday Press, 1967), p. 268.

13. Gilbert Murray *The Rise of the Greek Epic* (New York: Oxford University Press, 1960), p. 26.

14. Ibid., p. 88.

15. Ibid., p. 90.

16. Milton was undoubtedly impressed by the social implications of St. Paul's message, where love, as it should be practiced, would negate further regulation of human conduct:

<blockquote>

And if *there be*

any other commandment, it is briefly comprehended in
this saying, namely, Thou shalt love thy neighbor as
thyself. Love worketh no ill to his neighbor: therefore love *is* the fulfilling of the law.

[Romans 13:9-10]
</blockquote>

17. Edward Fairfax rightly translated *grazia* as "love," thereby giving its original theological meaning of "grace." *Jerusalem Delivered* (New York: Capricorn Books, 1963), p. 289.

18. *From Homer to Menander* (Berkeley: University of California Press, 1951), p. 55.

19. Claude Lévi-Strauss, *Tristes Tropiques*, tr. John Russell (New York: Atheneum, 1967), p. 392.

20. E. M. W. Tillyard, "The Crisis of *Paradise Lost,*" in *Milton, "Paradise Lost": A Collection of Critical Essays*, ed. Louis L. Martz (Englewood Cliffs, N.J.: Prentice-Hall, 1966), p. 159.

21. Although the manner in which Tasso determines the witch's conversion to Christianity is unconvincing for some critics (A. Bartlett Giamatti, *The Earthly Paradise and the Renaissance Epic,* (Princeton, N.J.: Princeton University Press, 1969, p. 209), the resolution of this problem is a perfect example of baroque intermingling of sensual and religious elements.

22. "Relato, espíritu unificador en la Generación del año '30," *Revista Iberoamericana* 32, no. 62 (1966): 211.

Epilogue

The confluence of divine, human, and natural elements in the mystical "All in All" lends itself to some final considerations regarding epic tradition. What sustains the narrative and intensifies the drama is the portrayal of universal, timeless passions and values in contradistinctive positions which create friction, dissension, war, or any other manifestation of violent behavior. To oppose justice there are the symbols of iniquity; to confront the faithful are the treacherous; to motivate a protagonist is love or hate—all overshadowed by the eternal struggle to preserve life and the inevitable encounter with death. Upon the epic's monumental stage these oppositions clash and interact, and are frequently resolved by patterns and techniques which are related to ecumenism, harmony, consubstantiation, or systasis. In *Paradise Lost*, the apparent contrariety between good and evil which results in the Fall is resolved by means of a *felix culpa* motif that reunites man and woman with their Creator, just as passion and reason are ideally expected to merge in order to yield spiritual harmony. The systatic pattern of forming complementary opposites such as male-female, human-natural, temptation-will power, terminates in a union that is greater or more perfect than the mere sum of the parts. When Trojans and Latins are integrated as the *Aeneid* fortells, they do so to produce a *tertium quid*, a great empire whose fame and accomplishments will exceed those of both cultures prior to fusion. The nations also represent another

258

duality, and a very important one—that of nature and man syncretized by their respective symbols, Lavinia and Aeneas, whose last-born son, Silvius, will be reared in the forest as his elemental ancestors would prefer before he assumes a major role in the founding of a new civilization.

Human and natural synergism became particularly evident as a style or theme in the Renaissance period, when Virgil's influence was prevalent and the bucolic atmosphere described in pastoral poetry contrasted with the environment of its courtly practitioners. The desire to return to an earthly Paradise away from the metropolis that represented progress was as much a part of that Renaissance society as it was during the Augustan era. Torquato Tasso focuses his theme of salvation on a city, but still manages to offer his characters refuge in rustic havens away from the basic scene of action. Erminia, in a frantic attempt to salve her wounds of unrequited love, temporarily finds consolation among a group of shepherds; however, more thematically significant is the ambivalence of the knights who forsake Jerusalem to enjoy the illusory Isle of Love, where Armida's garden and the pleasures of sensual abandonment flourish. The most prominent case of resolved human and natural opposition in *Gerusalemme Liberata* is to be found in the ultimate union of woods and Crusaders, formerly antagonists, which are reconciled by Rinaldo, whose repentance and purged state permit destruction of the evil powers inhabiting the enchanted forest. This act opens the way for constructive efforts to deliver Jerusalem, since the two forces, human and natural, circumscribed by providential approval, combine material and craftsmanship to build the engines that eventually free the Holy City.

A systatic dialectic may also be applied to the production of greater evil rather than good, as occurs in Dante's *Inferno*. Natural and human elements blend to intensify the ugliness of vice, and the effect lies in an amalgamation of violent landscape and gruesome bestial entities uniting in turn with perverted souls to yield an even more unholy totality. The most impressive example demonstrating such negative consubstantiation is described in Canto 25, when serpent and thief coalesce to form the awesome aberration witnessed by the poets. So too, the modern author Aguilera-Malta merges human and zoomorphic attributes in stylistic alchemy, and produces transformations of a similar order to create the malefactor Candelario Mariscal and his tropical counterpart, the crocodile. The ambivalent role of nature becomes even more significant when fire and water are also typologically substantiated in the Colonel and his name, to convey a regenerative potential which will be fulfilled in marriage with Dominga. This paradoxical but not irreconcilable combination of scabrous sinner and innocent virgin is further complicated by the joint efforts of paganism and Christianity which on the surface appear as an antithetical pair but are united, as happens time and again in epic tradition.

Nature can console man, work cooperatively with him, or become a dominating, hostile force. The polarization of natural and human elements which began with man's disobedience reaches a literary climax during the twentieth century in the Latin American fiction called regional, telluric, Creole, or *indigenista*. This opposition is what generally has given that literature a characteristic tone of fatality, which places man in a precarious position or in tragic circumstances. Such a state is reminiscent of the authentic epic hero's destiny as it was manipulated by supernal powers which also controlled the course of natural phenomena. The interaction of man and his environment has a romantic interpretation as well as a realistic sociopolitical and economic one; both aspects have been re-created by the writers of Latin American regional fiction. Similarly, Virgil presents in his works the idyllic, harmonious interrelationship of the shepherds and the land he loves, where communal activity blends perfectly with the pastoral setting. A parallel can easily be drawn between the *loci amoeni* of the *Eclogues* and the tranquil surroundings of the *cholo* in Ecuador before his islands were disturbed by intruders. Economic and literary fusion is obvious in Virgil's *Georgics*, which deals with the practical concerns of the farmer and his means of livelihood. So, too, the Latin American writer of telluric works includes his presentation of diurnal chores as a means of dramatizing the spiritual as well as economic bond that exists between peasant and natural environment.

Such is the case in *Don Goyo* and *La isla virgen*, in which Demetrio Aguilera-Malta details the routines of the *cholo* and intimately combines human and natural energies to produce a stable, cohesive unit guided by the strong, patriarchal figure of Don Goyo. But external human factors such as war, colonization, or urbanization enter to disrupt the ordered life of the *cholos* and establish man and nature as antinomous forces. When the relationship reaches such an antithetical level, the conclusion is one of agricultural failure, human suffering, and the eventual demise of the social structure or the nation itself. Man and nature become antagonists, and the dissociation of one-time symbionts has the same effect on Virgil's farmers as it does on Aguilera-Malta's peasants and lower classes. Don Goyo's tribe deteriorates, and Panama falls prey to spiritual and moral afflictions when the rural areas are deserted for the lucrative rewards of the canal. The same consequences are forecast by Virgil, who witnessed the abandonment of the countryside for the city and the drain of energy created by the extra-natural pursuits and intestine political strife.

The Latin poet's admiration for the farmer is the same as Aguilera-Malta's for the indigenous masses of his country and of the world. In the works of both writers can be found another anthropocentric dichotomy generated by the familiar opposition man-nature. It is that of class distinction which contrasts peasant and landowner, laborer and privileged aristocrat, the indigent and the affluent. Respect for the common man permeates the *Georgics* and recurs in the

Aeneid, when the immediate cause of war, the death of a stag, arouses the farmers, who courageously respond to the Trojans and fight with rudimentary implements against the arms of professional soldiers. In the same manner Aguilera-Malta molds his collective heroic image out of the working class, proletariat, and peasant, whose virtues are idealized all the more by the productive function they have in their society. In *Canal Zone, España leal, ¡Madrid!*, and *Una cruz en la Sierra Maestra* they stand as mass heroes confronting the forces of tyranny, whose moral deficiency often is based on the very lack of contact with the soil and disdain for the labor involved in the cultivation of the land. Thus nature is instrumental in the development of social oppositions which are related as well to the dichotomy of good and evil, or justice and injustice as symbolized by the antithetical pair hero-antihero.

Human contrariety brought about by moral differences is frequently viewed as a political, economic, or military power struggle in which the hero is champion of positive conduct and ideals. The antagonist is generally associated with brute force or barbarity and participates in the action as a type that violates, enslaves, victimizes, or destroys the less powerful. The despotic character may be Antinous in Penelope's household, Dido's brother, Pygmalion, or Mezentius, the exiled king in the *Aeneid*, who joins Turnus's army. For the Christian epicists Islam itself was tyranny: Marsiles in the *Chanson de Roland* and Aladino in Tasso's epic are specific examples of ignominious sovereignty. For Adam, Michael outlines the devastating effects of Nimrod and the Egyptian pharaohs upon his descendants. Evil in a position of absolute authority persists in Aguilera-Malta's military oppressors or dictators, abusive landowners, sadistic conquerors, and perverted men of science and law. All stand in sharp contrast to the spiritually stronger but martially weaker collective hero.

The irrepressible drive toward financial or political supremacy defines most demonic autocrats who oppose the equanimous hero of rational, temperate, and flexible character. His virtues frequently are accompanied by a democratic spirit which draws him closer to his followers and elicits even the admiration of adversaries. The Cid's already magnanimous reputation is enhanced when he asks his men for their opinion ("dezidme, cavalleros, cómmo vos plaze de far" (*Cid* 670), and the same policy unites Francisco de Orellana or Balboa and his men as they face the unknown in their New World adventures. Goffredo's noble stature increases as he accedes not only to divine or preternatural advice, but to the human exhortations of the Crusaders, who plead for Rinaldo's return.

The just leader is the model of reconciled appetite and reason, since he reflects a spiritual triumph which his despotic opponent can never achieve so long as passion rules his soul. The unjust liege symbolizes capitulation to the mighty forces of appetite, and whether the condition is dealt with psychically or politically, subjugation of the nobler element cannot be celebrated by the epicist, for oppression stifles and violence destroys. What the majordomo, Guayamabe, suggests in *La isla virgen* is essentially the only means for eliminating differences, whether they divide man and his neighbor, or man and nature: patience and understanding will prove fruitful; coercion and the imposition of will can only bring disaster. Ironically, Satan himself confirms the *cholo*'s thesis:

> . . .Who overcomes
> By force, hath overcome but half his foe.
>
> [*P.L.* 1. 648-49]

Tyranny and injustice, however, are basic to the paradoxical structure of Milton's poem and to all literature that is apocalyptic in character. Despite the havoc and destruction wrought by the perpetrators of evil and war, there is something positive that is generated. It is a dream of returning to the Golden Age or progressing forward toward the Fifth Empire—a vision sustained primarily by a balance between nature and man in an atmosphere of love and tranquility. It may be encountered as a Utopian projection of the model society, or as an internally blissful state which, according to the Archangel, will determine a "paradise, happier far" than its Edenic predecessor. Approached once more with Virgil in mind, the relationship of man and his environment may be summarized as a convergence of fundamental themes that attracted and preoccupied the author of the *Aeneid* as well as many a poet and philosopher since his time:

Cecini pascua, rura, duces.

It would indeed be a divinely inspired song that could celebrate as an accomplished feat the ideal union between munificent nature, the people who cultivate it and artfully realize its potential, and those leaders, rather than "warriors," whose sense of justice fosters the principles of harmony which is the essence of epic spirit.

Selected Bibliography

Demetrio Aguilera-Malta:
Works and Editions

Demetrio Aguilera-Malta's short stories, novels, and plays or excerpts therefrom have appeared in many periodicals and anthologies published in Latin America, the United States, and Europe. Some of his writings have been translated into English, French, Italian, Czech, Russian, etc. The English translations of his major works are included below.

Short Stories

Los que se van: cuentos del cholo i del montuvio. (With Joaquín Gallegos Lara and Enrique Gil Gilbert.) Guayaquil: Zea y Paladines, 1930.
———. 2nd ed. Introduction by Benjamin Carrión. Quito: Casa de la Cultura Ecuatoriana, 1955.

Novels

Don Goyo: novela americana. Madrid: Cénit, 1933.
———. 2nd ed. Quito: Antorcha, 1938.
———. 3rd ed. Guayaquil: Casa de la Cultura Ecuatoriana, Núcleo del Guayas, 1955.
———. 4th ed. Buenos Aires: Platina, 1958.
———. In *Fiesta in November: Stories from Latin America.*

Edited Angel Flores; introduction by Katherine Anne Porter; translated by Enid Eder Perkins. Boston: Houghton-Mifflin, 1942, pp. 120-228.

C.Z. (Canal Zone): los yanquis en Panamá. Santiago, Chile: Ercilla, 1935.

———. 2nd ed., rev. Mexico: Andrea, 1966.

———. 3rd ed. Mexico: Joaquín Mortiz, 1977.

¡Madrid!: reportaje novelado de una retaguardia heroica. Barcelona: Orión, 1936. (Also 2nd and 3rd eds.)

———. 4th ed. Prologue by Luis Alberto Sánchez. Santiago, Chile: Ercilla, 1937.

———. 5th and 6th eds. Guayaquil: Populares, 1938.

———. Excerpt in *Los que fueron a España.* Buenos Aires: Jorge Alvarez, 1966, pp. 123-27.

La isla virgen. Prologue by Angel F. Rojas. Guayaquil: Vera y Cía., 1942.

———. 2nd ed., rev. Prologue by Angel F. Rojas. Quito: Casa de la Cultura Ecuatoriana, 1954.

———. Excerpt in Willis Knapp Jones, *Spanish American Literature in Translation.* New York: Ungar, 1963, pp. 204-208.

Una cruz en la Sierra Maestra. Buenos Aires: Sophos, 1960.

La caballeresa del sol: el gran amor de Bolívar. Episodios americanos, I. Madrid: Guadarrama, 1964.
Manuela (La caballeresa del sol). Translated and introduced by Willis Knapp Jones. Carbondale: Southern Illinois University Press, 1967.

El Quijote de El Dorado: Orellana y el Río de las Amazonas. Episodios americanos, II. Madrid: Guadarrama, 1965.

Un nuevo mar para el rey: Balboa, Anayansi y el Océano Pacífico. Episodios americanos, III. Madrid: Guadarrama, 1965.

Siete lunas y siete serpientes. Mexico: Fondo de Cultura Económica, 1970.

———. "Seven Serpents and Seven Moons" [excerpt]. Translated by Gregory Rabassa. *Mundus Artium* 9, no. 1 (1976): 140-45.

El secuestro del general. Mexico: Joaquín Mortiz, 1973

Jaguar. Mexico: Grijalbo, 1977.

Homenaje a Demetrio Aguilera-Malta. Sus cincuenta años de narrador. Mexico: Grijalbo, 1978. Commemorative edition in three volumes of *Don Goyo, La isla virgen,* and *Siete lunas y siete serpientes.*

Theater

España leal; tragedia en un prólogo y tres actos, el último dividido en dos cuadros. Quito: Talleres Gráficos de Educación, 1938.

"Lázaro: caricaturas; tres escenas y un prólogo." *Revista del Colegio Nacional Vicente Rocafuerte* (Guayaquil) 2, no. 3 (1941).

"Amor y vino." (With Willis Knapp Jones.) *Revista Casa de la Cultura Ecuatoriana* (Quito) 2, no. 3 (1946): 292-311.

"Sangre azul." (With Willis Knapp Jones.) *Anales de la Universidad de Guayaquil,* 1946.
Also published in English, French, and Portuguese, Washington: Pan American Union, 1948.

Dos comedias fáciles ("Sangre azul" and "El pirata fantasma," with Willis Knapp Jones.) Boston: Houghton-Mifflin, 1950.

"No bastan los átomos." *Revista Casa de la Cultura Ecuatoriana* (Guayaquil) 7, no. 15 (1954): 333-412.

No bastan los átomos and *Dientes blancos.* (In one volume.) Quito: Casa de la Cultura Ecuatoriana, 1955.

———. "White Teeth" (*Dientes blancos*). Translated by Robert Losada, Jr. In *Odyssey Review* (New York) 3, no. 1 (1963): 19-26.

El tigre: pieza en un acto dividido en tres cuadros. Quito: Casa de la Cultura Ecuatoriana, 1956.

———. "El tigre." In Willis Knapp Jones. *Antología del teatro hispanoamericano.* Mexico: Studium, 1958.

———. "El tigre." In Carlos Solórzano *Antología del teatro hispanoamericano.* Vol. 2. Mexico: Fondo de Cultura Económica, 1964, pp. 7-27.

Honorarios. Quito: Casa de la Cultura Ecuatoriana, 1957.

Trilogía ecuatoriana: teatro breve ("Honorarios," "Dientes blancos," and "El tigre"). Prologue by Emmanuel Carballo. Mexico: Andrea, 1959.

Infierno negro: pieza en dos actos. Xalapa: Universidad Veracruzana, 1967.

———. "Black Hell" (*Infierno negro*). Translated by Elizabeth Lowe. In *Modern International Drama* 10, no. 21 (Spring 1977): 9-42.

"Una mujer para cada acto." (With Velia Márquez.) In Velia Márquez *Tres comedias.* Mexico: Finisterre, Colección de Teatro Hispanoamericano, 1970.

Teatro completo. ("España leal," "Lázaro," "No bastan los átomos," "Honorarios," "Dientes blancos," "El tigre," "Fantoche," "Muerte, S. A.," "Infierno negro.") Mexico: Finisterre, Colección de Teatro Hispanoamericano, 1970.

Essays

Demetrio Aguilera-Malta's writings have appeared in numerous periodicals throughout the world and are estimated to total more than 2,000 items. Among the Latin American magazines and newspapers to which he has contributed are *Diario de Panamá, La Estrella de Panamá, Hoy* (Panama), *Revista Universidad de San Carlos* (Guatemala), *Mundo* (Mexico), and a weekly column in the Sunday supplement "El Gallo Ilustrado" of *El Día* (Mexico). In Ecuador he was editor of *Ideal* (1924) and *Trópico* (1938), a monthly journal on art, literature, and history. Articles, poems, drawings as well as excerpts from his fiction and drama have also been published there in *Cromos, Letras del Ecuador, Voluntad, Savia*, etc. The list below, which is by no means exhaustive, contains some of Aguilera-Malta's major articles, essays, monographs, prologues to and reviews of other authors' works.

"De la cultura y de la libertad en Hispano-América" *Diario de Panamá.* May 1, 1930.

"Savia" *Diario de Panama.* 1931. (A regular colum in the newspaper with some thirty articles published.)

Leticia: notas y comentarios de un periodista ecuatoriano. Panama: Benedetti Hmnos., 1932.

"Oscar Cerruto y su *Aluvión de fuego*, gran novela de la Guerra del Chaco." *La Revista Americana de Buenos Aires* 13 (1936): 132-34.

La revolución española a través de dos estampas de Antonio Eden. Quito: Imprenta Fernández, 1938.

"Tránsito de la poesía afrocubana." *Revista Colegio Nacional de Vicente Rocafuerte*, no. 51 (1940): 31-42.

"América, continente del futuro." *Revista Colegio Nacional de Vicente Rocafuerte*, no. 51 (1940): 76-80.

"Biografía y paisaje de nuestro hombre insular." *Revista Colegio Nacional de Vicente Rocafuerte*, no. 52 (1940): 114-23.

"Discurso a los viejos profesores." *Revista Colegio Nacional de Vicente Rocafuerte*, no. 54 (1942): 315-16.

Prologue to Joaquín Gallegos Lara. *La ultima erranza.* Mexico, 1947.

"A propósito del teatro en la República Dominicana." *Boletín de la Unión Panamericana* 81 (1947).

"*Las tres ratas* de Pareja y Diezcanseco: novela cinematográfica." *Revista del Núcleo del Azuay de la Casa de la Cultura Ecuatoriana* (Cuenca) 6, no. 9 (1954).

"José de la Cuadra: un intento de evocación." *Letras del Ecuador*, no. 101 (1955): 21.

"Biografía apasionada del cine: prehistoria—la edad del disco." *Boletín Bibliográfico Bolivariano* (Medellín), no. 47 (1957).

"Benjamín Carrión, exégeta de la vida ecuatoriana." *La Gaceta* (Mexico) 5, no. 63 (1959): 2.

"El problema limítrofe ecuatoriano-peruano." *Cuadernos Americanos* 20, no. 3 (1961): 38-54.

"El teatro: un nuevo aspecto de Manuel Andújar." *Nación*, July 8, 1962, pp. 3-4.

"La crítica y nuestros libros: Agustín Yáñez y la novela americana." *La Gaceta* (Mexico) 9, nos. 99-100 (1962): 4.

Prologue to Manuel Andújar, *El primer juicio final.* Mexico: Andrea, 1962, pp. 7-11.

Prologue to Othón Castillo. *Sed en el puerto.* Mexico: Andrea, 1962.

Review of Agustín Yáñez, *Las tierras flacas*. *Revista Ibero-americana* 29 (1963): 192-93.

"Primeras visitas de Don Quijote a América." *Cuadernos de Bellas Artes* (Mexico) 5, no. 5 (1964): 33-40.

Review of Seymour Menton, *El cuento hispanoamericano*. *Letras del Ecuador* 19, no. 129 (1964): 13, 20.

Los generales de Bolívar. Mexico: Secretaría de Educación Pública, Subsecretaría de Asuntos Culturales, 1965.

"Primer viaje de Pizarro a Sudamérica." *Cuadernos Americanos* 25, no. 2 (1966): 238-59.

Prologue to Pedro Díaz Seijas, *Rómulo Gallegos: realidad y símbolo*. Mexico: B. Costa-Amic, 1967, pp. ix-xiii.

"Charla con Seymour Menton: el cuento hispanoamericano." *Mundo Nuevo*, no. 56 (February 1971): 49-52.

"Diálogo con Fernando Alegría: novelas, novelistas y críticos." *Mundo Nuevo*, no. 56 (February 1971): 45-48.

Miscellaneous

"Páginas de amor: poemas." *Cromos* (Guayaquil), April 15, 1924.

Primavera interior: poemas en prosas y versos. (With Jorge Pérez Concha.) Guayaquil: Tipografía de la Sociedad Filantrópica del Guayas, 1927.

"Cantaban las abejas." *Savia* (Ecuador), June 19, 1927. (Poetry).

"El libro de los mangleros." Mimeograph. Guayaquil, 1929. (Poetry and drawings.)

Panamá—Folklore. Panama: Star and Herald, 1930. (14 original engravings.)

"Romance de Paca Solana." *Trópico*, no. 2 (1938): 5-6. (Poetry.)

"El pirata fantasma." *Ultimas Noticias* (Quito, 1947). (A novelized version of the play written with Willis Knapp Jones.)

"La cadena infinita." Film, Chile, 1949.

"Entre dos carnavales." Film, Brazil, 1951.

Translation of Lídia Besouchet, "El personaje y su obra: pieza en un acto." *Cuadernos de Bellas Artes* (Mexico) 4, no. 5 (1963): 50-72. (Brazilian play).

Cholerías—grabados. n.d. (Prints.)

Unpublished Works

"Campeonatomanía."

"Carbón."

"La cadena infinita."

"El continente de la esperanza."

"Un hombre y mil mujeres."

"México y tú."

"El sátiro encadenado."

"Vórtice."

Criticism and Studies of the Works of Demetrio Aguilera-Malta

The following bibliography is an addendum to the annotated bio-bibliography compiled by Pedro Frank de Andrea, *Demetrio Aguilera-Malta: Bibliografía*, "Hojas Volantes" de la Comunidad Latinoamericana de Escritores, Boletín no. 5, Mexico: Editorial Libros de México, 1969, 36 pp. The items listed below include selected books, articles, dissertations, interviews, and reviews published since 1969. Any duplications are only those of works or articles which have been specifically mentioned in this study.

"Adjunto cultural a la embajada ecuatoriana en el Brasil." *Letras del Ecuador* (Quito), no. 41 (1949): 12.

Aguilera, Octavio. "El mágico y doliente mundo de Santorontón." *Diario de Mallorca*, April 15, 1971.

Allen, Richard F. "La obra literaria de Demetrio Aguilera-Malta." *Mundo Nuevo* (Buenos Aires), November 1969, pp. 52-62.

——— and Eugene Decker. "*Infierno negro* and *Casa Grande e Senzala:* A Comparison in Social Conflict." *Papers on French-Spanish-Spanish-American-Luso-Brazilian Literary Relations.* Evanston, Ill.: Northwestern University Press, 1970, pp. 17-31.

Baguer, Francois. *"Infierno negro* con el grupo jaliscense."
Excelsior (Mexico), December 30, 1970.

Bellini, Giuseppe. *"El señor presidente* y la temática de la
dictadura en la nueva novela hispanoamericana." University
of Paris 10 (Nanterre), *Cahier* 1, June 1975.

―――."Magia e realtà nella narrativa di Demetrio Aguilera-
Malta." *Studi di Letteratura Ispano-Americana* (Milan) 4
(1972): 7-53.

Benites, Jesús Luis. "Gorilas." *Revista Mexicana de Cultura,*
supplement of *El Nacional* (Mexico), December 9, 1973.

Bermúdez, María Elvira. "Catolicismo, política y sexo." *Revista
Mexicana de Cultura,* supplement of *El Nacional* (Mexico),
April 21, 1974.

Borges, Alberto. "Las apasionantes opiniones de un escritor
ecuatoriano: entrevista a Demetrio Aguilera-Malta." *Vistazo*
(Guayaquil), December 1969.

Bravo de Ramsey, Nancy. "Demetrio Aguilera aconseja olvidar
la generación del treinta: entrevista." *El Universo* (Guayaquil), June 28, 1975.

Brushwood, John S. "El criollismo 'de esencias' en *Don Goyo*
y *Ecue-Yamba-O."* In C. G. Boulter, et al., editors. *Lectures
in Memory of Louise Taft Semple.* Norman: University of
Oklahoma Press for the University of Cincinnati, 1973,
pp. 215-25.

Caballero de Monocle. "Au revoir a Demetrio. La ciudad frente
al río." *El Telégrafo* (Guayaquil), February 2, 1969.

Campos, Jorge. "Demetrio Aguilera-Malta y su saga mágica."
Insula (Madrid), no. 302.

―――. "Otros dictadores." In *El año literario español.* Madrid:
Ed. Castalia, 1974.

*Carballo, Emmanuel. "Veinticinco años de don Goyo." México
en la Cultura,* literary supplement of *Novedades* (Mexico),
March 8, 1959.

Carrasco Vintimilla, Alfonso. "Una novela prohibida." *El Mer-
curio* (Cuenca), February 10, 1974.

Carrión, Alejandro. Review of *El tigre* and other plays. *Letras
del Ecuador* (Quito), no. 106 (1956): 25.

Carrión, Benjamín. "Homenaje a un gran libro de nuestra

literatura: XX anniversario de *Los que se van.*" *Letras del Ecuador* (Quito), no. 62 (1950): 3.

——. "Itinerario de una hazaña." *El Gallo Ilustrado*, literary supplement of *El Día* (Mexico), March 6, 1966, pp. 1-2.

——. "*El secuestro del general*, último libro de Aguilera-Malta." *Cuadernos del Guayas* (Guayaquil, 1974).

Carter, Boyd G. "La novelística de Aguilera-Malta: Enfoques y pareceres." *Chasqui* 3, no. 3 (1973): 66-70.

Castillo, Othón. "*Siete lunas y siete serpientes* de Demetrio Aguilera-Malta." *La Opinión* (Los Angeles), April 29, 1970.

Cerutti, Franco. "Demetrio Aguilera-Malta, un novelista ejemplar." *Ancora, La Nación* (San José, Costa Rica), September 25, 1976.

Cervera, Juan. "*Siete lunas y siete serpientes.*" *Vida Universitaria* (Monterrey), July 12, 1970.

Colín, José Luis. "Los valores sociales y espirituales de *El secuestro del general.*" *Revista Mexicana de Cultura*, supplement of *El Nacional* (Mexico), February 24, 1974.

Cortés Camarillo, Félix. "El libro y el ensayo: *Siete lunas y siete serpientes.*" *El Universal* (Mexico), April 19, 1970.

Crowe, Violeta. "Aguilera-Malta y *El secuestro del general.*" *Nosotros* (Mexico), December 28, 1973.

Cruz, Jorge. "Escritores sudamericanos en México." *Boletín de la Comunidad Latinoamericana de Escritores*, no. 14 (1974): 75-79.

Cuesta, Juan de la. "Representantes ecuatorianos de la cultura." *El Comercio* (Quito), January 17, 1969.

Danne, César. "Don Goyo y don Buca, el espejo y la imagen." *La Razón* (Guayaquil), February 4, 1969.

Davis, J. Cary. "The 'Episodios Americanos' of Aguilera-Malta." *Foreign Language Quarterly* 9, nos. i-ii (1970): 49-53; 9, nos. iii-iv (1971): 43-47.

"Demetrio Aguilera-Malta, *Siete lunas y siete serpientes.*" *Tiempo* (Mexico), November 30, 1970.

Domingo, Alberto. "*Secuestro,* la vida airada." *Siempre* (Mexico), February 27, 1974.

Espinoza Altamirano, Horacio. *El secuestro del general.*" *La Opinión* (Los Angeles), November 20, 1973.

Fabila Hernández, Sadot. "Mis novelas buscan la realidad integradora: Aguilera-Malta." *Cultura de Hoy*, supplement of *El Día* (Mexico), December 3, 1973.

Fama, Antonio. *"Realismo mágico en la narrativa de Aguilera-Malta.* Madrid: Playor, S.A., 1977.

"La figura del mes: Demetrio Aguilera-Malta." *Vistazo* (Guayaquil), January 1969.

Flor, Jorge. "Hombres y libros, *Siete lunas y siete serpientes.*" *El Telégrafo* (Guayaquil), November 28, 1971.

Gallegos Lara, Joaquín. "Retrato biográfico de Aguilera-Malta." *Mensaje de la Biblioteca Nacional del Ecuador* (Quito), Epoca 3, no. 1: 112-16.

González Calzada, Manuel. "La novela de una fauna política." *El Día* (Mexico), March 26, 1974.

Guillén, Fedro. *"El secuestro del general."* *Novedades* (Mexico), November 3, 1973.

Huerta, Efraín. "Deslindes, buenas lecturas." *Diario de México*, March 25, 1974.

H. V. S. "Demetrio Aguilera-Malta se encuentra en Quito." *El Comercio* (Quito), January 16, 1969.

Koldewyn, Philip. "Protesta guerrillera y mitológica: Novela nueva de Aguilera-Malta." *Nueva Narrativa Hispanoamericana* 5, nos. 1-2 (1975): 199-205.

"Un libro inquietante: *Siete lunas y siete serpientes* por Demetrio Aguilera-Malta." *Tiempo* (Mexico), December 28, 1970.

Luzuriaga, Gerardo A. "Aguilera-Malta se incorpora a la nueva narrativa." *Nueva Narrativa Hispanoamericana* 1, no. 2 (1971).

―――. *Del realismo al expresionismo: el teatro de Aguilera-Malta.* Madrid: Plaza Mayor, 1971.

―――. "La evolución estilística del teatro de Aguilera-Malta." *Latin American Theatre Review* 3/2 (Spring 1970): 39-44.

"¡Madrid!: reportaje de una retaguardia heroica." *Claridad* (Buenos Aires) 16, no. 316 (1937).

"El maestro ecuatoriano Demetrio Aguilera-Malta." *Nivel* (Mexico), June 30, 1971.

Martí, Elú. "Libros, *El secuestro del general."* *Cultural*, supplement *El Heraldo* (Mexico), February 10, 1974.

Martínez Espinoza, Ignacio. "El libro de hoy: *Siete lunas y siete serpientes.*" *La Presna* (Mexico), July 3, 1970.

Megenney, William W. "Problemas raciales y culturales en dos piezas de Aguilera-Malta." *Cuadernos Americanos*, no. 176 (1971): 221-28.

Menton, Seymour. Review of *Siete lunas y siete serpientes.* *Revista Iberoamericana* 36, no. 73 (1970): 677-80.

Monsanto, Carlos H. "*Infierno negro:* drama de protesta social." *Duquesne Hispanic Review* 10 (1971): 11-22.

Moreno, Daniel. "*El secuestro del general.*" *Revista Mexicana de Cultura,* supplement of *El Nacional,* March 31, 1974.

Navasal, José M. "Una nueva película chilena." *Letras del Ecuador*, nos. 50-52 (1949): 25. (On the film "La cadena infinita.")

Otero, José. "Aguilera-Malta, Demetrio: *Siete lunas y siete serpientes.*" *Hispania* 54 (1971): 404.

Perdomo, José. "La charla evocadora de Demetrio Aguilera-Malta, radiografía en tecnicolor." *El Telégrafo* (Guayaquil), January 2, 1969.

Perkins, Blasco. "Demetrio Aguilera-Malta: *Infierno negro.*" *Zona Franca* (Caracas), 5, no. 65 (1969): 53.

Pitty, D. L. "Ser antiimperialista resulta una actitud vital: Aguilera-Malta, entrevista." *El Gallo Ilustrado*, supplement of *El Día* (Mexico), October 26, 1975.

Ponce, Bernardo. "*El secuestro del general.*" *El Sol* (Mexico), June 10, 1970.

Rabassa, Clementine C. "El aire como materia literaria: la épica, la nueva narrativa y Demetrio Aguilera-Malta." *Nueva Narrativa Hispanoamericana* 4 (1974): 261-68.

———. "Hacia la 'Négritude': las ediciones *variorum de Dientes blancos.*" In *Homenaje a Andrés Iduarte.* Clear Creek, Ind.: The American Hispanist, Inc., 1976, pp. 285-300.

———. "Prolegómeno al tema del negro en la obra de Demetrio Aguilera-Malta." *Hojas Volantes de la Communidad Latino-americana de Escritores*, September 1974, pp. 22-25.

———. Review of *Del realismo al expressionismo: El teatro de Aguilera-Malta*, by Gerardo Luzuriaga. *Books Abroad* 46 (July 1972).

——. Review of *El secuestro del general*, by Demetrio Aguilera-Malta. *Journal of Spanish Studies: Twentieth Century* 3, no. 1 (1975): 85-86.

——. Review of *Siete lunas y siete serpientes*, by Demetrio Aguilera-Malta. *Books Abroad* 45 (Spring 1971), p. 285.

——. "A Zoomorfose e a Trajetória Epico-Cristã em *Siete lunas y siete serpientes* de Demetrio Aguilera-Malta." *Suplemento Literário de Minas Gerais* (Belo Horizonte), Ano 5, no. 207 (August 15, 1970): 10-11. (Portuguese version of *"Siete lunas y siete serpientes* de Demetrio Aguilera-Malta." *El Libro y la Vida,* literary supplement of *El Dia* (Mexico), no. 22 (May 10, 1970).

Real, Manuel de J. *"Don Goyo* en dimensión continental." *Vistazo* (Guayaquil) 19: 226.

Ríos, Edmundo de los. *"Siete lunas y siete serpientes* de Demetrio Aguilera-Malta." *Diorama de la Cultura,* literary supplement of *Excelsior* (Mexico), May 3, 1970.

——. *"Siete lunas y siete serpientes* de Demetrio Aguilera-Malta." *El Día* (Mexico), May 11, 1970.

Rivas Iturralde, Vladimiro. *"El secuestro del general,* la descomposición de la metáfora; cuatro notas sobre la narrativa ecuatoriana." *Revista de la Universidad de México* 28, no. 2 (July 1974).

Rodríguez C., Victoria. "Acierto literario, *El secuestro del general. Diez* (Mexico), November 30, 1973.

Rodríguez Castelo, Hernán. "Demetrio Aguilera-Malta por él mismo." *El Tiempo* (Quito), August 23, 1970.

——. "El libro de la semana: *Siete lunas y siete serpientes." El Tiempo* (Quito), September 8, 1970.

Salcedo, René. "En Ecuador no hay crisis literaria: hay receso. Entrevista con Demetrio Aguilera-Malta." *Tricolor,* supplement of *El Telégrafo* (Guayaquil), January 25, 1969.

Sainz, Gustavo. "Un novelista enjuicia a sus colegas de 1973: *El secuestro del general." La Onda,* supplement of *Novedades* (Mexico), December 30, 1973.

Sánchez, Luis Alberto. *"El secuestro del general." La Prensa* Lima, April 21, 1974.

Schanzer, George O. "Se han vuelto satíricos. Análisis comparativo de la trayectoria novelística de Manuel Mujica-Láinez y Demetrio Aguilera-Malta." *Revista de la Comunidad Latinoamericana de Escritores* (Mexico), no. 17 (1976).

Selva, Mauricio de la. *"El secuestro del general." Diorama de la Cultura*, supplement of *Excelsior* (Mexico), November 25, 1973.

Sibirsky, Saúl. Review of *Episodios americanos* 1, 2, 3. *Revista Iberoamericana* 22, no. 61 (1966): 176-79.

Siemens, William W. "The Devouring Female in Four Latin American Novels." *Essays in Literature* (Western Illinois University) 1 (1974): 176-79.

Torre, Gerardo de la. "Aguilera-Malta, *Siete lunas y siete serpientes." Revista Mexicana de Cultura*, supplement of *El Nacional* (Mexico), October 25, 1970.

Varela, Julián. "El secuestro de mi general." *El Telégrafo* (Guayaquil), December 9, 1973.

Villasenor, Raúl. "Demetrio Aguilera-Malta: *El secuestro del general." Vida Universitaria* (Monterrey), June 23, 1970.

Viteri, Eugenia. *"Los que se van*, un libro crucial." *Letras del Ecuador* (Casa de la Cultura Ecuatoriana, Quito), no. 152 (August 1972).

Zendejas, Francisco. *"El secuestro del general." Excelsior* (Mexico), October 17, 1973.

Latin American and Ecuador

Although the titles listed below do not specifically mention Aguilera-Malta, most include some interpretation or analysis of his works.

Alegría, Fernando. *Breve historia de la novela hispanoamericana.* Mexico: Andrea, 1959.

Allison, Wayne L. "A Thematic Analysis of the Contemporary Ecuadorian Novel." Dissertation, University of New Mexico, 1964.

Anderson-Imbert, Enrique. *Spanish-American Literature: A*

278   Demetrio Aguilera-Malta and Social Justice

History. Translated by John V. Falconieri. Detroit: Wayne State University Press, 1963.

Arias, Augusto. *Panorama de la literatura ecuatoriana.* Quito: Imprenta Nacional, 1936.

Barrera, Isaac J. *Historia de la literatura ecuatoriana.* 4 vols. Quito: Casa de la Cultura Ecuatoriana, 1955.

———. *La literatura del Ecuador. Las literaturas americanas,* vol. 6. Buenos Aires: Universidad de Buenos Aires, Facultad de Filosofía y Letras, Instituto de Literatura, Sección Argentina y Americana, 1947.

———. *Literatura ecuatoriana: apuntaciones históricas.* 3rd ed. Quito: Ed. Ecuatoriana, 1939.

Bellini, Giuseppe. *La Protesta nel romanzo ispano-americano del novecento.* Milan-Varese: Cisalpino, 1957.

———. *Storia e letteratura ispano-americana.* Milan: "La Goliardica," Edizioni Universitarie, 1954.

Brion, Marcel. *Bartolomé de las Casas.* Mexico: Divulgación, 1953.

Brushwood, John S. *The Spanish American Novel: A Twentieth-Century Survey.* Austin: University of Texas Press, 1975.

Carrión, Alejandro. *Diccionario de la literatura latino-americana: Ecuador.* Washington: Pan American Union, 1962.

Carrión, Benjamín. "Estudio preliminar" in José de la Cuadra. *Los monos enloquecidos.* Quito: Casa de la Cultura Ecuatoriana, 1951.

———. *El nuevo relato ecuatoriano.* 2 vols. Quito: Casa de la Cultura Ecuatoriana, 1950.

Chaves, Alfredo. *Fuentes principales de la bibliografía ecuatoriana contemporánea.* Quito: Casa de la Cultura Ecuatoriana, 1958.

Chocano, José Santos. *Alma América: poemas indo-españoles.* Prologue by Miguel de Unamuno. Madrid: Lib. General de Victoriano Suárez, 1906.

Cometta Manzoni, Aida. *El indio en la novela de América.* Buenos Aires: Futuro, SRL, 1960.

Crooks, Esther J. "Contemporary Ecuador in the Novel and Short Story." *Hispania* 23, no. 1 (1940): 85-88.

Cuadra, José de la. *Obras completas.* Quito: Casa de la Cultura Ecuatoriana, 1958.

Da Silva, Zenia Sacks. "The Contemporary Ecuadorian Novel." 2 vols. Dissertation, New York University, 1955.

Ferrandiz Albornoz, Francisco. "El novelista ecuatoriano." Prologue to Jorge Icaza. *Flagelo.* Quito: Imprenta Nacional, Publicaciones del Sindicato de Escritores y Artistas, 1936, pp. v-lx.

Franco, Jean. *An Introduction to Spanish-American Literature.* New York: Cambridge University Press, 1969.

Franklin, Albert B. "Ecuador's Novelists at Work." *The Inter-American Quarterly* 2, no. 4 (1940): 29-41.

Gallegos, Rómulo. *Doña Bárbara.* 4th ed. Barcelona: Araluce, 1929.

García, Antonio. *Pasado y presente del indio.* Bogotá: Centro, 1939.

Grases, Pedro. "De la novela en América." In *Dos estudios.* Caracas: Talleres de la C. A. Artes Gráficas, 1943.

Heise, Karl H. *El Grupo de Guayaquil: arte y técnica de sus novelas sociales.* Madrid: Playor, 1975.

Icaza, Jorge. *Huasipungo.* Quito: Imprenta Nacional, 1934.

―――. "Relato, espíritu unificador en la generación del año 30." *Revista Iberoamericana* 32, no. 62 (1966): 211-16.

Iduarte, Andrés. "Cervantes, Juan Haldudo y la justicia." In *Pláticas hispanoamericanas.* Mexico: Fondo de Cultura Económica, 1951, pp. 145-49.

Jackson, Richard. *The Black Image in Latin American Literature.* Albuquerque: University of New Mexico Press, 1976.

Jaramillo Alvarado, Pío. *El indio ecuatoriano.* Quito: Imprenta Nacional, 1936.

Jones, Cecil Knight. *A Bibliography of Latin American Bibliographies.* 2nd ed. Washington: U. S. Government Printing Office, 1942. ("Ecuador," pp. 185-92.)

Jones, Willis Knapp. "El drama en el Ecuador." *Anales de la Universidad de Guayaquil* 2, no. 2 (1950).

Latcham, Ricardo. "La historia del criollismo." In *El criollismo.* Santiago, Chile: Ed. Universitaria, n. d.

León, Luis A. "Bibliografía nacional y extranjera sobre el indio ecuatoriano." In *Cuestiones indígenas del Ecuador,* vol. 1. Quito: Casa de la Cultura Ecuatoriana, 1946.

Loveluck, Juan, editor. *La novela hispanoamericana.* 2nd ed. Concepción: Ed. Universitaria, 1966.

Luzuriaga, Gerardo. "La generación ecuatoriana del treinta y el teatro." *CLE* (Comunidad Latinoamericana de Escritores), no. 8 (Mexico, 1970): 18-24.

————. "Panorama del teatro ecuatoriano. Mimeographed. Iowa City, Iowa, 1967.

Mariátegui, José Carlos. *Siete ensayos de interpretación de la realidad peruana.* Lima: Biblioteca Amauta, 1928.

McCullough, David. *The Path Between the Seas. The Creation of the Panama Canal, 1870-1914.* New York: Simon and Schuster, 1977.

Mejía Sánchez, Ernesto. "Observaciones sobre la novela latino-americana contemporánea." In *La novela iberoamericana contemporánea.* XII Congreso Internacional de Literatura Iberoamericana. Caracas: Universidad Central de Venezuela, 1968, pp. 51-57.

Meléndez, Concha., *La novela indianista en Hispanoamérica.* 2nd ed. Río Piedras: Universidad de Puerto Rico, 1961.

Menton, Seymour. *El cuento hispanoamericano: antología critico-histórica.* 2nd ed. 2 vols. Mexico: Fondo de Cultura Económica, 1964.

Mera, Juan León. *Cumandá o un drama entre salvajes.* Buenos Aires: Espasa-Calpe, Colección Austral, 1951.

Montalvo, Juan. *Las catilinarias.* 2 vols. Paris: Garnier, 1929.

Ospina, Uriel. *Problemas y perspectivas de la novela americana.* Bogotá: Tercer Mundo, 1964.

Pareja Diezcanseco, Alfredo. *Historia del Ecuador.* Quito: Editorial Colón, 1962.

————. "Consideraciones sobre el hecho literario." *Revista Casa de la Cultura Ecuatoriana* (Quito), no. 6 (1948): 127-45.

Pillement, Georges. *Les Conteurs Hispano-Américains.* Paris: Librairie Delagrave, 1933.

Proaño, Ernesto B. *Figuras y antología de literatura ecuatoriana.* Quito: Colegio Salesiano "Don Bosco," 1960.

Rabassa, Clementine. Review of *The Black Image in Latin American Literature* by Richard L. Jackson. *Chasqui*, May 1977, pp. 104-108.

Reyes, Alfonso. "La epopeya del Canal." In *Norte y sur (1925-1942)*. Mexico: Leyenda, 1944.

Rivadeneira, Edmundo. *La moderna novela ecuatoriana*. Quito: Casa de la Cultura Ecuatoriana, 1958.

Rivera, José Eustasio. *La vorágine*. Critical study and biography by Juan Loveluck. Santiago, Chile: Zig-Zag, 1953.

Rodó, José Enrique. *Ariel*. Mexico: Novaro-México, 1957.

Rodríguez Castelo, Hernán. "Teatro ecuatoriano." *Cuadernos Hispanoamericanos*, no. 172 (1964): 81-119.

Rojas, Angel F. *La novela ecuatoriana*. Mexico: Fondo de Cultura Económica, 1948.

Sacoto, Antonio. *The Indian in the Ecuadorian Novel*. New York: Las Américas, 1967.

Sánchez, Luis Alberto. *Proceso y contenido de la novela hispanoamericana*. Madrid: Gredos, 1953.

———. *Vida y pasión de la cultura en América*. Santiago, Chile: Biblioteca América, 1936.

Sarmiento, Domingo F. *Facundo: civilización y barbarie*. Garden City, N.Y.: Doubleday, 1961.

Saz, Agustín del. *Teatro hispanoamericano*. Vol. 2. Barcelona: Vergara, 1963.

Schwartz, Kessel. "The Contemporary Novel of Ecuador." Dissertation, Columbia University, 1953.

———. *A New History of Spanish American Fiction*. 2 vols. Miami: University of Miami Press, 1972.

Siegel, Reuben. "The Group of Guayaquil: A Study in Contemporary Ecuadorian Fiction." Dissertation, University of Wisconsin, 1951.

Smith, Gaddis. Review of *The Path Between the Seas*, by David McCullough. *The New York Times Book Review*, June 19, 1977, pp. 1, 39.

Solórzano, Carlos. *Teatro latinoamericano en el siglo XX*. Mexico: Pormaca, 1964.

Torres-Rioseco, Arturo, editor. *La novela iberoamericana*.

Memoria del Quinto Congreso del Instituto Internacional de Literatura Iberoamericana. Albuquerque: University of New Mexico Press, 1952.

Ubler, Kanil. *El indio en la novela de América.* Buenos Aires: Futuro, 1960.

Uslar-Pietri, Arturo. "Lo criollo en la literatura hispanoamericana." *Cuadernos Americanos* 49, no. 1 (1950): 266-78.

Uzcátegui, Emilio. "Ecuador's Novels and Novelists." *Américas* (Washington, D. C.: Pan American Union) 16 (May 1944): 29-34.

Verdugo, Iber H. "La actual novela hispanoamericana." *Mundo Nuevo,* no. 28 (1968): 75-83.

Viteri, Atanasio. *El cuento ecuatoriano moderno.* Quito: Talleres Tipográficos Modernos Nacionales, n. d.

Yáñez, Agustín. *El contenido social de la literatura iberoamericana. Jornadas,* vol. 14. Mexico: El Colegio de México, 1944.

The Epic and Related Works

Abercrombie, Lascelles. *The Epic.* 2nd ed. London: Secker, Ltd., 1922.

Andersson, Theodore Murdock. *Early Epic Scenery: Homer, Virgil, and the Medieval Legacy.* Ithaca: Cornell University Press, 1976.

Ariosto, Ludovico. *Orlando Furioso.* Edited Nicola Zingarelli. 2nd ed. Milan: Ulrico Hoepli, 1943.

Aristotle. *Aristotle.* Selections and translation Philip Wheelwright. New York: Odyssey Press, 1951.

Beowulf. Translated by Lucien Dean Pearson; edited, introduction and notes by Rowland L. Collins. Bloomington: Indiana University Press, 1965.

Bowra, C. M. *From Virgil to Milton.* London: Macmillan, 1962.

Brecht, Bertolt. *"Baal," "A Man's a Man," and "The Elephant Calf": Early Plays by Bertolt Brecht.* Adapted by Eric Bentley. New York: Grove Press, 1964.

Brodeur, Arthur Gilchrist. *The Art of "Beowulf."* Berkeley-Los Angeles: University of California Press, 1959.

Burns, Norman T., and Christopher J. Reagan, editors. *Concepts of the Hero in the Middle Ages and the Renaissance.* Albany: State University of New York Press, 1975.

Camões, Luís Vaz de. *Os Lusíadas* in *Obras Completas,* vols. 4-5. Introduction and notes by Hernâni Cidade. Lisbon: Sá da Costa, 1947.

Campbell, Joseph. *The Hero with a Thousand Faces.* Cleveland: World, 1956.

Cantar de Mio Cid. Edited by Ramón Menéndez Pidal. 3 vols. Madrid: Espasa-Calpe, 1956.

La Chanson de Roland. Edited by Léon Gautier. Tours: Alfred Mame et Fils, 1884.

————. *The Song of Roland.* Translated by C. K. Scott Moncrieff; introduction by G. K. Chesterton; note on technique by George Saintsbury. Ann Arbor: University of Michigan Press, 1966.

Cidade, Hernâni. *Luís de Camões.* Lisbon: Arcádia, 1961.

Clarke, Howard W. *The Art of the "Odyssey."* Englewood Cliffs, N.J.: Prentice-Hall, 1967.

Commager, Steele, editor. *Virgil: A Collection of Critical Essays.* Englewood Cliffs, N.J.: Prentice-Hall, 1966.

Daiches, David. *Milton.* New York: Norton, 1966.

Dante Alighieri. *La Divina Commedia.* Notes by Dino Provenzal. Verona: Mondadori, 1938.

————. *The "Divine Comedy" of Dante Alighieri.* Translation and notes by John D. Sinclair. Vol. 1, *Inferno.* New York: Oxford University Press, 1959.

Duggan, Joseph J. *"The Song of Roland": Formulaic Style and Poetic Craft.* Berkeley-Los Angeles: University of California Press, 1973.

Dürrenmatt, Friedrich. *"Problems of the Theatre," an Essay and "The Marriage of Mr. Mississippi," a Play by Friedrich Dürrenmatt.* Translated by Gerhard Nellhaus. New York: Grove Press, 1964.

Ebel, Henry. *After Dionysus: An Essay on Where We Are Now.* Rutherford, N. J.: Fairleigh Dickinson University Press, 1972.

The Epic of Gilgamesh. Introduction by N. K. Sanders. Baltimore: Penguin Books, 1966.

Ercilla y Zúñiga, Alonso de. *La Araucana.* Selection, prologue, and notes Juan Loveluck. Santiago, Chile: Zig-Zag, 1958.

Fixler, Michael. *Milton and the Kingdoms of God.* Evanston, Ill.: Northwestern University Press, 1964.

Frazer, Sir James George. *The Golden Bough: A Study in Magic and Religion.* 3rd ed., 12 vols. London: Macmillan, 1919-1920.

Giamatti, A. Bartlett. *The Earthly Paradise and the Renaissance Epic.* Princeton, N. J.: Princeton University Press, 1969.

Gordon, Cyrus H. *Before the Bible: The Common Background of Greek and Hebrew Civilisations.* New York: Harper and Row, 1962.

Greene, Thomas. *The Descent from Heaven: A Study in Epic Continuity.* New Haven: Yale University Press, 1963.

Gunther, Peter A. "Mental Inertia and Environmental Decay: The End of an Era." *The Living Wilderness* (Washington, D. C.) 34, no. 109 (1970): 3-5.

Guthrie, W. K. C. *The Greek Philosophers: From Thales to Aristotle.* New York: Harper, 1960.

Hägin, Peter. *The Epic Hero and the Decline of Heroic Poetry: A Study of the Neo-Classical English Epic with Special Reference to Milton's "Paradise Lost."* The Cooper Monographs on English and American Language and Literature, no. 8. Berne: Francke Verlag, 1964.

Hamilton, Edith. *Mythology.* New York: New American Library, 1954.

Hesiod. *Hesiod: "The Works and Days," "Theogony," "The Shield of Herakles."* Translated by Richmond Lattimore. Ann Arbor: University of Michigan Press, 1968.

The Holy Bible, Old and New Testaments. King James Version New York: American Bible Society, 1962.

Homer. *Iliad.* With translation by A. T. Murray. 2 vols. London: Heinemann, 1924-1925. (Loeb Classical Library)

———. *The "Iliad" of Homer.* Translation and introduction by Richmond Lattimore. Chicago: Chicago University Press, 1951.

————. *Odyssey.* With translation by A. T. Murray. 2 vols. London: Heinemann, 1919-1928. (Loeb Classical Library)

————. *The Odyssey.* Translation and introduction by E. V. Rieu. New York: Penguin, 1947.

————. *The "Odyssey" of Homer.* Translation and introduction by Richmond Lattimore. New York: Harper and Row, 1968.

Johnson, Lemuel. *The Devil, the Gargoyle, and the Buffoon: The Negro as Metaphor in Western Literature.* Port Washington: N. Y.: Kennikat Press, 1971.

Johnson, William Roger. *Darkness Visible: A Study of Vergil's "Aeneid."* Berkeley-Los Angeles: University of California Press, 1976.

Lévi-Strauss, Claude. *Totemism.* Translated by Rodney Needham. Boston: Beacon Press, 1963.

————. *Tristes Tropiques.* Translated by John Russell. New York: Atheneum, 1967.

Levy, Gertrude Rachel. *The Sword from the Rock.* London: Faber and Faber, 1953.

Lewis, C. S. *A Preface to "Paradise Lost."* London: Oxford University Press, 1960.

Lieb, Michael. *The Dialectics of Creation: Patterns of Birth and Regeneration in "Paradise Lost."* Amherst: University of Massachusetts Press, 1970.

Lucan. *The "Pharsalia" of Lucan.* Translated by Sir Edward Ripley. 2 vols. London: Arthur L. Humphreys, 1919.

McNamee, Maurice B. *Honor and the Epic Hero: A Study of the Shifting Concept of Magnanimity in Philosophy and Epic Poetry.* New York: Holt, Rinehart and Winston, 1959.

Marchant, R. A. *Beasts of Fact and Fable.* New York: Roy, 1962.

Martz, Louis L., editor. *Milton, "Paradise Lost": A Collection of Critical Essays.* Englewood Cliffs: N. J.: Prentice-Hall, 1966.

Menéndez Pidal, Ramón. *Romancero hispánico: hispano-portugués, americano y sefardí, teoría e historia.* 2 vols. Madrid: Espasa-Calpe, 1953.

————. *En Torno al "Poema del Cid."* Barcelona: Editora y Distribuidora Hispano Americana, 1963.

Milton, John. *Paradise Lost*. Introduction and notes by Merritt Y. Hughes. New York: Odyssey Press, 1935.

Murray, Gilbert. *The Rise of the Greek Epic*. New York: Oxford University Press, 1960.

Musa, Mark, editor. *Essays on Dante*. Bloomington: Indiana University Press, 1964.

Nicolson, Marjorie. *John Milton: A Reader's Guide to His Poetry*. New York: Noonday Press, 1967.

O'Neill, Eugene. *The Emperor Jones*. New York: Noble and Noble, 1958.

Ovid. *Metamorphoses*. Translated by Horace Gregory. New York: New American Library, 1960.

Patrides, C. A., editor. *Approaches to "Paradise Lost": The York Tercentenary Lectures*. London: Edward Arnold, 1968.

Petrocchi, Giorgio. *I Fantasmi di Tancredi: Saggi sul Tasso e sul Rinascimento*. Cattanissetta-Rome: S. Sciascia, 1972.

Pierce, Frank. *La poesía épica del Siglo de Oro*. Translated by J. C. Cayol de Bethencourt. 2nd ed., rev. Madrid: Gredos, 1968.

Plato. *The "Republic" of Plato*. Translation, introduction, and notes by Francis MacDonald Cornford. New York-London: Oxford University Press, 1957.

Post, L. A. *From Homer to Menander*. Berkeley: University of California Press, 1951.

Rabassa, Clementine. "Cynegetics and Irony in the Thematic Unity of the *Lusiads*." *Luso-Brazilian Review* 10, no. 2 (December 1973): 197-207.

Sholod, Barton. *Charlemagne in Spain: The Cultural Legacy of Roncesvalles*. Geneva: Librairie Droz, 1966.

Sobejano, Gonzalo. *El epíteto en la lírica española*. Madrid: Gredos, 1956.

Steadman, John. *Epic and Tragic Structure in "Paradise Lost."* Chicago: University of Chicago Press, 1976.

Steiner, George, and Robert Fagles, editors. *Homer: A Collection of Critical Essays*. Englewood Cliffs, N. J.: Prentice-Hall, 1962.

Tasso, Torquato. *La "Gerusalemme Liberata" di Torquato Tasso*.

New revised edition by Pietro Papini; notes by Severino Ferrari. Florence: Sansoni, 1940.

————. *Jerusalem Delivered.* Translated by Edward Fairfax; introduction by John Charles Nelson. New York: Capricorn Books, 1963.

Thompson, David. *Dante's Epic Journeys.* Baltimore: Johns Hopkins University Press, 1974.

Tillyard, E. M. W. *The English Epic and Its Background.* London: Chatto and Windus, 1954.

————. *The Epic Strain in the English Novel.* Fair Lawn, N. J.: Essential Books, 1958.

Tolkien, J. R. R. *"Beowulf": The Monsters and the Critics. Proceedings of the British Academy,* vol. 22. London: Humphrey Milford Amen House, 1936.

Virgil. *The "Aeneid" of Virgil.* Translated by C. Day Lewis. Garden City, N. Y.: Doubleday, 1952.

————. *The Aeneid.* Translated by James H. Mantinband. New York: Ungar, 1964.

————. *Eclogues, Georgics, and Aeneid.* With translation by H. Rushton Fairclough. 2 vols. London: Heinemann, 1916-1922. (Loeb Classical Library)

————. *The Eclogues and Georgics.* Translated by C. Day Lewis. Garden City, N.Y.: Doubleday, 1964.

Waldock, A. J. A. *"Paradise Lost" and Its Critics.* London: Cambridge University Press, 1961.

Webster, T. B. L. *From Mycenae to Homer.* New York: Praeger, 1958.

Whitman, Cedric H. *Homer and the Homeric Tradition.* Cambridge: Harvard University Press, 1958.

Wilkie, Brian. *Romantic Poets and Epic Tradition.* Madison-Milwaukee: University of Wisconsin Press, 1965.

Woodhull, Marianna. *The Epic of "Paradise Lost."* New York: The Knickerbocker Press, 1907.

Index

863
R112d

Rabassa, Clementine
Christos.

Demetrio Aguilera-
Malta and social
justice

DATE			
MAY 1 1 84			